Basic Electrical Engineering

Basic Electrical Engineering

Mathew West
Sara Miles

KNOWLEDGE
BAKERS

KNOWLEDGE BAKERS

Cataloging in Publication Data--DK
Courtesy: D.K. Agencies (P) Ltd. <docinfo@dkagencies.com>

West, Mathew (*Writer on electrical engineering*), **author.**
Basic electrical engineering / Mathew West, Sara Miles.
pages cm
Includes bibliographical references and index.
ISBN 9789391502058

1. Electrical engineering. I. Miles, Sara (Writer on electrical engineering), author. II. Title.

LCC TK145.W47 2023 | DDC 621.3 23

ISBN: 978-93-91502-05-8

9 789391 502058

Published by : **Knowledge Bakers**
Pune, India
Email: knowledgebakers2019@gmail.com

Digitally Printed at : **Replika Press Pvt. Ltd.**

Preface

Humans have an intimate relationship with electricity, to the point that it's virtually impossible to separate your life from it. Sure, you can flee from the world of crisscrossing power lines and live your life completely off the grid, but even at the loneliest corners of the world, electricity exists. If it's not lighting up the storm clouds overhead or crackling in a static spark at your fingertips, then it's moving through the human nervous system, animating the brain's will in every flourish, breath and unthinking heartbeat. Electricity powers our world and our bodies. Harnessing its energy is both the domain of imagined sorcery and humdrum, everyday life — from Emperor Palpatine toasting Luke Skywalker, to the simple act of ejecting the "Star Wars" disc from your PC. Electrical engineering is the field deals with the study and application of electricity, electronics and electromagnetism. The field first became an identifiable occupation in the late nineteenth century after commercialization of the electric telegraph and electrical power supply. It now covers a range of subtopics including power, electronics, control systems, signal processing and telecommunications.

Electrical engineering may include electronic-engineering. Where a distinction is made, usually outside of the United States, electrical engineering is considered to deal with the problems associated with systems such as electric power transmission and electrical machines, whereas electronic engineering deals with the study of electronic systems including computers, communication systems, integrated circuits, and radar. Electrical engineering has many subdisciplines, the most popular of which are listed below. Although there are electrical engineers who focus exclusively on one of these subdisciplines, many deal with a combination of them. Sometimes certain fields, such as electronic engineering and computer engineering, are considered separate disciplines in their own right. From a different point-of-view, electrical engineers are usually concerned with using electricity to transmit electric power, while electronic engineers are concerned with using electricity to process information. The subdisciplines can overlap, for example, in the growth of power electronics, and the study of behaviour of large electrical grids under the control of digital computers and electronics.

The present book covers the basic theory and practice of electronics related to electricity. It goes on to explain the fundamental principles and components, relating them constantly to real-world examples. Sections on tools and troubleshooting give engineers deeper understanding and the know-how to create and maintain their own electronic design projects. The author builds a genuine understanding of the fundamentals and shows how they can be applied to a range of engineering problems. This book on Basic Electrical Engineering has been prepared in a novel format by keeping in mind the basic trend of the students. The idea is to make understand what exactly the students should learn from the subject point of view. The book is equally useful as a reference for bank of questions and answers.

Dr Mathew West
Dr Sara Miles

Contents

1

Introduction

Mathematics in Electronics

Electrical Engineering careers usually include courses in Calculus (single and multivariable), Complex Analysis, Differential Equations (both ordinary and partial), Linear Algebra and Probability. Fourier Analysis and Z-Transforms are also subjects which are usually included in electrical engineering programs. Of these subjects, Calculus and Differential equations are usually prerequisites for the Physics courses required in most electrical engineering programs (mainly Mechanics, Electromagnetism & Semiconductor Physics). Complex Analysis has direct applications in Circuit Analysis, while Fourier Analysis is needed for all Signals & Systems courses, as are Linear Algebra and Z-Transform.

Basic Applications

A number of electrical laws apply to all electrical networks. These include

- Faraday's law of induction: Any change in the magnetic environment of a coil of wire will cause a voltage (emf) to be "induced" in the coil.
- Gauss's Law: The total of the electric flux out of a closed surface is equal to the charge enclosed divided by the permittivity.
- Kirchhoff's current law: the sum of all currents entering a node is equal to the sum of all currents leaving the node or the sum of total current at a junction is zero
- Kirchhoff's voltage law: the directed sum of the electrical potential differences around a circuit must be zero.

- Ohm's law: the voltage across a resistor is the product of its resistance and the current flowing through it.at constant temperature.
- Norton's theorem: any two-terminal collection of voltage sources and resistors is electrically equivalent to an ideal current source in parallel with a single resistor.
- Thevenin's theorem: any two-terminal combination of voltage sources and resistors is electrically equivalent to a single voltage source in series with a single resistor.
- Millman's theorem: the voltage on the ends of branches in parallel is equal to the sum of the currents flowing in every branch divided by the total equivalent conductance.
- See also Analysis of resistive circuits.

Circuit analysis is the study of methods to solve linear systems for an unknown variable.

Circuit Analysis

Signal Analysis

- Fourier analysis. Deconstructing a periodic waveform into its constituent frequencies; see also: Fourier theorem, Fourier transform.
- Nyquist-Shannon sampling theorem.
- Information theory. Sets fundamental limits on how information can be transmitted or processed by any system.

Electronic Circuit Simulation

Electronic circuit simulation uses mathematical models to replicate the behaviour of an actual electronic device or circuit. Simulation software allows for modelling of circuit operation and is an invaluable analysis tool. Due to its highly accurate modelling capability, many Colleges and Universities use this type of software for the teaching of electronics technician and electronics engineering programs. Electronics simulation software engages the user by integrating them into the learning experience. These kinds of interactions actively engage learners to analyze, synthesize, organise, and evaluate content and result in learners constructing their own knowledge.

Simulating a circuit's behaviour before actually building it can greatly improve design efficiency by making faulty designs known as such, and providing insight into the behaviour of electronics circuit designs. In particular, for integrated circuits, the tooling (photomasks) is expensive, breadboards are impractical, and probing the behaviour of internal signals is extremely difficult. Therefore almost all IC design relies heavily on simulation. The most well known analog simulator is SPICE. Probably the best known digital simulators are those based on Verilog and VHDL.

Some electronics simulators integrate a schematic editor, a simulation engine, and on-screen waveforms, and make "what-if" scenarios easy and instant. They also typically contain extensive model and device libraries. These models typically include IC specific transistor models such as BSIM, generic components such as resistors, capacitors, inductors and transformers, user defined models (such as controlled current and voltage sources, or models in Verilog-A or VHDL-AMS). Printed circuit board (PCB) design requires specific models as well, such as transmission lines for the traces and IBIS models for driving and receiving electronics.

Types

While there are strictly analog electronics circuit simulators, popular simulators often include both analog and event-driven digital simulation capabilities, and are known as mixed-mode simulators. This means that any simulation may contain components that are analog, event driven (digital or sampled-data), or a combination of both. An entire mixed signal analysis can be driven from one integrated schematic. All the digital models in mixed-mode simulators provide accurate specification of propagation time and rise/fall time delays. The event driven algorithm provided by mixed-mode simulators is general purpose and supports non-digital types of data. For example, elements can use real or integer values to simulate DSP functions or sampled data filters. Because the event driven algorithm is faster than the standard SPICE matrix solution, simulation time is greatly reduced for circuits that use event driven models in place of analog models.

Mixed-mode simulation is handled on three levels; (a) with primitive digital elements that use timing models and the built-in 12 or 16 state digital logic simulator, (b) with subcircuit models that use the actual transistor topology of the integrated circuit, and finally, (c) with In-line Boolean logic expressions.

Exact representations are used mainly in the analysis of transmission line and signal integrity problems where a close inspection of an IC's I/O characteristics is needed. Boolean logic expressions are delay-less functions that are used to provide efficient logic signal processing in an analog environment.

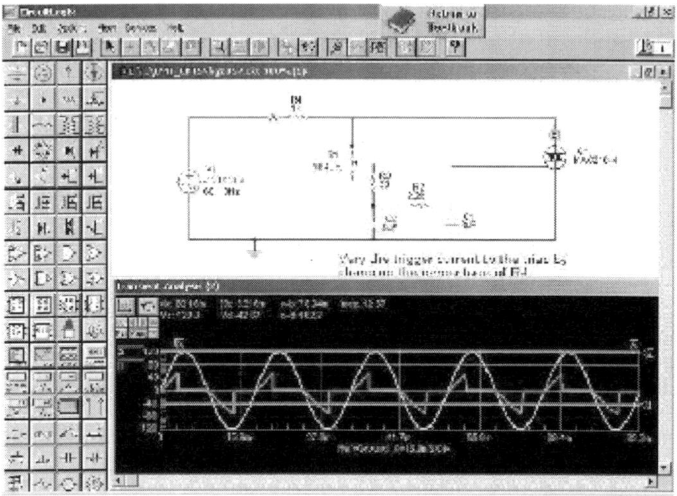

Figure: *CircuitLogix mixed-mode simulator.*

These two modelling techniques use SPICE to solve a problem while the third method, digital primitives, use mixed mode capability. Each of these methods has its merits and target applications.

In fact, many simulations (particularly those which use A/D technology) call for the combination of all three approaches. No one approach alone is sufficient.

Another type of simulation used mainly for power electronics represent piecewise linear algorithms. These algorithms use an analog (linear) simulation until a power electronic switch changes its state. At this time a new analog model is calculated to be used for the next simulation period. This methodology both enhances simulation speed and stability significantly.

Electronic Packaging

Electronic packaging is a major discipline within the field of electronic engineering, and includes a wide variety of technologies. It refers to enclosures and protective features built into the product itself, and not to shipping containers. It applies both to end products and to components.

Packaging Techniques

Sheet Metal: Punched and formed sheet metal is one of the oldest types of electronic packaging. It can be mechanically strong, provides electromagnetic shielding when the product requires that feature, and is easily made for prototypes and small production runs with little custom tooling expense. Fairly professional results are possible in a home workshop.

Cast Metal: Gasketed metal castings are sometimes used to package electronic equipment for exceptionally severe environments, such as in heavy industry, aboard ship, or deep under water. Aluminium die castings are more common than iron or steel sand castings.

Machined Metal: Electronic packages are sometimes made by machining solid blocks of metal, usually aluminium, into complex shapes. They are fairly common in microwave assemblies for aerospace use, where precision transmission lines require complex metal shapes, in combination with hermetically sealed housings. Quantities tend to be small; sometimes only one unit of a custom design is required. Piece part costs are high, but there is little or no cost for custom tooling, and first-piece deliveries can take as little as half a day. The tool of choice is a numerically controlled vertical milling machine, with automatic translation of computer-aided design (CAD) files to toolpath command files.

Molded Plastic: Molded plastic cases and structural parts can be made by a variety of methods, offering tradeoffs in piece part cost, tooling cost, mechanical and electrical properties, and ease of assembly. Examples are injection molding, transfer molding, vacuum forming, and die cutting. Pl can be post-processed to provide conductive surfaces when confused.

Potting: Formally called "encapsulation", potting consists of immersing the part or assembly in a liquid resin, and then curing it. Potting can be done in a pre-molded potting shell, or directly in a mold. Today it is most widely used to protect semiconductor components from moisture and mechanical damage, and to serve as a mechanical structure holding the lead frame and the chip together. In earlier times it was often used to discourage reverse engineering of proprietary products built as printed circuit modules. It is also commonly used in high voltage products to allow live parts to be placed much closer together, so that the product can be smaller; also, to keep dirt and conductive contaminants such as impure water out of sensitive areas. Another use is to protect deep-submergence items such as sonar transducers from collapsing under extreme pressure, by filling all voids. Potting can be rigid or soft. When void-free potting is required, it's common practice to place the product in a vacuum chamber while the resin is still liquid, hold a vacuum for several minutes to draw the air out of internal cavities and the resin itself, then release the vacuum. Atmospheric pressure collapses the voids and forces the liquid resin into all internal spaces. Vacuum potting works best with resins that cure by polymerization, rather than solvent evaporation.

Porosity Sealing or Impregnation: Porosity Sealing or Resin Impregnation is similar to potting, but doesn't use a shell or a mold. Parts are submerged in a polymerizable monomer or solvent-based low viscosity plastic solution. The pressure above the fluid is lowered to a full vacuum. After the vacuum is released, the fluid flows into the part. When the part is withdrawn from the resin bath, it is drained and/or cleaned and then cured.

Curing can consist of polymerizing the internal resin or evaporating the solvent, which leaves an insulating dielectric material between different voltage components. Porosity sealing (Resin Impregnation) fills all interior spaces, and may or may not leave a thin coating on the surface, depending on the wash/rinse performance. The main application of vacuum impregnation porosity sealing is in boosting the dielectric strength of transformers, solenoids, lamination stacks or coils, and some high voltage components. It prevents ionization from forming between closely spaced live surfaces and initiating failure.

Conformal Coating: Conformal coating is a thin insulating coating applied by various methods. It provides mechanical and chemical protection of delicate components. It's widely used on mass-produced items such as axial-lead resistors, and sometimes on printed circuit boards. It can be very economical, but somewhat difficult to achieve consistent process quality. See Conformal coating, Parylene.

Glob-top

Glob-top is a variant of conformal coating used in chip-on-board assembly (COB). It consists of a drop of specially formulated resin deposited over a semiconductor chip and its wire bonds, to provide mechanical support and exclude contaminants such as fingerprint residues which could disrupt circuit operation.

Hermetic Metal/Glass Cases: Hermetic metal packaging began life in the vacuum tube industry, where a totally leak-proof housing was essential to operation. This industry developed the glass-seal electrical feedthrough, using alloys such as Kovar to match the coefficient of expansion of the sealing glass so as to minimise mechanical stress on the critical metal-glass bond as the tube warmed up. Some later tubes used metal cases and feedthroughs, and only the insulation around the individual feedthroughs used glass. Today, glass-seal packages are used mostly in critical components and assemblies for aerospace use, where leakage must be prevented even under extreme changes in temperature, pressure, and humidity.

Hermetic Ceramic Packages: Packages consisting of a lead frame embedded in a vitreous paste layer between flat ceramic top and bottom covers are more convenient than metal/glass packages for some products, but give equivalent performance. Examples are integrated circuit chips in ceramic Dual In-line Package form, or complex hybrid assemblies of chip components on a ceramic base plate. This type of packaging can also be divided into two main types: multilayer ceramic packages (like LTCC and HTCC) and pressed ceramic packages.

Printed Circuit Assemblies: Printed circuits are primarily a technology for connecting components together, but they also provide mechanical structure. In some products, such as computer accessory boards, they're all the structure there is. This makes them part of the universe of electronic packaging.

Design Considerations

An engineer or designer must balance many objectives and practical considerations when selecting packaging methods.

- Hazards to be protected against: mechanical damage, exposure to weather and dirt, electromagnetic interference, etc.
- Heat dissipation requirements
- Tradeoffs between tooling capital cost and per-unit cost
- Tradeoffs between time to first delivery and production rate
- Availability and capability of suppliers
- User interface design and convenience

- Ease of access to internal parts when required for maintenance
- Product safety, and compliance with regulatory standards
- Aesthetics, and other marketing considerations
- Service life and reliability

Reliability Evaluation

A typical reliability qualification includes the following types of environmental stresses:

- Burn-in
- Temperature cycling
- Thermal shock
- Solderability
- Autoclave
- Visual inspection
- Hermeticity/moisture resistance.

2

Analysis of Series

Parallel and Series-parallel Circuits Excited by Independent Voltage Sources

What are "Series" and "Parallel" Circuits?

Circuits consisting of just one battery and one load resistance are very simple to analyze, but they are not often found in practical applications. Usually, we find circuits where more than two components are connected together. There are two basic ways in which to connect more than two circuit components: *series* and *parallel*. First, an example of a series circuit:

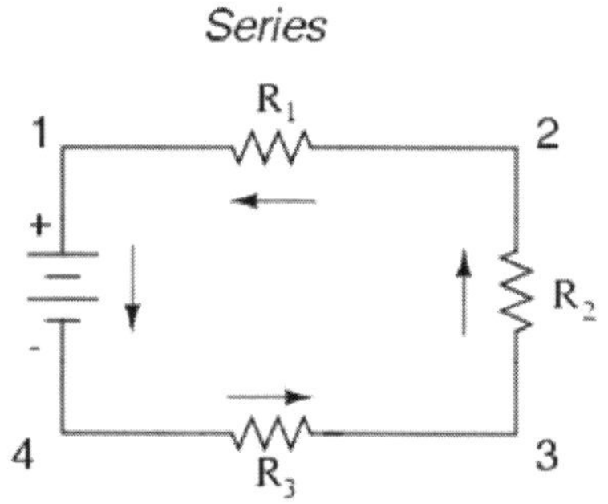

Here, we have three resistors (labelled R_1, R_2, and R_3), connected in a long chain from one terminal of the battery to the other. (It should be noted that the subscript labelling — those little numbers to the lower-right of the letter "R" — are unrelated to the resistor values in ohms. They serve only to identify one resistor from another.) The defining characteristic of a series circuit is that there is only one path for electrons to flow. In this circuit the electrons flow in a counter-clockwise direction, from point 4 to point 3 to point 2 to point 1 and back around to 4.

Now, let's look at the other type of circuit, a parallel configuration:

Parallel

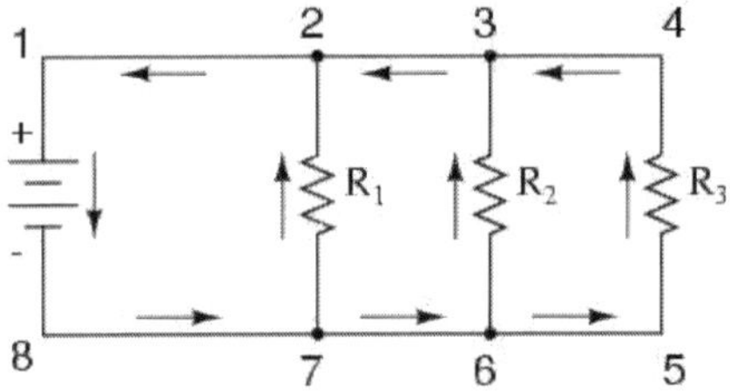

Again, we have three resistors, but this time they form more than one continuous path for electrons to flow. There's one path from 8 to 7 to 2 to 1 and back to 8 again. There's another from 8 to 7 to 6 to 3 to 2 to 1 and back to 8 again. And then there's a third path from 8 to 7 to 6 to 5 to 4 to 3 to 2 to 1 and back to 8 again. Each individual path (through R_1, R_2, and R_3) is called a *branch.*

The defining characteristic of a parallel circuit is that all components are connected between the same set of electrically common points. Looking at the schematic diagram, we see that points 1, 2, 3, and 4 are all electrically common. So are points 8, 7, 6, and 5. Note that all resistors as well as the battery are connected between these two sets of points.

And, of course, the complexity doesn't stop at simple series and parallel either! We can have circuits that are a combination of series and parallel, too:

Series-parallel

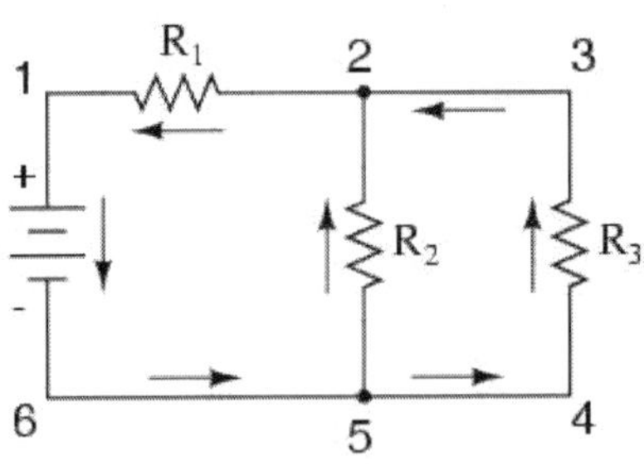

In this circuit, we have two loops for electrons to flow through: one from 6 to 5 to 2 to 1 and back to 6 again, and another from 6 to 5 to 4 to 3 to 2 to 1 and back to 6 again. Notice how both current paths go through R_1 (from point 2 to point 1). In this configuration, we'd say that R_2 and R_3 are in parallel with each other, while R_1 is in series with the parallel combination of R_2 and R_3.

This is just a preview of things to come. Don't worry! We'll explore all these circuit configurations in detail, one at a time!

The basic idea of a "series" connection is that components are connected end-to-end in a line to form a single path for electrons to flow:

Series connection

only one path for electrons to flow!

The basic idea of a "parallel" connection, on the other hand, is that all components are connected across each other's leads. In a purely parallel circuit, there are never more than two sets of electrically common points, no matter how many components are connected. There are many paths for electrons to flow, but only one voltage across all components:

Parallel connection

These points are electrically common

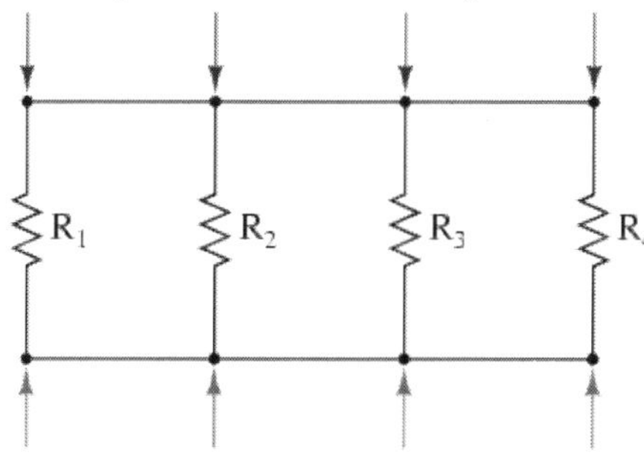

These points are electrically common

Series and parallel resistor configurations have very different electrical properties. We'll explore the properties of each configuration in the sections to come.

- In a series circuit, all components are connected end-to-end, forming a single path for electrons to flow.
- In a parallel circuit, all components are connected across each other, forming exactly two sets of electrically common points.
- A "branch" in a parallel circuit is a path for electric current formed by one of the load components (such as a resistor).

Simple Series Circuits

Let's start with a series circuit consisting of three resistors and a single battery:

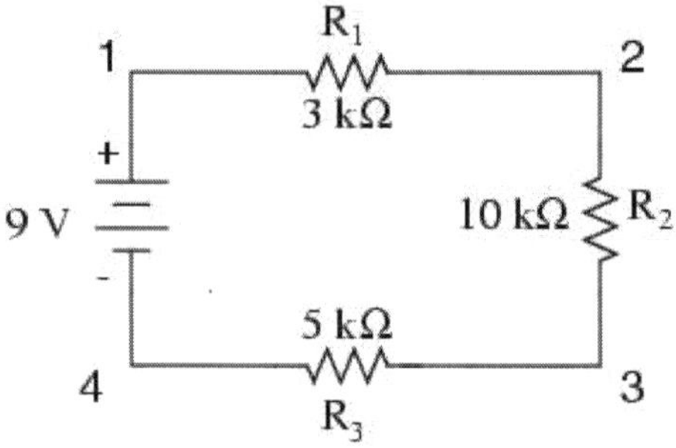

The first principle to understand about series circuits is that the amount of current is the same through any component in the circuit. This is because there is only one path for electrons to flow in a series circuit, and because free electrons flow through conductors like marbles in a tube, the rate of flow (marble speed) at any point in the circuit (tube) at any specific point in time must be equal.

From the way that the 9 volt battery is arranged, we can tell that the electrons in this circuit will flow in a counter-clockwise direction, from point 4 to 3 to 2 to 1 and back to 4. However, we have one source of voltage and three resistances. How do we use Ohm's Law here?

An important caveat to Ohm's Law is that all quantities (voltage, current, resistance, and power) must relate to each other in terms of the same two points in a circuit. For instance, with a single-battery, single-resistor circuit, we could easily calculate any quantity because they all applied to the same two points in the circuit:

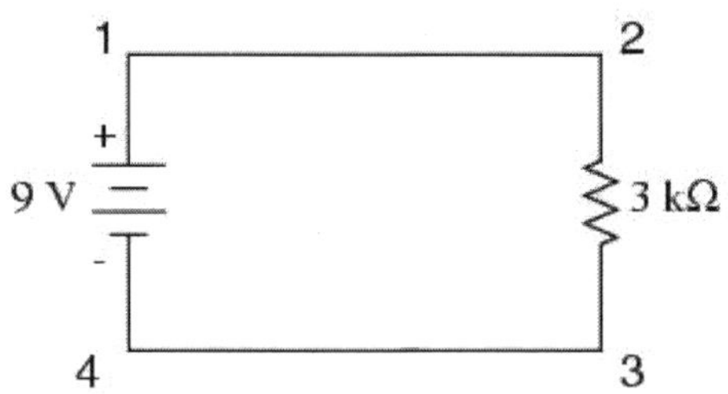

$$I = \frac{E}{R}$$

$$I = \frac{9\ volts}{3\,k\Omega} = 3\,m\Omega$$

Since points 1 and 2 are connected together with wire of negligible resistance, as are points 3 and 4, we can say that point 1 is electrically common to point 2, and that point 3 is electrically common to point 4. Since we know we have 9 volts of electromotive force between points 1 and 4 (directly across the battery), and since point 2 is common to point 1 and point 3 common to point 4, we must also have 9 volts between points 2 and 3 (directly across the resistor). Therefore, we can apply Ohm's Law (I = E/R) to the current through the resistor, because we know the voltage (E) across the resistor and the resistance (R) of that resistor. All terms (E, I, R) apply to the same two points in the circuit, to that same resistor, so we can use the Ohm's Law formula with no reservation.

However, in circuits containing more than one resistor, we must be careful in how we apply Ohm's Law. In the three-resistor example circuit below, we know that we have 9 volts between points 1 and 4, which is the amount of electromotive force trying to push electrons through the series combination of R_1, R_2, and R_3. However, we cannot take the value of 9 volts and divide it by 3k, 10k or 5k Ω to try to find a current value, because we don't know how much voltage is across any one of those resistors, individually.

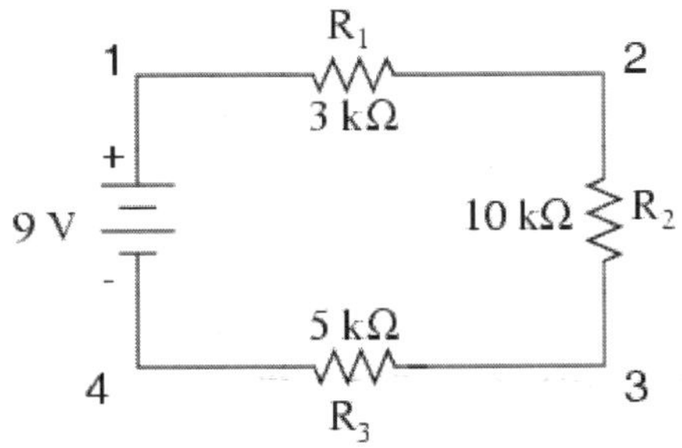

The figure of 9 volts is a *total* quantity for the whole circuit, whereas the figures of 3k, 10k, and 5k Ω are *individual* quantities for individual resistors. If we were to plug a figure for total voltage into an Ohm's Law equation with a figure for individual resistance, the result would not relate accurately to any quantity in the real circuit.

For R_1, Ohm's Law will relate the amount of voltage across R_1 with the current through R_1, given R_1's resistance, 3kΩ:

$$I_{R1} = \frac{E_{R1}}{3\,k\Omega} \qquad E_{R1} = I_{R1}(3\,k\Omega)$$

But, since we don't know the voltage across R_1 (only the total voltage supplied by the battery across the three-resistor series combination) and we don't know the current through R_1, we can't do any calculations with either formula. The same goes for R_2 and R_3: we can apply the Ohm's Law equations if and only if all terms are representative of their respective quantities between the same two points in the circuit.

So what can we do? We know the voltage of the source (9 volts) applied across the series combination of R_1, R_2, and R_3, and we know the resistances of each resistor, but since those quantities aren't in the same context, we can't use Ohm's Law to determine the circuit current. If only we knew what the *total* resistance was for the circuit: then we could calculate *total* current with our figure for *total* voltage (I=E/R).

This brings us to the second principle of series circuits: the total resistance of any series circuit is equal to the sum of the individual resistances. This should make intuitive sense: the more resistors in series that the electrons must flow through, the more difficult it will be for those electrons to flow. In the example problem, we had a 3 kΩ, 10 kΩ, and 5 kΩ resistor in series, giving us a total resistance of 18 kΩ:

$$R_{total} = R_1 + R_2 + R_3$$

$$R_{total} = 3\,k\Omega + 10\,k\Omega + 5\,k\Omega$$

$$R_{total} = 18\,k\Omega$$

In essence, we've calculated the equivalent resistance of R_1, R_2, and R_3 combined. Knowing this, we could re-draw the circuit with a single equivalent resistor representing the series combination of R_1, R_2, and R_3:

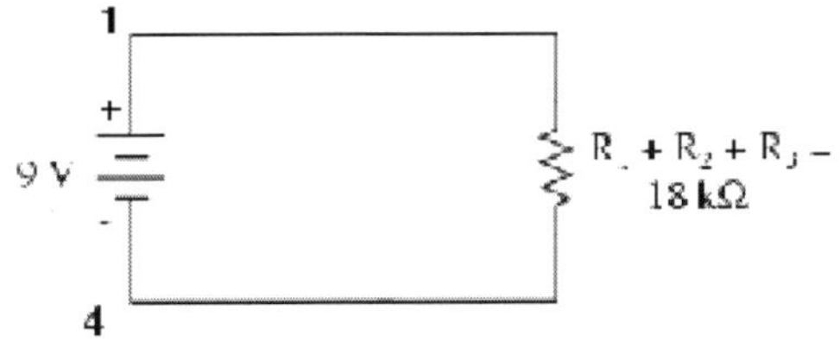

Now we have all the necessary information to calculate circuit current, because we have the voltage between points 1 and 4 (9 volts) and the resistance between points 1 and 4 (18 kΩ):

$$I_{total} = \frac{E_{total}}{R_{total}}$$

$$I_{total} = \frac{9\text{ volts}}{18\,k\Omega} = 500\,\mu A$$

Knowing that current is equal through all components of a series circuit (and we just determined the current through the battery), we can go back to our original circuit schematic and note the current through each component:

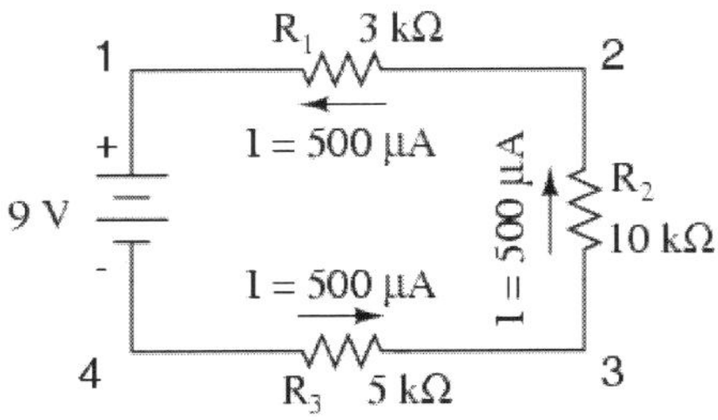

Now that we know the amount of current through each resistor, we can use Ohm's Law to determine the voltage drop across each one (applying Ohm's Law in its proper context):

$$E_{R1} = I_{RI}R_{I} \quad E_{R2} = I_{R2}R_{2} \quad E_{R3} = I_{R3}R_{3}$$

$$E_{R1} = (500\mu A)(3\,k\Omega) = 1.5V$$

$$E_{R2} = (500\mu A)(10\,k\Omega) = 5\,V$$

$$E_{R3} = (500\mu A)(5\,k\Omega) = 2.5\,V$$

Notice the voltage drops across each resistor, and how the sum of the voltage drops (1.5 + 5 + 2.5) is equal to the battery (supply) voltage: 9 volts. This is the third principle of series circuits: that the supply voltage is equal to the sum of the individual voltage drops.

However, the method we just used to analyze this simple series circuit can be streamlined for better understanding. By using a table to list all voltages, currents, and resistances in the circuit, it becomes very easy to see which of those quantities can be properly related in any Ohm's Law equation:

	R_1	R_2	R_3	Total	
E					Volts
I					Amps
R					Ohms
	↑ *Ohm's Law*	↑ *Ohm's Law*	↑ *Ohm's Law*	↑ *Ohm's Law*	

The rule with such a table is to apply Ohm's Law only to the values within each vertical column. For instance, E_{R1} only with I_{R1} and

R_1; E_{R2} only with I_{R2} and R_2; etc. You begin your analysis by filling in those elements of the table that are given to you from the beginning:

	R_1	R_2	R_3	Total	
E				**9**	Volts
I					Amps
R	**3k**	**10k**	**5k**		Ohms

As you can see from the arrangement of the data, we can't apply the 9 volts of E_T (total voltage) to any of the resistances (R_1, R_2, or R_3) in any Ohm's Law formula because they're in different columns. The 9 volts of battery voltage is *not* applied directly across R_1, R_2, or R_3. However, we can use our "rules" of series circuits to fill in blank spots on a horizontal row. In this case, we can use the series rule of resistances to determine a total resistance from the *sum* of individual resistances:

	R_1	R_2	R_3	Total	
E				9	Volts
I					Amps
R	3k	10k	5k	**18k**	Ohms

Rule of series circuits
$R_T = R_1 + R_2 + R_3$

Now, with a value for total resistance inserted into the rightmost ("Total") column, we can apply Ohm's Law of I=E/R to total voltage and total resistance to arrive at a total current of 500 μA:

	R_1	R_2	R_3	Total	
E				9	Volts
I				**500μ**	Amps
R	3k	10k	5k	18k	Ohms

Ohm's Law

Then, knowing that the current is shared equally by all components of a series circuit (another "rule" of series circuits), we can fill in the currents for each resistor from the current figure just calculated:

	R_1	R_2	R_3	Total	
E				9	Volts
I	**500µ**	**500µ**	**500µ**	**500µ**	Amps
R	3k	10k	5k	18k	Ohms

Rule of series circuits
$I_T = I_1 = I_2 = I_3$

Finally, we can use Ohm's Law to determine the voltage drop across each resistor, one column at a time:

	R_1	R_2	R_3	Total	
E	**1.5**	**5**	**2.5**	9	Volts
I	500µ	500µ	500µ	500µ	Amps
R	3k	10k	5k	18k	Ohms
	Ohm's Law	*Ohm's Law*	*Ohm's Law*		

Just for fun, we can use a computer to analyze this very same circuit automatically. It will be a good way to verify our calculations and also become more familiar with computer analysis. First, we have to describe the circuit to the computer in a format recognizable by the software. The SPICE programme we'll be using requires that all electrically unique points in a circuit be numbered, and component placement is understood by which of those numbered points, or "nodes," they share. For clarity, I numbered the four corners of our example circuit 1 through 4. SPICE, however, demands that there be a node zero somewhere in the circuit, so I'll re-draw the circuit, changing the numbering scheme slightly:

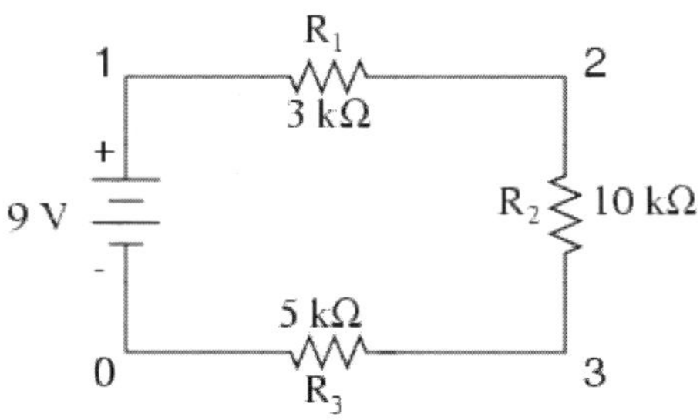

All I've done here is re-numbered the lower-left corner of the circuit 0 instead of 4. Now, I can enter several lines of text into a computer file describing the circuit in terms SPICE will understand, complete with a couple of extra lines of code directing the programme to display voltage and current data for our viewing pleasure. This computer file is known as the *netlist* in SPICE terminology:

```
series circuit
v1 1 0
r1 1 2 3k
r2 2 3 10k
r3 3 0 5k
.dc v1 9 9 1
.print dc v(1,2) v(2,3) v(3,0)
.end
```

Now, all I have to do is run the SPICE programme to process the netlist and output the results:

```
v1             v(1,2)        v(2,3)        v(3)          i(v1)
9.000E+00      1.500E+00     5.000E+00     2.500E+00     -5.000E-04
```

This printout is telling us the battery voltage is 9 volts, and the voltage drops across R_1, R_2, and R_3 are 1.5 volts, 5 volts, and 2.5 volts, respectively. Voltage drops across any component in SPICE are referenced by the node numbers the component lies between, so v(1,2) is referencing the voltage between nodes 1 and 2 in the circuit, which are the points between which R_1 is located. The order of node numbers is important: when SPICE outputs a figure for v(1,2), it regards the polarity the same way as if we were holding a voltmeter with the red test lead on node 1 and the black test lead on node 2.

We also have a display showing current (albeit with a negative value) at 0.5 milliamps, or 500 microamps. So our mathematical analysis has been vindicated by the computer. This figure appears as a negative number in the SPICE analysis, due to a quirk in the way SPICE handles current calculations.

In summary, a series circuit is defined as having only one path for electrons to flow. From this definition, three rules of series circuits follow: all components share the same current; resistances add to equal a larger, total resistance; and voltage drops add to equal a larger, total voltage. All of these rules find root in the definition of a series circuit. If you understand that definition fully, then the rules are nothing more than footnotes to the definition.

- Components in a series circuit share the same current: $I_{Total} = I_1 = I_2 = \ldots I_n$
- Total resistance in a series circuit is equal to the sum of the individual resistances: $R_{Total} = R_1 + R_2 + \ldots R_n$

- Total voltage in a series circuit is equal to the sum of the individual voltage drops: $E_{Total} = E_1 + E_2 + ... E_n$

Simple Parallel Circuits

Let's start with a parallel circuit consisting of three resistors and a single battery:

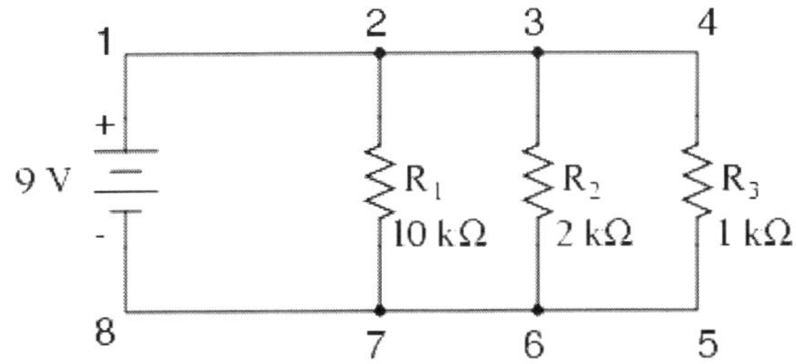

The first principle to understand about parallel circuits is that the voltage is equal across all components in the circuit. This is because there are only two sets of electrically common points in a parallel circuit, and voltage measured between sets of common points must always be the same at any given time. Therefore, in the above circuit, the voltage across R_1 is equal to the voltage across R_2 which is equal to the voltage across R_3 which is equal to the voltage across the battery. This equality of voltages can be represented in another table for our starting values:

	R_1	R_2	R_3	Total	
E	9	9	9	9	Volts
I					Amps
R	10k	2k	1k		Ohms

Just as in the case of series circuits, the same caveat for Ohm's Law applies: values for voltage, current, and resistance must be in the same context in order for the calculations to work correctly. However, in the above example circuit, we can immediately apply Ohm's Law to each resistor to find its current because we know the voltage across each resistor (9 volts) and the resistance of each resistor:

$$I_{R1} = \frac{E_{R1}}{R_1} \quad I_{R2} = \frac{E_{R2}}{R_2} \quad I_{R3} = \frac{E_{R3}}{R_3}$$

$$I_{R1} = \frac{9V}{10k\Omega} = 0.9mA$$

$$I_{R2} = \frac{9V}{2k\Omega} = 4.5mA$$

$$I_{R3} = \frac{9V}{1k\Omega} = 9mA$$

	R_1	R_2	R_3	Total	
E	9	9	9	9	Volts
I	**0.9m**	**4.5m**	**9m**		Amps
R	10k	2k	1k		Ohms
	↑ Ohm's Law	↑ Ohm's Law	↑ Ohm's Law		

At this point we still don't know what the total current or total resistance for this parallel circuit is, so we can't apply Ohm's Law to the rightmost ("Total") column. However, if we think carefully about what is happening it should become apparent that the total current must equal the sum of all individual resistor ("branch") currents:

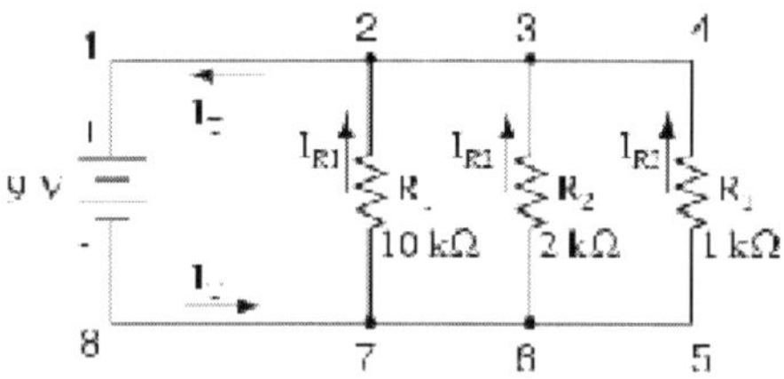

As the total current exits the negative (-) battery terminal at point 8 and travels through the circuit, some of the flow splits off at point 7 to go up through R_1, some more splits off at point 6 to go up through R_2, and the remainder goes up through R_3. Like a river branching into several smaller streams, the combined flow rates of all streams must equal the flow rate of the whole river.

The same thing is encountered where the currents through R_1, R_2, and R_3 join to flow back to the positive terminal of the battery (+) toward point 1: the flow of electrons from point 2 to point 1 must equal the sum of the (branch) currents through R_1, R_2, and R_3.

This is the second principle of parallel circuits: the total circuit current is equal to the sum of the individual branch currents. Using this principle, we can fill in the I_T spot on our table with the sum of I_{R1}, I_{R2}, and I_{R3}:

	R_1	R_2	R_3	Total	
E	9	9	9	9	Volts
I	0.9m	4.5m	9m	**14.4m**	Amps ←
R	10k	2k	1k		Ohms

Rule of parallel circuits
$I_{total} = I_1 + I_2 + I_3$

Finally, applying Ohm's Law to the rightmost ("Total") column, we can calculate the total circuit resistance:

	R_1	R_2	R_3	Total	
E	9	9	9	9	Volts
I	0.9m	4.5m	9m	14.4m	Amps
R	10k	2k	1k	**625**	Ohms

$$R_{total} = \frac{E_{total}}{I_{total}} = \frac{9\text{ V}}{14.4\text{ mA}} = 625\ \Omega$$

↑ *Ohm's Law*

Please note something very important here. The total circuit resistance is only 625 Ω: *less* than any one of the individual resistors. In the series circuit, where the total resistance was the sum of the individual resistances, the total was bound to be *greater* than any one of the resistors individually.

Here in the parallel circuit, however, the opposite is true: we say that the individual resistances *diminish* rather than *add* to make the total. This principle completes our triad of "rules" for parallel circuits, just as series circuits were found to have three rules for voltage, current, and resistance. Mathematically, the relationship between total resistance and individual resistances in a parallel circuit looks like this:

$$R_{total} = \frac{1}{\frac{1}{R_1} + \frac{1}{R_2} + \frac{1}{R_3}}$$

The same basic form of equation works for *any* number of resistors connected together in parallel, just add as many 1/R terms on the denominator of the fraction as needed to accommodate all parallel resistors in the circuit.

Just as with the series circuit, we can use computer analysis to double-check our calculations. First, of course, we have to describe our example circuit to the computer in terms it can understand. I'll start by re-drawing the circuit:

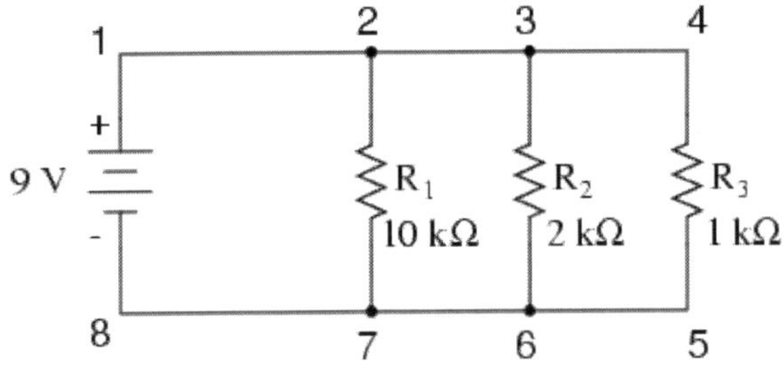

Once again we find that the original numbering scheme used to identify points in the circuit will have to be altered for the benefit of SPICE. In SPICE, all electrically common points must share identical node numbers. This is how SPICE knows what's connected to what, and how. In a simple parallel circuit, all points are electrically common in one of two sets of points. For our example circuit, the wire connecting the tops of all the components will have one node number and the wire connecting the bottoms of the components will have the other. Staying true to the convention of including zero as a node number, I choose the numbers 0 and 1:

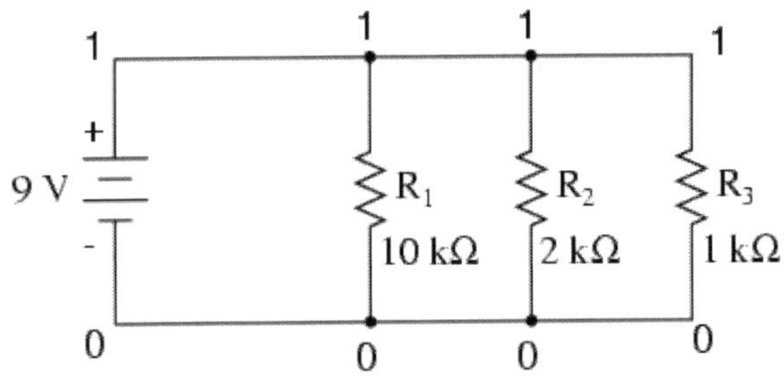

An example like this makes the rationale of node numbers in SPICE fairly clear to understand. By having all components share common sets of numbers, the computer "knows" they're all connected in parallel with each other.

In order to display branch currents in SPICE, we need to insert zero-voltage sources in line (in series) with each resistor, and then reference our current measurements to those sources. For whatever reason, the creators of the SPICE programme made it so that current could only be calculated *through* a voltage source. This is a somewhat annoying demand of the SPICE simulation programme. With each of these "dummy" voltage sources added, some new node numbers must be created to connect them to their respective branch resistors:

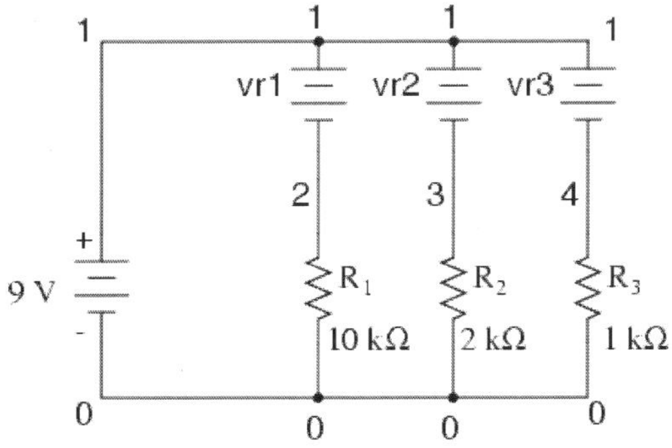

NOTE: vr1, vr2, and vr3 are all "dummy" voltage sources with values of 0 volts each!!

The dummy voltage sources are all set at 0 volts so as to have no impact on the operation of the circuit. The circuit description file, or *netlist*, looks like this:

```
Parallel circuit
v1 1 0
r1 2 0 10k
r2 3 0 2k
r3 4 0 1k
vr1 1 2 dc 0
vr2 1 3 dc 0
vr3 1 4 dc 0
.dc v1 9 9 1
.print dc v(2,0) v(3,0) v(4,0)
.print dc i(vr1) i(vr2) i(vr3)
.end
```

Running the computer analysis, we get these results (I've annotated the printout with descriptive labels):

```
v1             v(2)          v(3)          v(4)
9.000E+00      9.000E+00     9.000E+00     9.000E+00
battery        R1 voltage    R2 voltage    R3 voltage
voltage

v1             i(vr1)        i(vr2)        i(vr3)
9.000E+00      9.000E-04     4.500E-03     9.000E-03
battery        R1 current    R2 current    R3 current
voltage
```

These values do indeed match those calculated through Ohm's Law earlier: 0.9 mA for I_{R1}, 4.5 mA for I_{R2}, and 9 mA for I_{R3}. Being connected in parallel, of course, all resistors have the same voltage dropped across them (9 volts, same as the battery).

In summary, a parallel circuit is defined as one where all components are connected between the same set of electrically common points. Another way of saying this is that all components are connected across each other's terminals. From this definition, three rules of parallel circuits follow: all components share the same voltage; resistances diminish to equal a smaller, total resistance; and branch currents add to equal a larger, total current. Just as in the case of series circuits, all of these rules find root in the definition of a parallel circuit. If you understand that definition fully, then the rules are nothing more than footnotes to the definition.

- Components in a parallel circuit share the same voltage: $E_{Total} = E_1 = E_2 = \ldots E_n$
- Total resistance in a parallel circuit is *less* than any of the individual resistances: $R_{Total} = 1 / (1/R_1 + 1/R_2 + \ldots 1/R_n)$
- Total current in a parallel circuit is equal to the sum of the individual branch currents: $I_{Total} = I_1 + I_2 + \ldots I_n$.

Conductance

When students first see the parallel resistance equation, the natural question to ask is, "Where did *that* thing come from?" It is truly an odd piece of arithmetic, and its origin deserves a good explanation.

Resistance, by definition, is the measure of *friction* a component presents to the flow of electrons through it. Resistance is symbolized by the capital letter "R" and is measured in the unit of "ohm." However, we can also think of this electrical property in terms of its inverse: how *easy* it is for electrons to flow through a component, rather than how *difficult*. If *resistance* is the word we use to symbolize the measure of how difficult it is for electrons to flow, then a good word to express how easy it is for electrons to flow would be *conductance*.

Mathematically, conductance is the reciprocal, or inverse, of resistance:

$$\text{Conductance} = \frac{1}{\text{Resistance}}$$

The greater the resistance, the less the conductance, and vice versa. This should make intuitive sense, resistance and conductance being opposite ways to denote the same essential electrical property. If two components' resistances are compared and it is found that component "A" has one-half the resistance of component "B," then we could alternatively express this relationship by saying that component "A" is *twice* as conductive as component "B." If component "A" has but one-third the resistance of component "B," then we could say it is *three times* more conductive than component "B," and so on.

Carrying this idea further, a symbol and unit were created to represent conductance. The symbol is the capital letter "G" and the unit is the *mho*, which is "ohm" spelled backwards (and you didn't think electronics engineers had any sense of humor!). Despite its appropriateness, the unit of the mho was replaced in later years by the unit of *siemens* (abbreviated by the capital letter "S"). This decision to change unit names is reminiscent of the change from the temperature unit of degrees *Centigrade* to degrees *Celsius*, or the change from the unit of frequency *c.p.s.* (cycles per second) to *Hertz*. If you're looking for a pattern here, Siemens, Celsius, and Hertz are all surnames of famous scientists, the names of which, sadly, tell us less about the nature of the units than the units' original designations.

The unit of siemens is never expressed without the last letter "s." In other words, there is no such thing as a unit of "siemen" as there is in the case of the "ohm" or the "mho." The reason for this is the proper spelling of the respective scientists' surnames. The unit for electrical resistance was named after someone named "Ohm," whereas the unit for electrical conductance was named after someone named "Siemens," therefore it would be improper to "singularize" the latter unit as its final "s" does not denote plurality.

Back to our parallel circuit example, we should be able to see that multiple paths (branches) for current reduces total resistance for the whole circuit, as electrons are able to flow easier through the whole network of multiple branches than through any one of those branch resistances alone. In terms of *resistance*, additional branches result in a lesser total (current meets with less opposition). In terms of *conductance*, however, additional branches results in a greater total (electrons flow with greater conductance):

Total parallel resistance is *less* than any one of the individual branch resistances because parallel resistors resist less together than they would separately:

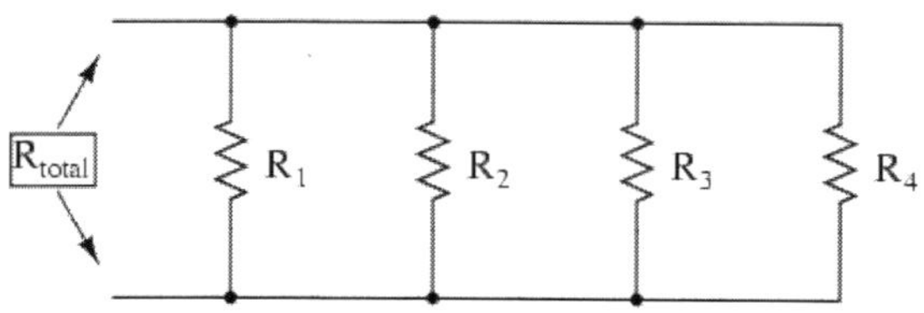

R_{total} is less than R_1, R_2, R_3, or R_4 individually

Total parallel conductance is *greater* than any of the individual branch conductances because parallel resistors conduct better together than they would separately:

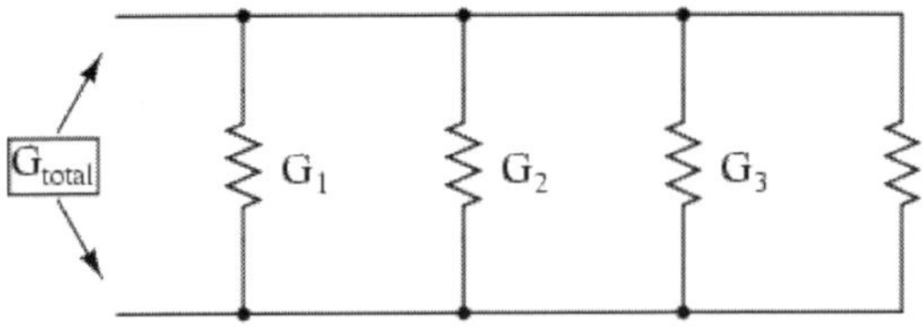

G_{total} is greater than G_1, G_2, G_3, or G_4 individually

To be more precise, the total conductance in a parallel circuit is equal to the sum of the individual conductances:

$$G_{total} = G_1 + G_2 + G_3 + G_4$$

If we know that conductance is nothing more than the mathematical reciprocal (1/x) of resistance, we can translate each term of the above formula into resistance by substituting the reciprocal of each respective conductance:

$$\frac{1}{R_{total}} = \frac{1}{R_1} + \frac{1}{R_2} + \frac{1}{R_3} + \frac{1}{R_4}$$

Solving the above equation for total resistance (instead of the reciprocal of total resistance), we can invert (reciprocate) both sides of the equation:

$$\frac{1}{R_{total}} = \frac{1}{\frac{1}{R_1} + \frac{1}{R_2} + \frac{1}{R_3} + \frac{1}{R_4}}$$

So, we arrive at our cryptic resistance formula at last! Conductance (G) is seldom used as a practical measurement, and so the above formula is a common one to see in the analysis of parallel circuits.

- Conductance is the opposite of resistance: the measure of how *easy* it is for electrons to flow through something.
- Conductance is symbolized with the letter "G" and is measured in units of *mhos* or *Siemens*.
- Mathematically, conductance equals the reciprocal of resistance: G = 1/R

Power Calculations

When calculating the power dissipation of resistive components, use any one of the three power equations to derive the answer from values of voltage, current, and/or resistance pertaining to each component:

Power equations

$$P = IE \quad P = \frac{E^2}{R} \quad P = I^2R$$

This is easily managed by adding another row to our familiar table of voltages, currents, and resistances:

	R_1	R_2	R_3	Total	
E					Volts
I					Amps
R					Ohms
P					Watts

Power for any particular table column can be found by the appropriate Ohm's Law equation (*appropriate* based on what figures are present for E, I, and R in that column).

An interesting rule for total power versus individual power is that it is additive for *any* configuration of circuit: series, parallel, series/parallel, or otherwise. Power is a measure of rate of work, and since power dissipated *must* equal the total power applied by the source(s) (as per the Law of Conservation of Energy in physics), circuit configuration has no effect on the mathematics.

- Power is additive in *any* configuration of resistive circuit: $P_{Total} = P_1 + P_2 + \ldots P_n$

Correct Use of Ohm's Law

One of the most common mistakes made by beginning electronics students in their application of Ohm's Laws is mixing the contexts of voltage, current, and resistance. In other words, a student might mistakenly use a value for I through one resistor and the value for E across a set of interconnected resistors, thinking that they'll arrive at the resistance of that one resistor. Not so! Remember this important rule: The variables used in Ohm's Law equations must be *common* to the same two points in the circuit under consideration. I cannot overemphasize this rule. This is especially important in series-parallel combination circuits where nearby components may have different values for both voltage drop *and* current.

When using Ohm's Law to calculate a variable pertaining to a single component, be sure the voltage you're referencing is solely across that single component and the current you're referencing is solely through that single component and the resistance you're referencing is solely for that single component. Likewise, when calculating a variable pertaining to a set of components in a circuit, be sure that the voltage, current, and resistance values are specific to that complete set of components only! A good way to remember this is to pay close attention to the *two points* terminating the component or set of components being analyzed, making sure that the voltage in question is across those two points, that the current in question is the electron flow from one of those points all the way to the other point, that the resistance in question is the equivalent of a single resistor between those two points, and that the power in question is the total power dissipated by all components between those two points.

The "table" method presented for both series and parallel circuits in this chapter is a good way to keep the context of Ohm's Law correct for any kind of circuit configuration. In a table like the one shown below, you are only allowed to apply an Ohm's Law equation for the values of a single *vertical* column at a time:

	R_1	R_2	R_3	Total	
E					Volts
I					Amps
R					Ohms
P					Watts
	↑ Ohm's Law	↑ Ohm's Law	↑ Ohm's Law	↑ Ohm's Law	

Deriving values *horizontally* across columns is allowable as per the principles of series and parallel circuits:

For series circuits:

	R_1	R_2	R_3	Total	
E	———	———	———	→ Add	Volts
I	———	———	———	→ Equal	Amps
R	———	———	———	→ Add	Ohms
P	———	———	———	→ Add	Watts

$$E_{total} = E_1 + E_2 + E_3$$

$$I_{total} = I_1 = I_2 = I_3$$

$$R_{total} = R_1 + R_2 + R_3$$

$$P_{total} = P_1 + P_2 + P_3$$

For parallel circuits:

	R_1	R_2	R_3	Total	
E	→	→	→	Equal	Volts
I	→	→	→	Add	Amps
R	→	→	→	Diminish	Ohms
P	→	→	→	Add	Watts

$$E_{total} = E_1 = E_2 = E_3$$

$$I_{total} = I_1 + I_2 + I_3$$

$$R_{total} = \frac{1}{\frac{1}{R_1} + \frac{1}{R_2} + \frac{1}{R_3}}$$

$$P_{total} = P_1 + P_2 + P_3$$

Not only does the "table" method simplify the management of all relevant quantities, it also facilitates cross-checking of answers by making it easy to solve for the original unknown variables through other methods, or by working backwards to solve for the initially given values from your solutions.

For example, if you have just solved for all unknown voltages, currents, and resistances in a circuit, you can check your work by adding a row at the bottom for power calculations on each resistor, seeing whether or not all the individual power values add up to the total power.

If not, then you must have made a mistake somewhere! While this technique of "cross-checking" your work is nothing new, using the table to arrange all the data for the cross-check(s) results in a minimum of confusion.

- Apply Ohm's Law to vertical columns in the table.
- Apply rules of series/parallel to horizontal rows in the table.
- Check your calculations by working "backwards" to try to arrive at originally given values (from your first calculated answers), or by solving for a quantity using more than one method (from different given values).

Component Failure Analysis

The job of a technician frequently entails "troubleshooting" (locating and correcting a problem) in malfunctioning circuits. Good troubleshooting is a demanding and rewarding effort, requiring a thorough understanding of the basic concepts, the ability to formulate hypotheses (proposed explanations of an effect), the ability to judge the value of different hypotheses based on their probability (how likely one particular cause may be over another), and a sense of creativity in applying a solution to rectify the problem.

While it is possible to distill these skills into a scientific methodology, most practiced troubleshooters would agree that troubleshooting involves a touch of art, and that it can take years of experience to fully develop this art.

An essential skill to have is a ready and intuitive understanding of how component faults affect circuits in different configurations. We will explore some of the effects of component faults in both series and parallel circuits here, then to a greater degree at the end of the "Series-Parallel Combination Circuits" chapter.

Let's start with a simple series circuit:

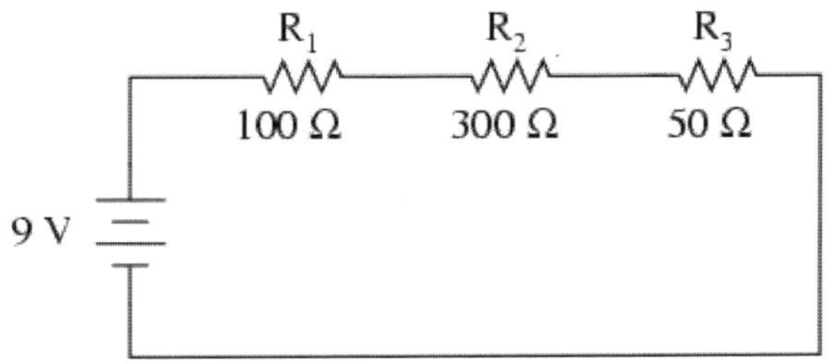

With all components in this circuit functioning at their proper values, we can mathematically determine all currents and voltage drops:

	R_1	R_2	R_3	Total	
E	2	6	1	9	Volts
I	20m	20m	20m	20m	Amps
R	100	300	50	450	Ohms

Now let us suppose that R_2 fails shorted. *Shorted* means that the resistor now acts like a straight piece of wire, with little or no resistance. The circuit will behave as though a "jumper" wire were connected across R_2 (in case you were wondering, "jumper wire" is a common term for a temporary wire connection in a circuit). What causes the shorted condition of R_2 is no matter to us in this example; we only care about its effect upon the circuit:

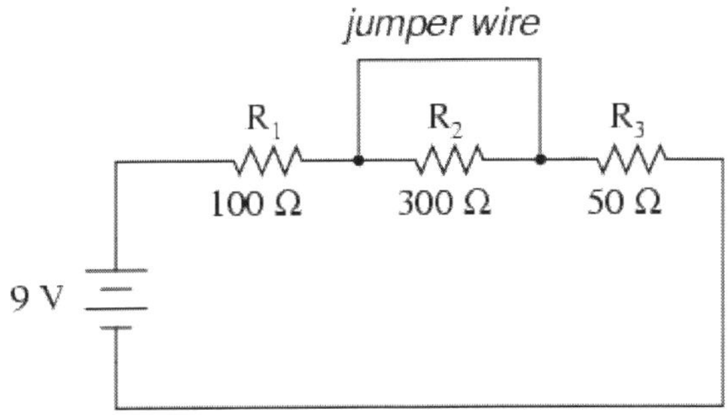

With R_2 shorted, either by a jumper wire or by an internal resistor failure, the total circuit resistance will *decrease*. Since the voltage output by the battery is a constant (at least in our ideal simulation here), a decrease in total circuit resistance means that total circuit current *must increase*:

	R_1	R_2	R_3	Total	
E	6	0	3	9	Volts
I	60m	60m	60m	60m	Amps
R	100	0	50	150	Ohms

↑ *Shorted resistor* (under R_2)

As the circuit current increases from 20 milliamps to 60 milliamps, the voltage drops across R_1 and R_3 (which haven't changed resistances) increase as well, so that the two resistors are dropping the whole 9 volts. R_2, being bypassed by the very low resistance of the jumper wire, is effectively eliminated from the circuit, the resistance from one lead to the other having been reduced to zero. Thus, the voltage drop across R_2, even with the increased total current, is zero volts.

On the other hand, if R_2 were to fail "open" — resistance increasing to nearly infinite levels — it would also create wide-reaching effects in the rest of the circuit:

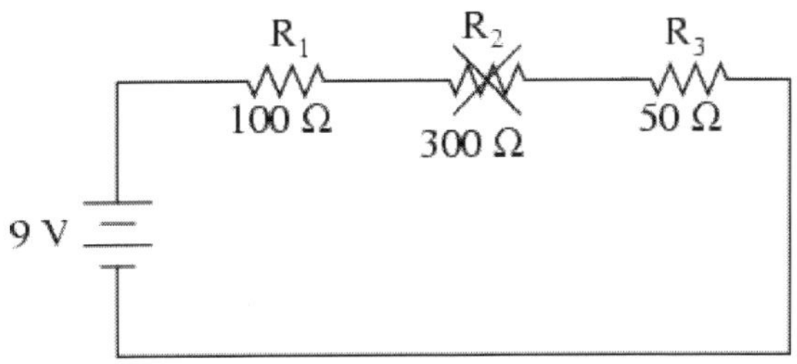

	R_1	R_2	R_3	Total	
E	0	9	0	9	Volts
I	0	0	0	0	Amps
R	100	∞	50	∞	Ohms

↑ *Open resistor* (R_2)

With R_2 at infinite resistance and total resistance being the sum of all individual resistances in a series circuit, the total current decreases to zero. With zero circuit current, there is no electron flow to produce voltage drops across R_1 or R_3. R_2, on the other hand, will manifest the full supply voltage across its terminals.

We can apply the same before/after analysis technique to parallel circuits as well. First, we determine what a "healthy" parallel circuit should behave like.

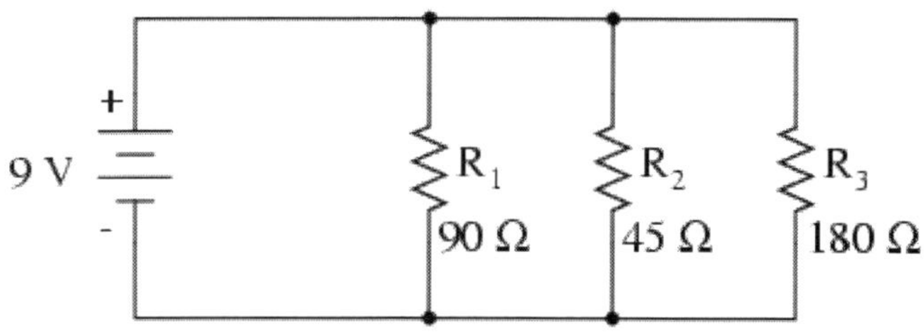

	R_1	R_2	R_3	Total	
E	9	9	9	9	Volts
I	100m	200m	50m	350m	Amps
R	90	45	180	25.714	Ohms

Supposing that R_2 opens in this parallel circuit, here's what the effects will be:

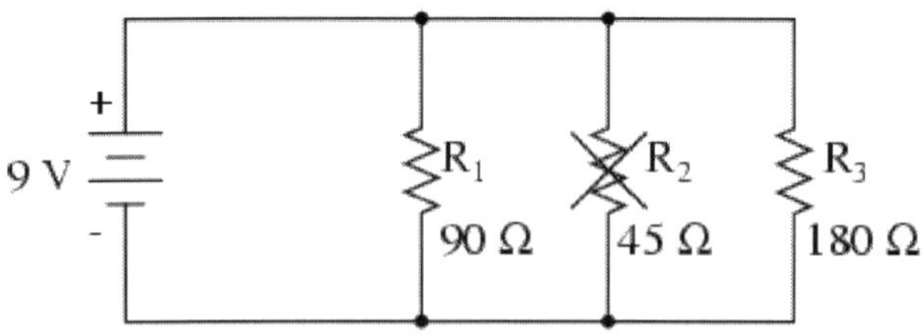

	R_1	R_2	R_3	Total	
E	9	9	9	9	Volts
I	100m	0	50m	150m	Amps
R	90	∞	180	60	Ohms

↑ *Open resistor* (R_2)

Notice that in this parallel circuit, an open branch only affects the current through that branch and the circuit's total current. Total voltage — being shared equally across all components in a parallel circuit, will be the same for all resistors. Due to the fact that the voltage source's tendency is to hold voltage *constant*, its voltage will not change, and being in parallel with all the resistors, it will hold all the resistors' voltages the same as they were before: 9 volts. Being that voltage is the only common parameter in a parallel circuit, and the other resistors haven't changed resistance value, their respective branch currents remain unchanged.

This is what happens in a household lamp circuit: all lamps get their operating voltage from power wiring arranged in a parallel fashion. Turning one lamp on and off (one branch in that parallel circuit closing and opening) doesn't affect the operation of other lamps in the room, only the current in that one lamp (branch circuit) and the total current powering all the lamps in the room:

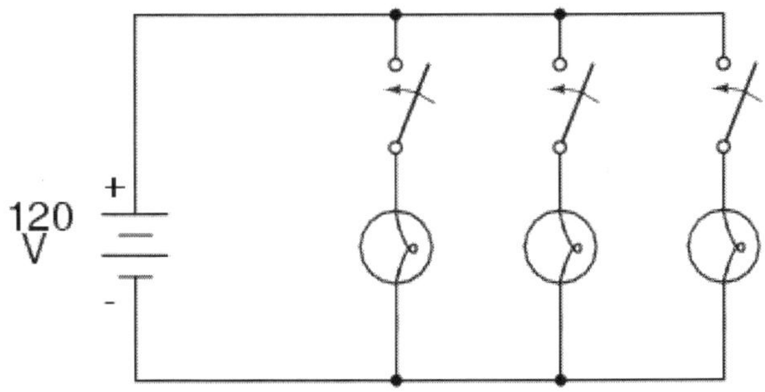

In an ideal case (with perfect voltage sources and zero-resistance connecting wire), shorted resistors in a simple parallel circuit will also have no effect on what's happening in other branches of the circuit. In real life, the effect is not quite the same, and we'll see why in the following example:

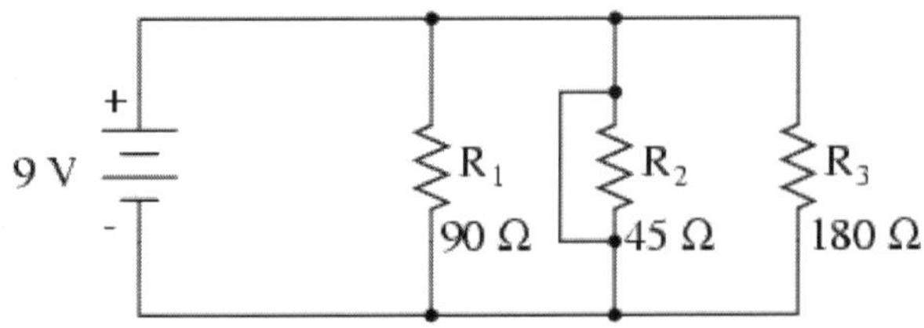

R_2 "shorted" with a jumper wire

	R_1	R_2	R_3	Total	
E	9	9	9	9	Volts
I	100m	∞	50m	∞	Amps
R	90	0	180	0	Ohms

↑ *Shorted resistor* (under the R_2 column)

A shorted resistor (resistance of 0 Ω) would theoretically draw infinite current from any finite source of voltage (I=E/0). In this case, the zero resistance of R_2 decreases the circuit total resistance to zero Ω as well, increasing total current to a value of infinity. As long as the voltage source holds steady at 9 volts, however, the other branch currents (I_{R1} and I_{R3}) will remain unchanged.

The critical assumption in this "perfect" scheme, however, is that the voltage supply will hold steady at its rated voltage while supplying an infinite amount of current to a short-circuit load. This is simply not realistic. Even if the short has a small amount of resistance (as opposed to absolutely zero resistance), no *real* voltage source could arbitrarily supply a huge overload current and maintain steady voltage at the same time. This is primarily due to the internal resistance intrinsic to all electrical power sources, stemming from the inescapable physical properties of the materials they're constructed of:

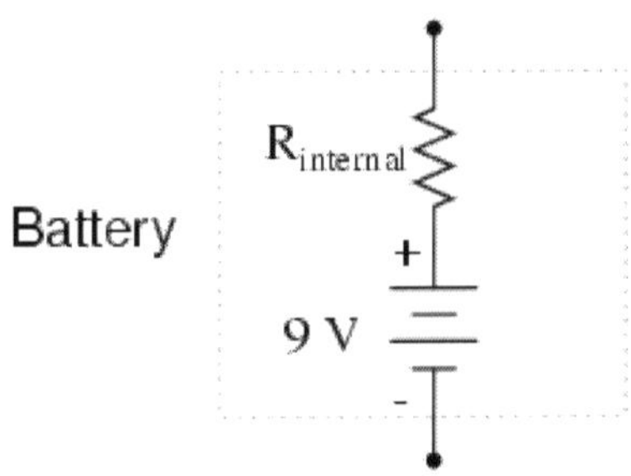

These internal resistances, small as they may be, turn our simple parallel circuit into a series-parallel combination circuit. Usually, the internal resistances of voltage sources are low enough that they can be safely ignored, but when high currents resulting from shorted components are encountered, their effects become very noticeable. In this case, a shorted R_2 would result in almost all the voltage being dropped across the internal resistance of the battery, with almost no voltage left over for resistors R_1, R_2, and R_3:

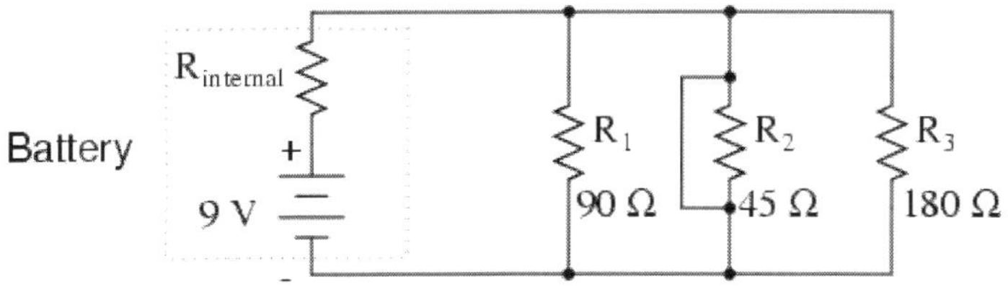

R_2 "shorted" with a jumper wire

	R_1	R_2	R_3	Total	
E	low	low	low	low	Volts
I	low	high	low	high	Amps
R	90	0	180	0	Ohms

↑ *Shorted resistor* (under R_2)

↑ *Supply voltage decrease due to voltage drop across internal resistance* (under Total)

Suffice it to say, intentional direct short-circuits across the terminals of any voltage source is a bad idea. Even if the resulting high current (heat, flashes, sparks) causes no harm to people nearby, the voltage source will likely sustain damage, unless it has been specifically designed to handle short-circuits, which most voltage sources are not.

Eventually in this book I will lead you through the analysis of circuits *without the use of any numbers*, that is, analyzing the effects of component failure in a circuit without knowing exactly how many volts the battery produces, how many ohms of resistance is in each resistor, etc. This section serves as an introductory step to that kind of analysis.

Whereas the normal application of Ohm's Law and the rules of series and parallel circuits is performed with numerical quantities (*"quantitative"*), this new kind of analysis without precise numerical figures is something I like to call *qualitative* analysis. In other words, we will be analyzing the *qualities* of the effects in a circuit rather than the precise *quantities*. The result, for you, will be a much deeper intuitive understanding of electric circuit operation.

- To determine what would happen in a circuit if a component fails, re-draw that circuit with the equivalent resistance of the failed component in place and re-calculate all values.
- The ability to intuitively determine what will happen to a circuit with any given component fault is a *crucial* skill for any electronics troubleshooter to develop. The best way to learn is to experiment with circuit calculations and real-life circuits, paying close attention to what changes with a fault, what remains the same, and *why*!
- A *shorted* component is one whose resistance has dramatically decreased.
- An *open* component is one whose resistance has dramatically increased. For the record, resistors tend to fail open more often than fail shorted, and they almost never fail unless physically or electrically overstressed (physically abused or overheated).

Building Simple Resistor Circuits

In the course of learning about electricity, you will want to construct your own circuits using resistors and batteries. Some options are available in this matter of circuit assembly, some easier than others. In this section, I will explore a couple of fabrication techniques that will not only help you build the circuits shown in this chapter, but also more advanced circuits.

If all we wish to construct is a simple single-battery, single-resistor circuit, we may easily use *alligator clip* jumper wires like this:

Jumper wires with "alligator" style spring clips at each end provide a safe and convenient method of electrically joining components together.

If we wanted to build a simple series circuit with one battery and three resistors, the same "point-to-point" construction technique using jumper wires could be applied:

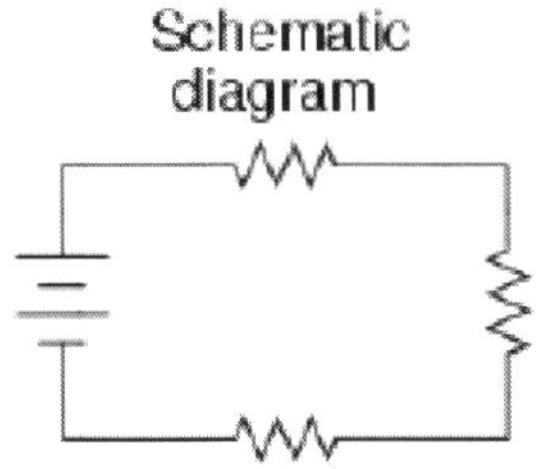

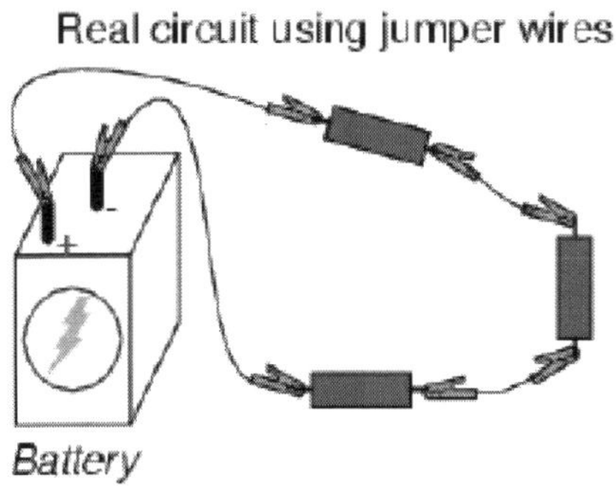

This technique, however, proves impractical for circuits much more complex than this, due to the awkwardness of the jumper wires and the physical fragility of their connections. A more common method of temporary construction for the hobbyist is the *solderless breadboard*, a device made of plastic with hundreds of spring-loaded connection sockets joining the inserted ends of components and/or 22-gauge solid wire pieces. A photograph of a real breadboard is shown here, followed by an illustration showing a simple series circuit constructed on one:

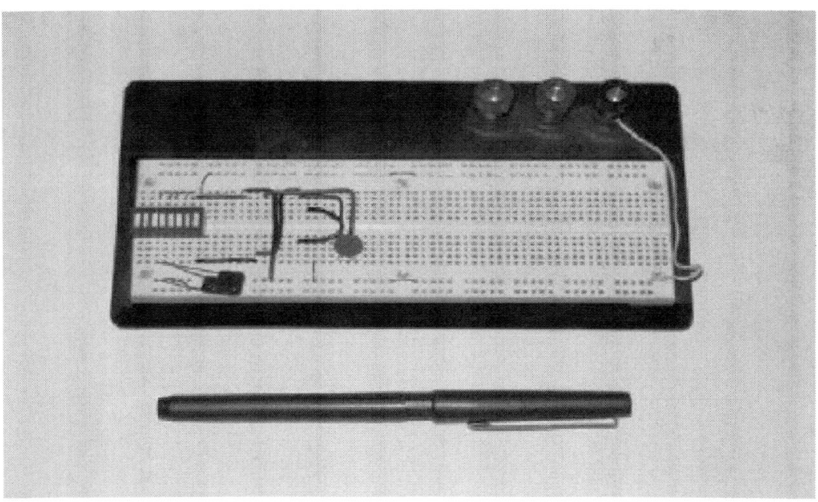

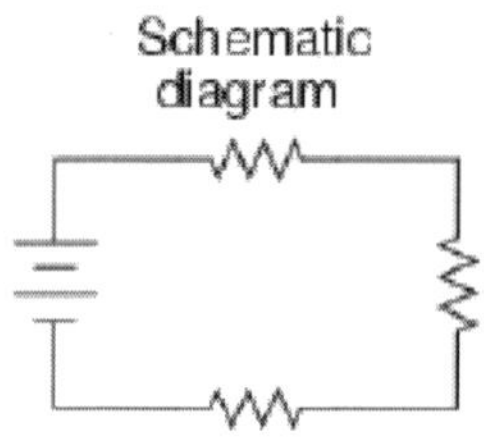

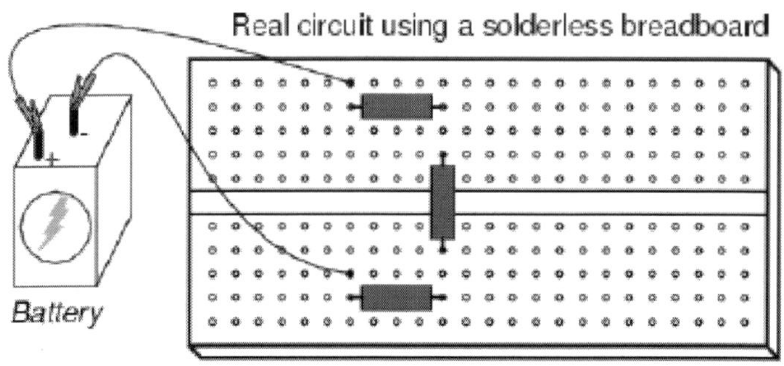

Underneath each hole in the breadboard face is a metal spring clip, designed to grasp any inserted wire or component lead. These metal spring clips are joined underneath the breadboard face, making connections between inserted leads. The connection pattern joins every five holes along a vertical column (as shown with the long axis of the breadboard situated horizontally):

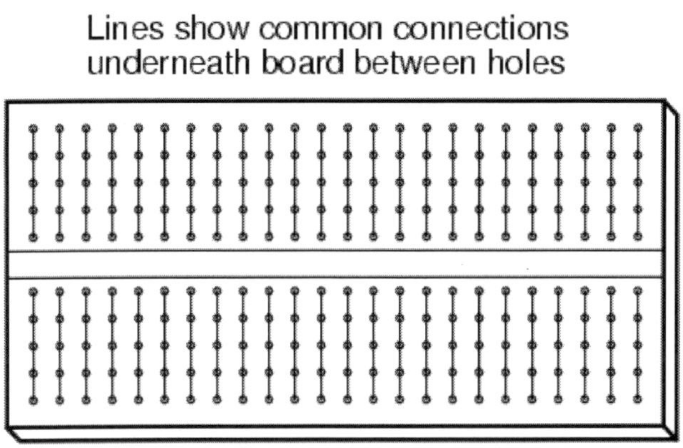

Thus, when a wire or component lead is inserted into a hole on the breadboard, there are four more holes in that column providing potential connection points to other wires and/or component leads. The result is an extremely flexible platform for constructing temporary circuits. For example, the three-resistor circuit just shown could also be built on a breadboard like this:

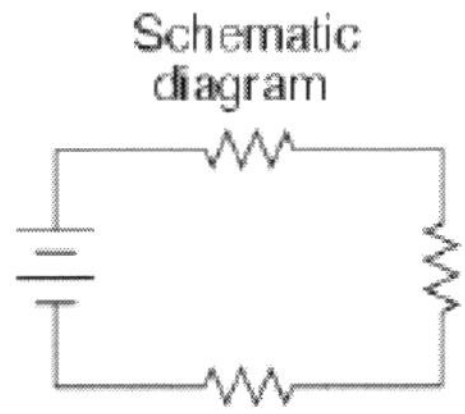

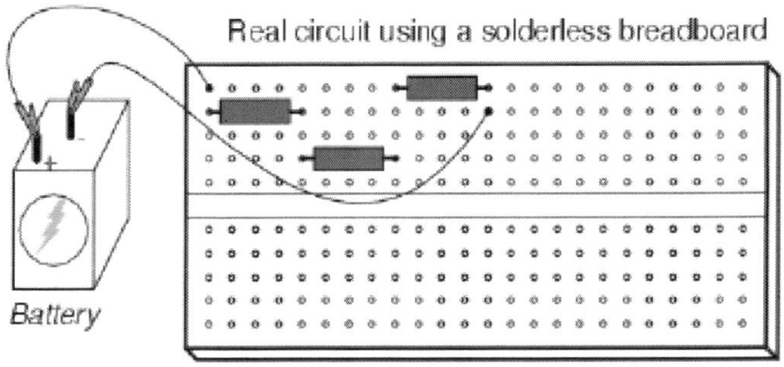

A parallel circuit is also easy to construct on a solderless breadboard:

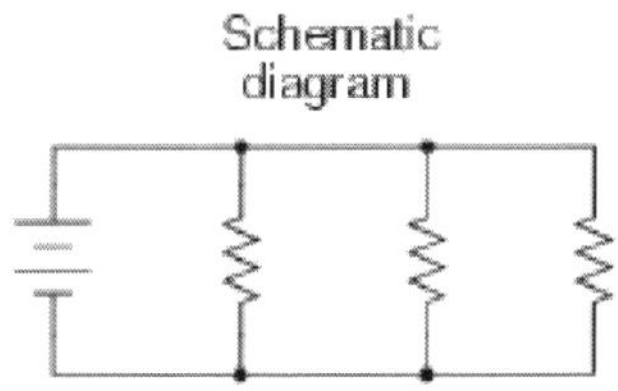

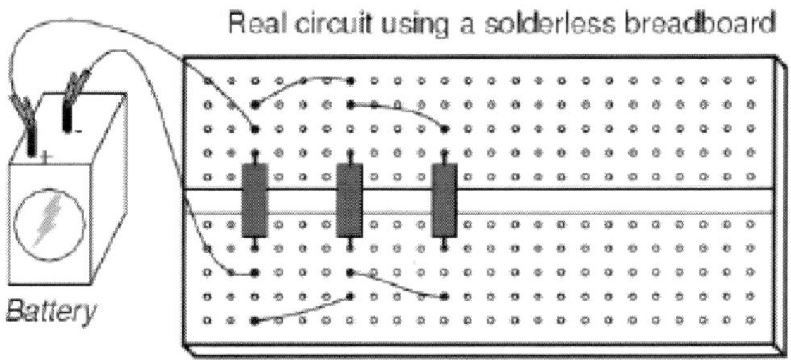

Breadboards have their limitations, though. First and foremost, they are intended for *temporary* construction only. If you pick up a breadboard, turn it upside-down, and shake it, any components plugged into it are sure to loosen, and may fall out of their respective holes. Also, breadboards are limited to fairly low-current (less than 1 amp) circuits. Those spring clips have a small contact area, and thus cannot support high currents without excessive heating.

For greater permanence, one might wish to choose soldering or wire-wrapping. These techniques involve fastening the components and wires to some structure providing a secure mechanical location (such as a phenolic or fibreglass board with holes drilled in it, much like a breadboard without the intrinsic spring-clip connections), and then attaching wires to the secured component leads. Soldering is a form of low-temperature welding, using a tin/lead or tin/silver alloy that melts to and electrically bonds copper objects. Wire ends soldered to component leads or to small, copper ring "pads" bonded on the surface of the circuit board serve to connect the components together. In wire wrapping, a small-gauge wire is tightly wrapped around component leads rather than soldered to leads or copper pads, the tension of the wrapped wire providing a sound mechanical and electrical junction to connect components together.

An example of a *printed circuit board*, or *PCB*, intended for hobbyist use is shown in this photograph:

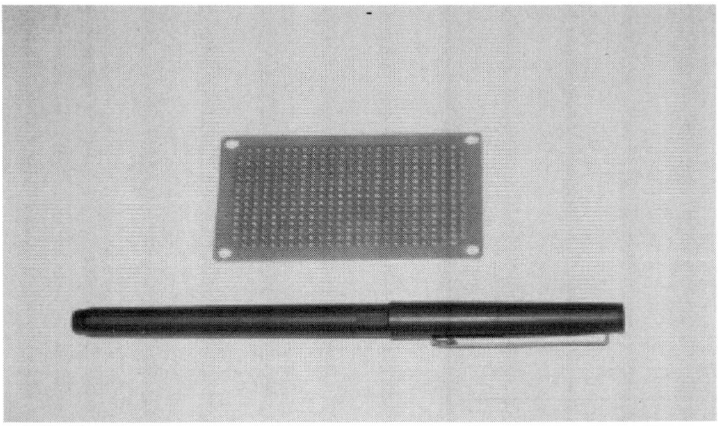

This board appears copper-side-up: the side where all the soldering is done. Each hole is ringed with a small layer of copper metal for bonding to the solder. All holes are independent of each other on this particular board, unlike the holes on a solderless breadboard which are connected together in groups of five. Printed circuit boards with the same 5-hole connection pattern as breadboards can be purchased and used for hobby circuit construction, though.

Production printed circuit boards have *traces* of copper laid down on the phenolic or fibreglass substrate material to form pre-engineered connection pathways which function as wires in a circuit. An example of such a board is shown here, this unit actually a "power supply" circuit designed to take 120 volt alternating current (AC) power from a household wall socket and transform it into low-voltage direct current (DC). A resistor appears on this board, the fifth component counting up from the bottom, located in the middle-right area of the board.

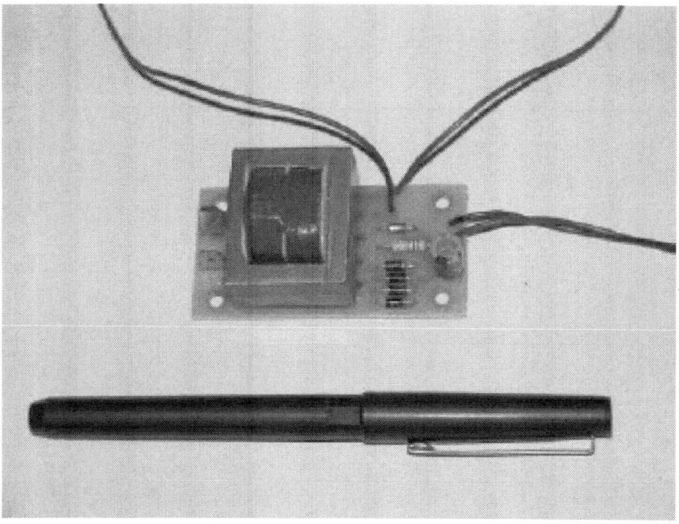

A view of this board's underside reveals the copper "traces" connecting components together, as well as the silver-coloured deposits of solder bonding the component leads to those traces:

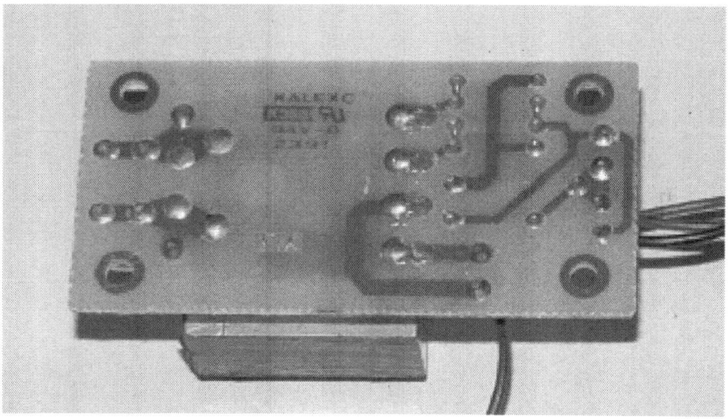

A soldered or wire-wrapped circuit is considered permanent: that is, it is unlikely to fall apart accidently. However, these construction techniques are sometimes considered *too* permanent. If anyone wishes to replace a component or change the circuit in any substantial way, they must invest a fair amount of time undoing the connections. Also, both soldering and wire-wrapping require specialized tools which may not be immediately available.

An alternative construction technique used throughout the industrial world is that of the *terminal strip*. Terminal strips, alternatively called *barrier strips* or *terminal blocks*, are comprised of a length of nonconducting material with several small bars of metal embedded within. Each metal bar has at least one machine screw or other fastener under which a wire or component lead may be secured. Multiple wires fastened by one screw are made electrically common to each other, as are wires fastened to multiple screws on the same bar. The following photograph shows one style of terminal strip, with a few wires attached.

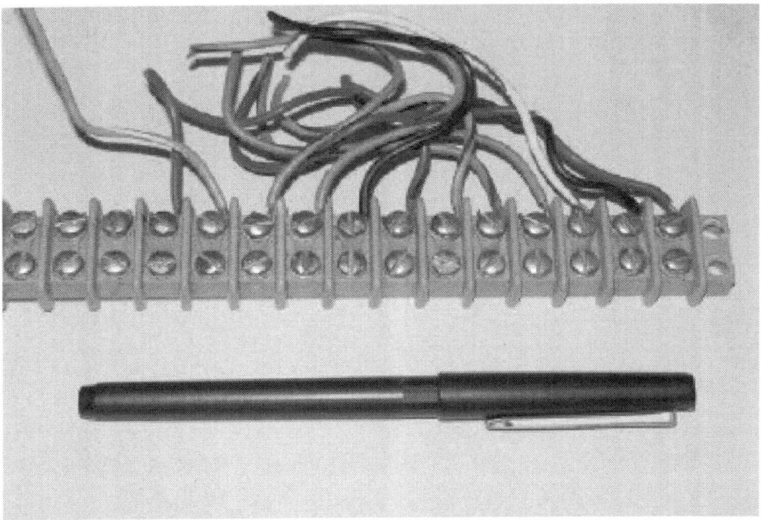

Another, smaller terminal strip is shown in this next photograph. This type, sometimes referred to as a "European" style, has recessed screws to help prevent accidental shorting between terminals by a screwdriver or other metal object:

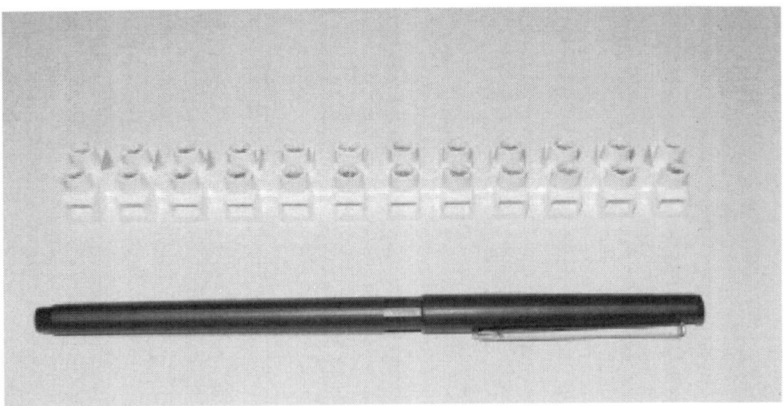

In the following illustration, a single-battery, three-resistor circuit is shown constructed on a terminal strip:

Series circuit constructed on a terminal strip

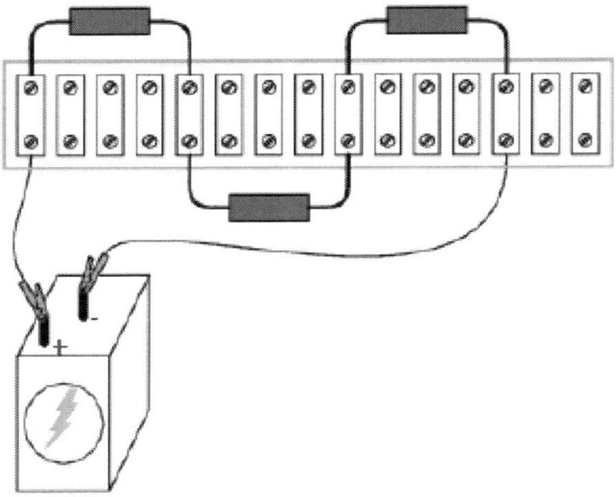

If the terminal strip uses machine screws to hold the component and wire ends, nothing but a screwdriver is needed to secure new connections or break old connections.

Some terminal strips use spring-loaded clips — similar to a breadboard's except for increased ruggedness — engaged and disengaged using a screwdriver as a push tool (no twisting involved). The electrical connections established by a terminal strip are quite robust, and are considered suitable for both permanent and temporary construction.

One of the essential skills for anyone interested in electricity and electronics is to be able to "translate" a schematic diagram to a real circuit layout where the components may not be oriented the same way.

Schematic diagrams are usually drawn for maximum readability (excepting those few noteworthy examples sketched to create maximum confusion!), but practical circuit construction often demands a different component orientation.

Building simple circuits on terminal strips is one way to develop the spatial-reasoning skill of "stretching" wires to make the same connection paths. Consider the case of a single-battery, three-resistor parallel circuit constructed on a terminal strip:

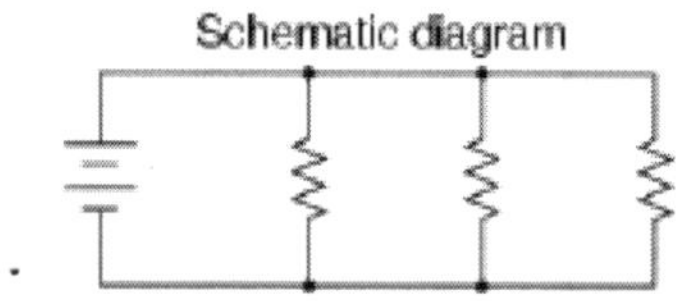

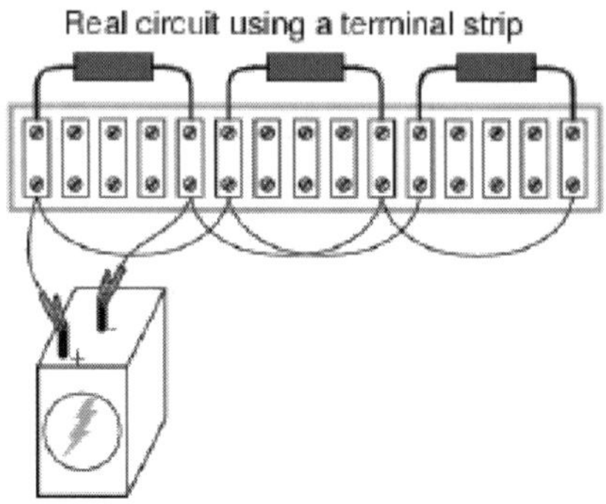

Progressing from a nice, neat, schematic diagram to the real circuit — especially when the resistors to be connected are physically arranged in a *linear* fashion on the terminal strip — is not obvious to many, so I'll outline the process step-by-step. First, start with the clean schematic diagram and all components secured to the terminal strip, with no connecting wires:

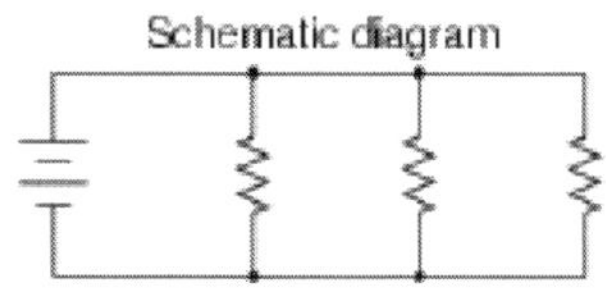

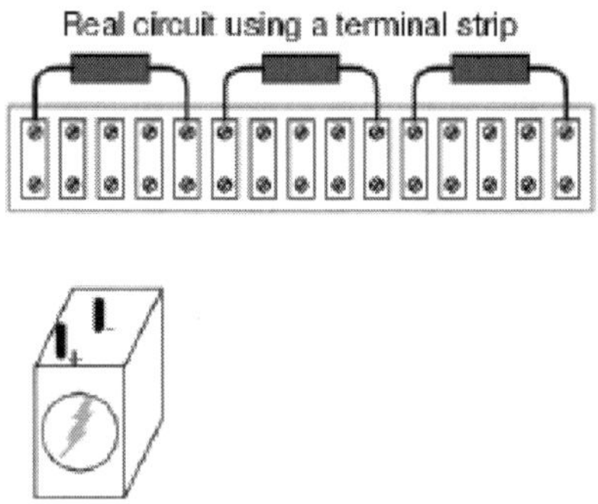

Next, trace the wire connection from one side of the battery to the first component in the schematic, securing a connecting wire between the same two points on the real circuit. I find it helpful to over-draw the schematic's wire with another line to indicate what connections I've made in real life:

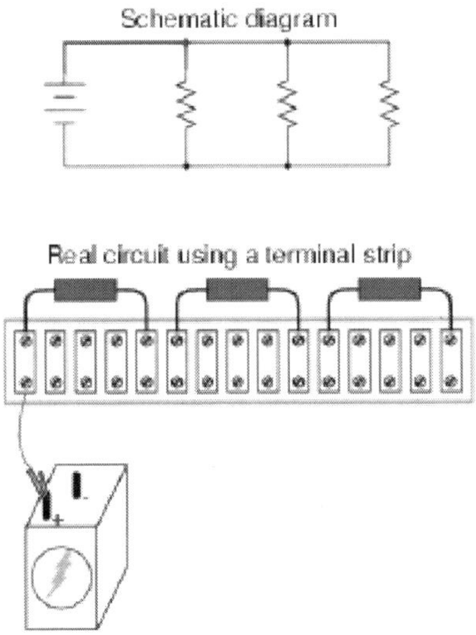

Continue this process, wire by wire, until all connections in the schematic diagram have been accounted for. It might be helpful to regard common wires in a SPICE-like fashion: make all connections to a common wire in the circuit as one step, making sure each and every component with a connection to that wire actually has a connection to that wire before proceeding to the next. For the next step, I'll show how the top sides of the remaining two resistors are connected together, being common with the wire secured in the previous step:

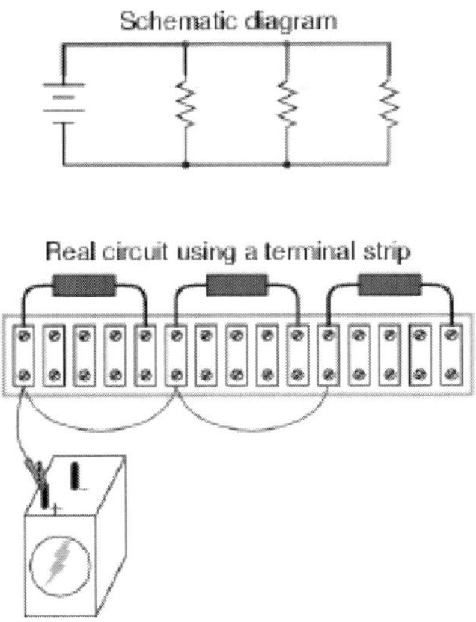

With the top sides of all resistors (as shown in the schematic) connected together, and to the battery's positive (+) terminal, all we have to do now is connect the bottom sides together and to the other side of the battery:

Schematic diagram

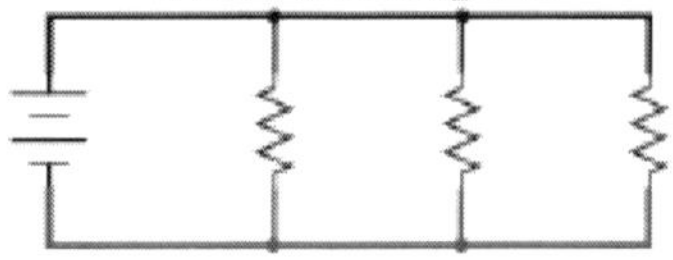

Real circuit using a terminal strip

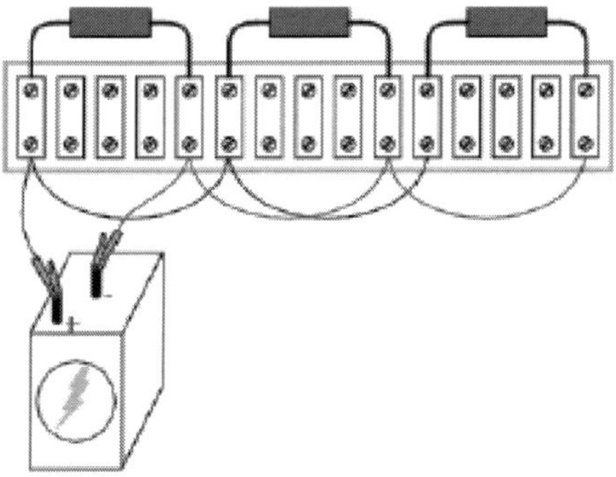

Typically in industry, all wires are labelled with number tags, and electrically common wires bear the same tag number, just as they do in a SPICE simulation. In this case, we could label the wires 1 and 2:

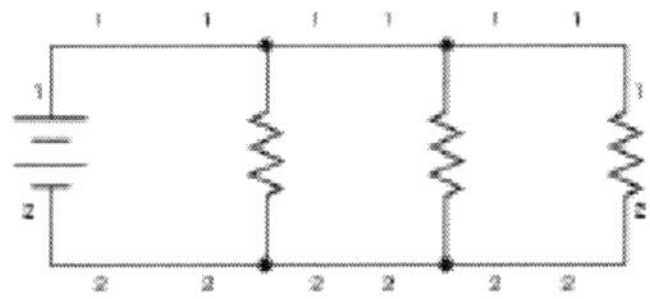

Common wire numbers representing electrically common points

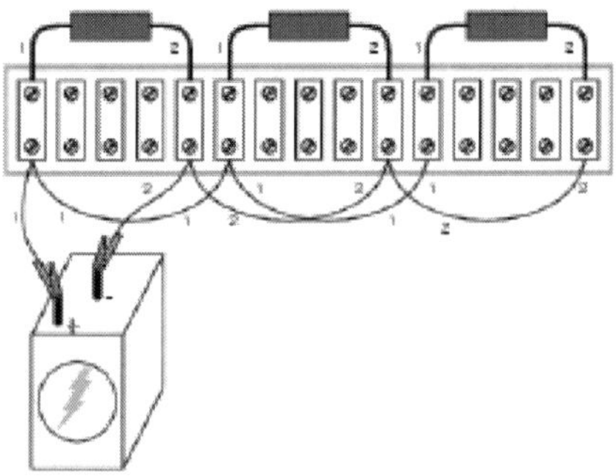

Another industrial convention is to modify the schematic diagram slightly so as to indicate actual wire connection points on the terminal strip. This demands a labelling system for the strip itself: a "TB" number (terminal block number) for the strip, followed by another number representing each metal bar on the strip.

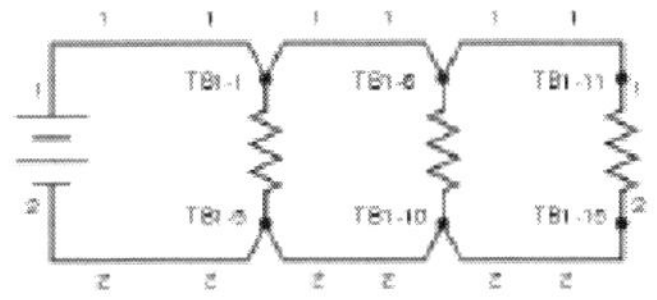

Terminal strip bars labeled and connection points referenced in diagram

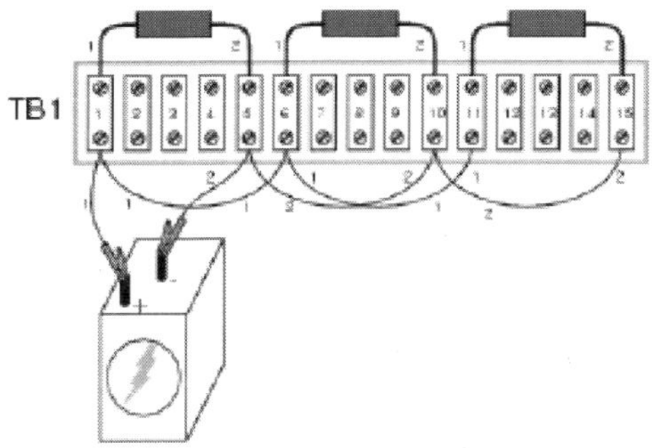

This way, the schematic may be used as a "map" to locate points in a real circuit, regardless of how tangled and complex the connecting wiring may appear to the eyes. This may seem excessive for the simple, three-resistor circuit shown here, but such detail is absolutely necessary for construction and maintenance of large circuits, especially when those circuits may span a great physical distance, using more than one terminal strip located in more than one panel or box.

Power and Energy

In physics, power is the rate at which energy is transferred, used, or transformed. The unit of power is the joule per second (J/s), known as the watt (in honour of James Watt, the eighteenth-century developer of the steam engine). For example, the rate at which a light bulb transforms electrical energy into heat and light is measured in watts—the more wattage, the more power, or equivalently the more electrical energy is used per unit time.

Energy transfer can be used to do work, so power is also the rate at which this work is performed. The same amount of work is done when carrying a load up a flight of stairs whether the person carrying it walks or runs, but more power is expended during the running because the work is done in a shorter amount of time. The output power of an electric motor is the product of the torque the motor generates and the angular velocity of its output shaft.

The power expended to move a vehicle is the product of the traction force of the wheels and the velocity of the vehicle.

The integral of power over time defines the work done. Because this integral depends on the trajectory of the point of application of the force and torque, this calculation of work is said to be path dependent.

Units

Figure: *Ansel Adams photograph of electrical wires of the Boulder Dam Power Units, 1941–1942*

The dimension of power is energy divided by time. The SI unit of power is the watt (W), which is equal to one joule per second. Other units of power include ergs per second (erg/s), horsepower (hp), metric horsepower (Pferdestärke (PS) or cheval vapeur, CV), and foot-pounds per minute. One horsepower is equivalent to 33,000 foot-pounds per minute, or the power required to lift 550 pounds by one foot in one second, and is equivalent to about 746 watts. Other units include dBm, a relative logarithmic measure with 1 milliwatt as reference; (food) calories per hour (often referred to as kilocalories per hour); Btu per hour (Btu/h); and tons of refrigeration (12,000 Btu/h).

Average Power

As a simple example, burning a kilogram of coal releases much more energy than does detonating a kilogram of TNT, but because the TNT reaction releases energy much more quickly, it delivers far more power than the coal. If ΔW is the amount of work performed during a period of time of duration Δt, the average power P_{avg} over that period is given by the formula

$$P_{avg} = \frac{\Delta W}{\Delta t}.$$

It is the average amount of work done or energy converted per unit of time. The average power is often simply called "power" when the context makes it clear.

The instantaneous power is then the limiting value of the average power as the time interval Δt approaches zero.

$$P = \lim_{\Delta t \to 0} P_{avg} = \lim_{\Delta t \to 0} \frac{\Delta W}{\Delta t} = \frac{dW}{dt}.$$

In the case of constant power P, the amount of work performed during a period of duration T is given by:

$$W = PT.$$

In the context of energy conversion, it is more customary to use the symbol E rather than W.

Mechanical Power

Power in mechanical systems is the combination of forces and movement. In particular, power is the product of a force on an object and the object's velocity, or the product of a torque on a shaft and the shaft's angular velocity.

Mechanical power is also described as the time derivative of work. In mechanics, the work done by a force F on an object that travels along a curve C is given by the line integral:

$$W_C = \int_C \mathbf{F} \cdot \mathrm{d}\mathbf{x}$$

Which, when the path is a straight line, can also be written as:

$$\int \mathbf{F} \cdot \mathbf{v} dt,$$

where x defines the path C and v is the velocity along this path. Applying the gradient theorem to the first equation (and remembering that force is the negative of the gradient of the potential energy) yields:

$$W_C = U(B) - U(A)$$

Where A and B are the beginning and end of the path along which the work was done.

Thus the power developed along a path is the time derivative of this:

$$P(t) = \frac{\mathrm{d}U(B)}{\mathrm{d}t} - \frac{\mathrm{d}U(A)}{\mathrm{d}t}$$

In one dimension and with a constant velocity, this can be simplified to:

$$P(t) = F \cdot v.$$

In rotational systems, power is the product of the torque τ and angular velocity ω,

$$P(t) = \boldsymbol{\tau} \cdot \boldsymbol{\omega},$$

where ω measured in radians per second.

In fluid power systems such as hydraulic actuators, power is given by

$$P(t) = pQ,$$

where p is pressure in pascals, or N/m^2 and Q is volumetric flow rate in m^3/s in SI units.

Mechanical Advantage

If a mechanical system has no losses then the input power must equal the output power. This provides a simple formula for the mechanical advantage of the system.

Let the input power to a device be a force F_A acting on a point that moves with velocity v_A and the output power be a force F_B acts on a point that moves with velocity v_B. If there are no losses in the system, then

$$P = F_A v_A = F_B v_B,$$

and the mechanical advantage of the system is given by

$$\mathrm{MA} = \frac{F_B}{F_A} = \frac{v_A}{v_B}.$$

A similar relationship is obtained for rotating systems, where T_A and ω_A are the torque and angular velocity of the input and T_B and ω_B are the torque and angular velocity of the output. If there are no losses in the system, then

$$P = T_A\omega_A = T_B\omega_B,$$

which yields the mechanical advantage

$$\text{MA} = \frac{T_B}{T_A} = \frac{\omega_A}{\omega_B}.$$

These relations are important because they define the maximum performance of a device in terms of velocity ratios determined by its physical dimensions.

Power in Optics

In optics, or radiometry, the term *power* sometimes refers to radiant flux, the average rate of energy transport by electromagnetic radiation, measured in watts. In other contexts, it refers to optical power, the ability of a lens or other optical device to focus light. It is measured in dioptres (inverse metres), and equals the inverse of the focal length of the optical device.

Electric Power

Electric power is the rate at which electric energy is transferred by an electric circuit. The SI unit of power is the watt, one joule per second.

Electric power is usually produced by electric generators, but can also be supplied by chemical sources such as electric batteries. Electric power is generally supplied to businesses and homes by the electric power industry. Electric power is usually sold by the kilowatt hour (3.6 MJ) which is the product of power in kilowatts multiplied by running time in hours. Electric utilities measure power using an electricity metre, which keeps a running total of the electric energy delivered to a customer.

Definition

Electric power, like mechanical power, is the rate of doing work, measured in watts, and represented by the letter P. The term *wattage* is used colloquially to mean "electric power in watts." The electric power in watts produced by an electric current I consisting of a charge of Q coulombs every t seconds passing through an electric potential (voltage) difference of V is

$$P = \text{work done per unit time} = \frac{QV}{t} = IV$$

where

Q is electric charge in coulombs

t is time in seconds

I is electric current in amperes

V is electric potential or voltage in volts

Electric power is equal to work unit.

Explanation

Electric power is transformed to other forms of power when electric charges move through an electric potential (voltage) difference, which occurs in electrical components in electric circuits. When electric charges move through a potential difference from a high voltage to a low voltage, the energy in the potential is converted to kinetic energy of the charges, which perform work on the device. Devices in which this occurs are called *passive* devices or *loads*; they consume electric power, converting it to other forms such as mechanical work, heat, light, etc. Examples are electrical appliances, such as light bulbs, electric motors, and electric heaters.

If the charges are forced to move by an outside force in the direction from a lower potential to a higher, work is being done *on* the charges, so power is transferred to the electric current from some other type of energy, such as mechanical energy or chemical energy. Devices in which this occurs are called *active* devices or *power sources*; sources of electric current, such as electric generators and batteries.

Passive Sign Sonvention

In electronics, which deals with more passive than active devices, electric power consumed in a device is defined to have a positive sign, while power produced by a device is defined to have a negative sign. This is called the *passive sign convention*.

Resistive Circuits

In the case of resistive (Ohmic, or linear) loads, Joule's law can be combined with Ohm's law ($V = I \cdot R$) to produce alternative expressions for the dissipated power:

$$P = I^2 R = \frac{V^2}{R},$$

where R is the electrical resistance.

Alternating Current

In alternating current circuits, energy storage elements such as inductance and capacitance may result in periodic reversals of the direction of energy flow. The portion of power flow that, averaged over a complete cycle of the AC waveform, results in net transfer of energy in one direction is known as real power (also referred to as active power). That portion of power flow due to stored energy, that returns to the source in each cycle, is known as reactive power. The real power P in watts consumed by a device is given by

$$P = \frac{1}{2} V_p I_p \cos\theta = V_{rms} I_{rms} \cos\theta$$

where

V_p is the peak voltage in volts

I_p is the peak current in amperes

V_{rms} is the root-mean-square voltage in volts

I_{rms} is the root-mean-square current in amperes

θ is the phase angle between the current and voltage sine waves

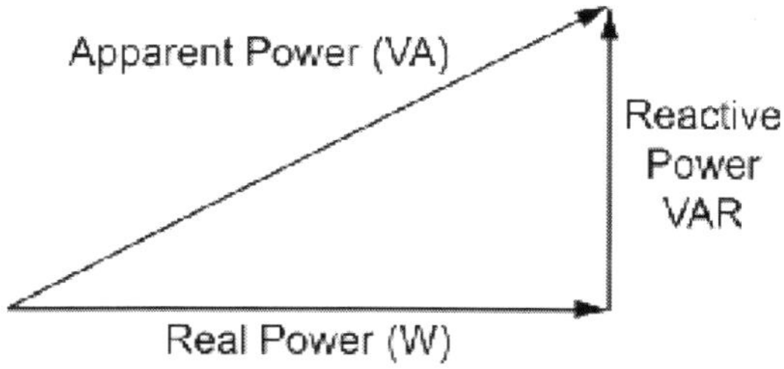

Figure: *Power triangle: The components of AC power*

The relationship between real power, reactive power and apparent power can be expressed by representing the quantities as vectors. Real power is represented as a horizontal vector and reactive power is represented as a vertical vector. The apparent power vector is the hypotenuse of a right triangle formed by connecting the real and reactive power vectors. This representation is often called the *power triangle.* Using the Pythagorean Theorem, the relationship among real, reactive and apparent power is:

$$(\text{apparent power})^2 = (\text{real power})^2 + (\text{reactive power})^2$$

Real and reactive powers can also be calculated directly from the apparent power, when the current and voltage are both sinusoids with a known phase angle θ between them:

$$(\text{real power}) = (\text{apparent power})\cos(\theta)$$

$$(\text{reactive power}) = (\text{apparent power})\sin(\theta)$$

The ratio of real power to apparent power is called power factor and is a number always between 0 and 1. Where the currents and voltages have non-sinusoidal forms, power factor is generalized to include the effects of distortion.

Electromagnetic Fields

Electrical power flows wherever electric and magnetic fields exist together and fluctuate in the same place. The simplest example of this is in electrical circuits, as the preceding section showed. In the general case, however, the simple equation $P = IV$ must be replaced by a more complex calculation, the integral of the cross-product of the electrical and magnetic field vectors over a specified area, thus:

$$P = \int_S (\mathbf{E} \times \mathbf{H}) \cdot \mathbf{dA}.$$

The result is a scalar since it is the *surface integral* of the *Poynting vector*.

Electric Power Supply

Electricity Generation

The fundamental principles of electricity generation were discovered during the 1820s and early 1830s by the British scientist Michael Faraday. His basic method is still used today: electricity is generated by the movement of a loop of wire, or disc of copper between the poles of a magnet. For electric utilities, it is the first process in the delivery of electricity to consumers. The other processes, electricity transmission, distribution, and electrical power storage and recovery using pumped-storage methods are normally carried out by the electric power industry. Electricity is most often generated at a power station by electromechanical generators, primarily driven by heat engines fuelled by chemical combustion or nuclear fission but also by other means such as the kinetic energy of flowing water and wind. There are many other technologies that can be and are used to generate electricity such as solar photovoltaics and geothermal power.

Battery Power

A battery is a device consisting of one or more electrochemical cells that convert stored chemical energy into electrical energy. Since the invention of the first battery (or "voltaic pile") in 1800 by Alessandro Volta and especially since the technically improved Daniell cell in 1836, batteries have become a common power source for many household and industrial applications. According to a 2005 estimate, the worldwide battery industry generates US$48 billion in sales each year, with 6% annual growth.

There are two types of batteries: primary batteries (disposable batteries), which are designed to be used once and discarded, and secondary batteries (rechargeable batteries), which are designed to be recharged and used multiple times. Batteries come in many sizes, from miniature cells used to power hearing aids and wristwatches to battery banks the size of rooms that provide standby power for telephone exchanges and computer data centres.

Electric Power Industry

The electric power industry provides the production and delivery of power, in sufficient quantities to areas that need electricity, through a grid connection. The grid distributes electrical energy to customers. Electric power is generated by central power stations or by distributed generation. Many households and businesses need access to electricity, especially in developed nations, the demand being scarcer in developing nations. Demand for electricity is derived from the requirement for electricity in order to operate domestic appliances, office equipment, industrial machinery and provide sufficient energy for both domestic and commercial lighting, heating, cooking and industrial processes. Because of this aspect of the industry, it is viewed as a public utility as infrastructure.

Peak Power and Duty Cycle

In the case of a periodic signal $s(t)$ of period T, like a train of identical pulses, the instantaneous power $p(t) = |s(t)|^2$ is also a periodic function of period T. The *peak power* is simply defined by:

$$P_0 = \max[p(t)].$$

The peak power is not always readily measurable, however, and the measurement of the average power P_{avg} is more commonly performed by an instrument. If one defines the energy per pulse as:

$$\epsilon_{\text{pulse}} = \int_0^T p(t)\,\mathrm{d}t$$

then the average power is:

$$P_{\text{avg}} = \frac{1}{T}\int_0^T p(t)\,\mathrm{d}t = \frac{\epsilon_{\text{pulse}}}{T}.$$

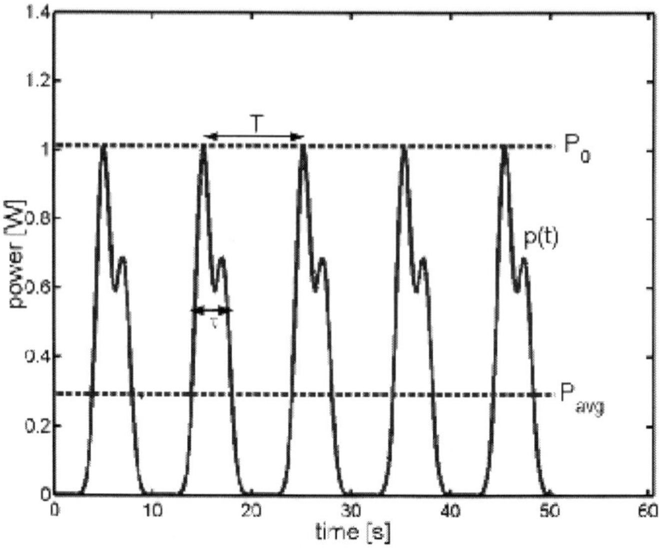

Figure: *In a train of identical pulses, the instantaneous power is a periodic function of time. The ratio of the pulse duration to the period is equal to the ratio of the average power to the peak power. It is also called the duty cycle.*

One may define the pulse length τ such that $P_0\tau = \epsilon_{\text{pulse}}$ so that the ratios

$$\frac{P_{\text{avg}}}{P_0} = \frac{\tau}{T}$$

are equal. These ratios are called the *duty cycle* of the pulse train.

3

Direct Current

Direct current (DC) is the unidirectional flow of electric charge. Direct current is produced by sources such as batteries, thermocouples, solar cells, and commutator-type electric machines of the dynamo type. Direct current may flow in a conductor such as a wire, but can also flow through semiconductors, insulators, or even through a vacuum as in electron or ion beams. The electric current flows in a constant direction, distinguishing it from alternating current (AC). A term formerly used for *direct current* was galvanic current.

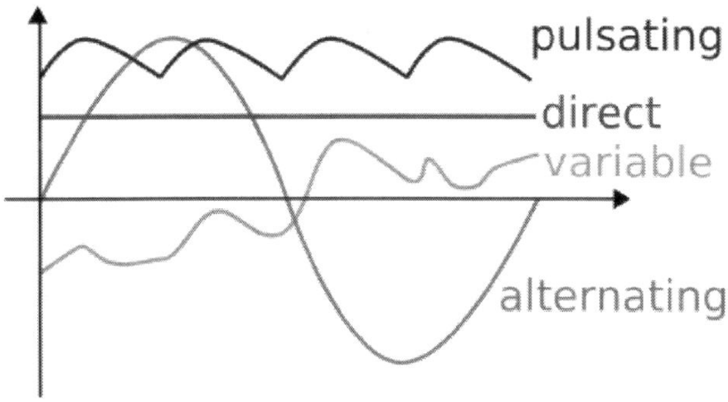

Figure: *Direct Current (red curve). The horizontal axis measures time; the vertical, current or voltage.*

The abbreviations *AC* and *DC* are often used to mean simply *alternating* and *direct*, as when they modify *current* or *voltage*.

Direct current may be obtained from an alternating current supply by use of a current-switching arrangement called a rectifier, which contains electronic elements (usually) or electromechanical elements (historically) that allow current to flow only in one direction. Direct current may be made into alternating current with an inverter or a motor-generator set.

The first commercial electric power transmission (developed by Thomas Edison in the late nineteenth century) used direct current. Because of the significant advantages of alternating current over direct current in transforming and transmission, electric power distribution is nearly all alternating current today. In the mid-1950s, HVDC transmission was developed, and is now an option instead of long-distance high voltage alternating current systems. For applications requiring direct current, such as third rail power systems, alternating current is distributed to a substation, which utilizes a rectifier to convert the power to direct current.

Direct current is used to charge batteries, and in nearly all electronic systems, as the power supply. Very large quantities of direct-current power are used in production of aluminium and other electrochemical processes. Direct current is used for some railway propulsion, especially in urban areas. High-voltage direct current is used to transmit large amounts of power from remote generation sites or to interconnect alternating current power grids.

Various Definitions

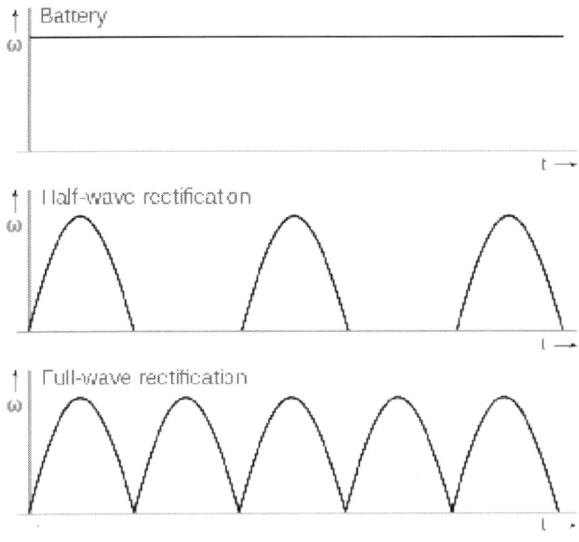

Figure: *Types of direct current.*

Within electrical engineering, the term *DC* is used to refer to power systems that use only one polarity of voltage or current, and to refer to the constant, zero-frequency, or slowly varying local mean value of a voltage or current. For example, the voltage across a DC voltage source is constant as is the current through a DC current source. The DC solution of an electric circuit is the solution where all voltages and currents are constant. It can be shown that any stationary voltage or current waveform can be decomposed into a sum of a DC component and a zero-mean time-varying component; the DC component is defined to be the expected value, or the average value of the voltage or current over all time.

Although DC stands for "direct current", DC often refers to "constant polarity". Under this definition, DC voltages can vary in time, as seen in the raw output of a rectifier or the fluctuating voice signal on a telephone line. Some forms of DC (such as that produced by a voltage regulator) have almost no variations in voltage, but may still have variations in output power and current.

Circuits

A direct current circuit is an electrical circuit that consists of any combination of constant voltage sources, constant current sources, and resistors. In this case, the circuit voltages and currents are independent of time. A particular circuit voltage or current does not depend on the past value of any circuit voltage or current. This implies that the system of equations that represent a DC circuit do not involve integrals or derivatives with respect to time.

If a capacitor or inductor is added to a DC circuit, the resulting circuit is not, strictly speaking, a DC circuit. However, most such circuits have a DC solution. This solution gives the circuit voltages and currents when the circuit is in DC steady state. Such a circuit is represented by a system of differential equations. The solution to these equations usually contain a time varying or transient part as well as constant or steady state part. It is this steady state part that is the DC solution. There are some circuits that do not have a DC solution. Two simple examples are a constant current source connected to a capacitor and a constant voltage source connected to an inductor.

In electronics, it is common to refer to a circuit that is powered by a DC voltage source such as a battery or the output of a DC power supply as a DC circuit even though what is meant is that the circuit is DC powered.

Applications

Direct-current installations usually have different types of sockets, connectors, switches, and fixtures, mostly due to the low voltages used, from those suitable for alternating current. It is usually important with a direct-current appliance not to reverse polarity unless the device has a diode bridge to correct for this (most battery-powered devices do not).

Figure: *This symbol is found on many electronic devices that either require or produce direct current.*

The Unicode symbol for direct current is U+2393 (“#). DC is commonly found in many extra-low voltage applications and some low-voltage applications, especially where these are powered by batteries, which can produce only DC, or solar power systems, since solar cells can produce only DC. Most automotive applications use DC, although the alternator is an AC device which uses a rectifier to produce DC. Most electronic circuits require a DC power supply. Applications using fuel cells (mixing hydrogen and oxygen together with a catalyst to produce electricity and water as byproducts) also produce only DC.

The vast majority of automotive applications use “12 V” DC power; a few have a 6-volt or a 42-volt electrical system.

Light aircraft electrical systems are typically 12 V or 28 V. Through the use of a DC-DC converter, high DC voltages such as 48V to 72V DC can be stepped down to 36V, 24V, 18V, 12V or 5V to supply different loads. In a telecommunications system operating at 48V DC, it is generally more efficient to step voltage down to 12V to 24VDC with a DC-DC converter and power equipment loads directly at their native DC input voltages versus operating a 48VDC to 120VAC inverter to provide power to equipment.

Many telephones connect to a twisted pair of wires, and use a bias tee to internally separate the AC component of the voltage between the two wires (the audio signal) from the DC component of the voltage between the two wires (used to power the phone).

Telephone exchange communication equipment, such as DSLAM, uses standard -48V DC power supply. The negative polarity is achieved by grounding the positive terminal of power supply system and the battery bank. This is done to prevent electrolysis depositions.

Ohm's Law

How Voltage, Current, and Resistance Relate

An electric circuit is formed when a conductive path is created to allow free electrons to continuously move. This continuous movement of free electrons through the conductors of a circuit is called a *current*, and it is often referred to in terms of "flow," just like the flow of a liquid through a hollow pipe.

The force motivating electrons to "flow" in a circuit is called *voltage*. Voltage is a specific measure of potential energy that is always relative between two points. When we speak of a certain amount of voltage being present in a circuit, we are referring to the measurement of how much *potential* energy exists to move electrons from one particular point in that circuit to another particular point. Without reference to *two* particular points, the term "voltage" has no meaning.

Free electrons tend to move through conductors with some degree of friction, or opposition to motion. This opposition to motion is more properly called *resistance*. The amount of current in a circuit depends on the amount of voltage available to motivate the electrons, and also the amount of resistance in the circuit to oppose electron flow. Just like voltage, resistance is a quantity relative between two points. For this reason, the quantities of voltage and resistance are often stated as being "between" or "across" two points in a circuit.

To be able to make meaningful statements about these quantities in circuits, we need to be able to describe their quantities in the same way that we might quantify mass, temperature, volume, length, or any other kind of physical quantity. For mass we might use the units of "kilogram" or "gram." For temperature we might use degrees Fahrenheit or degrees Celsius. Here are the standard units of measurement for electrical current, voltage, and resistance:

Quantity	***Symbol***	***Unit of Measurement***	***Unit Abbreviation***
Current	1	Ampere ("Amp")	A
Voltage	E or v	Volt	V
Resistance	R	Ohm	Ω

The "symbol" given for each quantity is the standard alphabetical letter used to represent that quantity in an algebraic equation. Standardized letters like these are common in the disciplines of physics and engineering, and are internationally recognized. The "unit abbreviation" for each quantity represents the alphabetical symbol used as a shorthand notation for its particular unit of measurement. And, yes, that strange-looking "horseshoe" symbol is the capital Greek letter Ω, just a character in a *foreign* alphabet (apologies to any Greek readers here).

Each unit of measurement is named after a famous experimenter in electricity: The *amp* after the Frenchman Andre M. Ampere, the *volt* after the Italian Alessandro Volta, and the *ohm* after the German Georg Simon Ohm.

The mathematical symbol for each quantity is meaningful as well. The "R" for resistance and the "V" for voltage are both self-explanatory, whereas "I" for current seems a bit weird. The "I" is thought to have been meant to represent "Intensity" (of electron flow), and the other symbol for voltage, "E," stands for "Electromotive force." From what research I've been able to do, there seems to be some dispute over the meaning of "I." The symbols "E" and "V" are interchangeable for the most part, although some texts reserve "E" to represent voltage across a source (such as a battery or generator) and "V" to represent voltage across anything else.

All of these symbols are expressed using capital letters, except in cases where a quantity (especially voltage or current) is described in terms of a brief period of time (called an "instantaneous" value). For example, the voltage of a battery, which is stable over a long period of time, will be symbolized with a capital letter "E," while the voltage peak of a lightning strike at the very instant it hits a power line would most likely be symbolized with a lower-case letter "e" (or lower-case "v") to designate that value as being at a single moment in time. This same lower-case convention holds true for current as well, the lower-case letter "i" representing current at some instant in time. Most direct-current (DC) measurements, however, being stable over time, will be symbolized with capital letters.

One foundational unit of electrical measurement, often taught in the beginnings of electronics courses but used infrequently afterwards, is the unit of the *coulomb*, which is a measure of electric charge proportional to the number of electrons in an imbalanced state. One coulomb of charge is equal to 6,250,000,000,000,000,000 electrons. The symbol for electric charge quantity is the capital letter "Q," with the unit of coulombs abbreviated by the capital letter "C." It so happens that the unit for electron flow, the amp, is equal to 1 coulomb of electrons passing by a given point in a circuit in 1 second of time. Cast in these terms, current is the *rate of electric charge motion* through a conductor.

As stated before, voltage is the measure of *potential energy per unit charge* available to motivate electrons from one point to another. Before we can precisely define what a "volt" is, we must understand how to measure this quantity we call "potential energy."

The general metric unit for energy of any kind is the *joule*, equal to the amount of work performed by a force of 1 newton exerted through a motion of 1 metre (in the same direction).

In British units, this is slightly less than 3/4 pound of force exerted over a distance of 1 foot. Put in common terms, it takes about 1 joule of energy to lift a 3/4 pound weight 1 foot off the ground, or to drag something a distance of 1 foot using a parallel pulling force of 3/4 pound. Defined in these scientific terms, 1 volt is equal to 1 joule of electric potential energy per (divided by) 1 coulomb of charge. Thus, a 9 volt battery releases 9 joules of energy for every coulomb of electrons moved through a circuit.

These units and symbols for electrical quantities will become very important to know as we begin to explore the relationships between them in circuits. The first, and perhaps most important, relationship between current, voltage, and resistance is called Ohm's Law, discovered by Georg Simon Ohm and published in his 1827 paper, *The Galvanic Circuit Investigated Mathematically*.

Ohm's principal discovery was that the amount of electric current through a metal conductor in a circuit is directly proportional to the voltage impressed across it, for any given temperature. Ohm expressed his discovery in the form of a simple equation, describing how voltage, current, and resistance interrelate:

$$E = I R$$

In this algebraic expression, voltage (E) is equal to current (I) multiplied by resistance (R). Using algebra techniques, we can manipulate this equation into two variations, solving for I and for R, respectively:

$$I = \frac{E}{R} \qquad R = \frac{E}{I}$$

Let's see how these equations might work to help us analyze simple circuits:

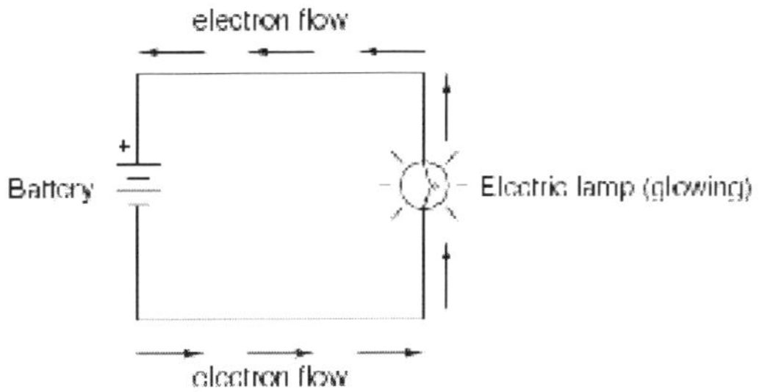

In the above circuit, there is only one source of voltage (the battery, on the left) and only one source of resistance to current (the lamp, on the right). This makes it very easy to apply Ohm's Law. If we know the values of any two of the three quantities (voltage, current, and resistance) in this circuit, we can use Ohm's Law to determine the third.

In this first example, we will calculate the amount of current (I) in a circuit, given values of voltage (E) and resistance (R):

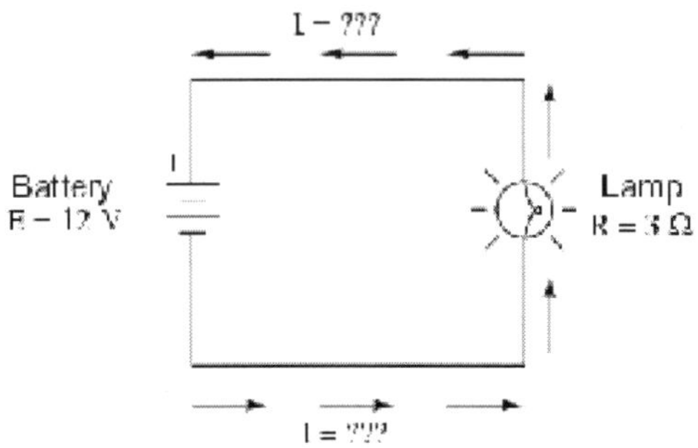

What is the amount of current (*I*) in this circuit?

$$I = \frac{E}{R} \qquad = \frac{12\text{ V}}{3\,\Omega} = 4\text{ A}$$

In this second example, we will calculate the amount of resistance (R) in a circuit, given values of voltage (E) and current (I):

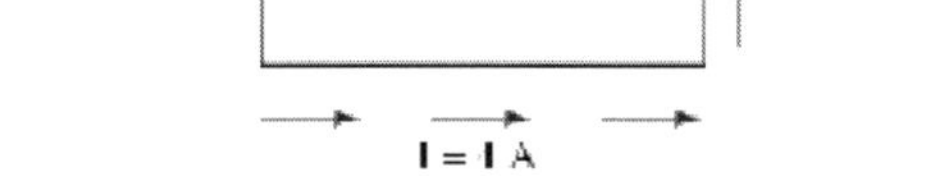

What is the amount of resistance (R) offered by the lamp?

$$R = \frac{E}{I} \qquad = \frac{36\text{ V}}{4\text{ A}} = 9\,\Omega$$

In the last example, we will calculate the amount of voltage supplied by a battery, given values of current (I) and resistance (R):

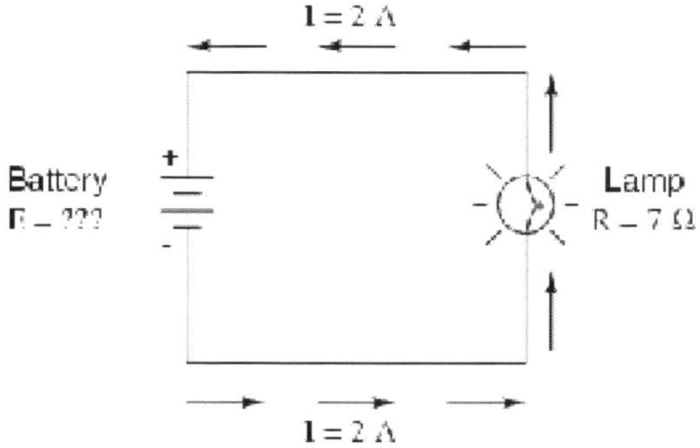

What is the amount of voltage provided by the battery?

$$E = IR = (2\text{ A})\,(7\text{ W}) = 14\text{ V}$$

Ohm's Law is a very simple and useful tool for analyzing electric circuits. It is used so often in the study of electricity and electronics that it needs to be committed to memory by the serious student. For those who are not yet comfortable with algebra, there's a trick to remembering how to solve for any one quantity, given the other two. First, arrange the letters E, I, and R in a triangle like this:

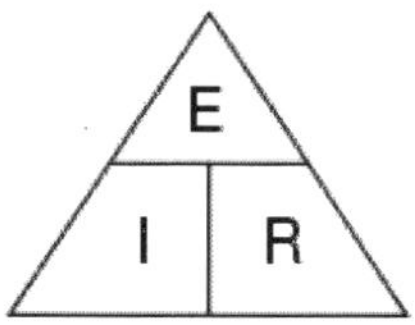

If you know E and I, and wish to determine R, just eliminate R from the picture and see what's left:

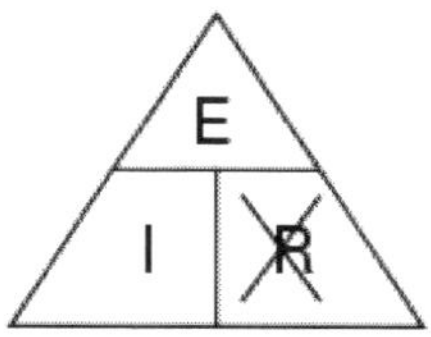

$$R = \frac{E}{I}$$

If you know E and R, and wish to determine I, eliminate I and see what's left:

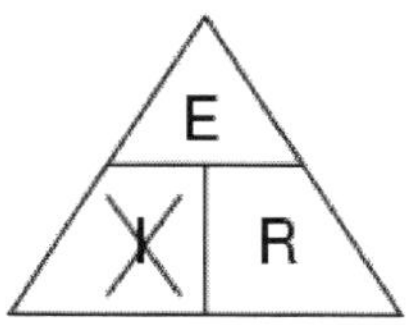

$$I = \frac{E}{R}$$

Lastly, if you know I and R, and wish to determine E, eliminate E and see what's left:

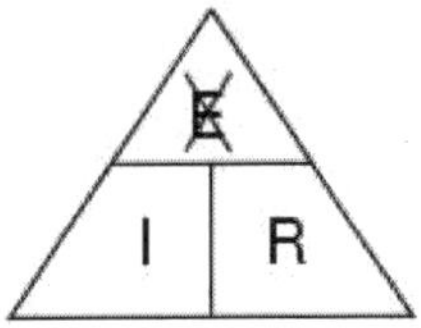

E = I R

Eventually, you'll have to be familiar with algebra to seriously study electricity and electronics, but this tip can make your first calculations a little easier to remember. If you are comfortable with algebra, all you need to do is commit E=IR to memory and derive the other two formulae from that when you need them!

- REVIEW:
- Voltage measured in *volts*, symbolized by the letters "E" or "V".
- Current measured in *amps*, symbolized by the letter "I".
- Resistance measured in *ohms*, symbolized by the letter "R".
- Ohm's Law: E = IR ; I = E/R ; R = E/I

An Analogy for Ohm's Law

Ohm's Law also makes intuitive sense if you apply it to the water-and-pipe analogy. If we have a water pump that exerts pressure (voltage) to push water around a "circuit" (current) through a restriction (resistance), we can model how the three variables interrelate. If the resistance to water flow stays the same and the pump pressure increases, the flow rate must also increase.

Pressure	= increase	Voltage	= increase
Flow rate	= increase	Current	= increase
Resistance	= same	Resistance	= same

$$\overset{\uparrow}{E} = \overset{\uparrow}{I}\, R$$

If the pressure stays the same and the resistance increases (making it more difficult for the water to flow), then the flow rate must decrease.

As odd as it may seem, the actual mathematical relationship between pressure, flow, and resistance is actually more complex for fluids like water than it is for electrons. If you pursue further studies in physics, you will discover this for yourself. Thankfully for the electronics student, the mathematics of Ohm's Law is very straightforward and simple.

- REVIEW:
- With resistance steady, current follows voltage (an increase in voltage means an increase in current, and vice versa).
- With voltage steady, changes in current and resistance are opposite (an increase in current means a decrease in resistance, and vice versa).
- With current steady, voltage follows resistance (an increase in resistance means an increase in voltage).

Power in Electric Circuits

In addition to voltage and current, there is another measure of free electron activity in a circuit: *power*. First, we need to understand just what power is before we analyze it in any circuits.

Power is a measure of how much work can be performed in a given amount of time. *Work* is generally defined in terms of the lifting of a weight against the pull of gravity. The heavier the weight and/or the higher it is lifted, the more work has been done. *Power* is a measure of how rapidly a standard amount of work is done.

For American automobiles, engine power is rated in a unit called "horsepower," invented initially as a way for steam engine manufacturers to quantify the working ability of their machines in terms of the most common power source of their day: horses. One horsepower is defined in British units as 550 ft-lbs of work per second of time. The power of a car's engine won't indicate how tall of a hill it can climb or how much weight it can tow, but it will indicate how *fast* it can climb a specific hill or tow a specific weight.

The power of a mechanical engine is a function of both the engine's speed and its torque provided at the output shaft. Speed of an engine's output shaft is measured in revolutions per minute, or RPM. Torque is the amount of twisting force produced by the engine, and it is usually measured in pound-feet, or lb-ft (not to be confused with foot-pounds or ft-lbs, which is the unit for work). Neither speed nor torque alone is a measure of an engine's power.

A 100 horsepower diesel tractor engine will turn relatively slowly, but provide great amounts of torque. A 100 horsepower motorcycle engine will turn very fast, but provide relatively little torque. Both will produce 100 horsepower, but at different speeds and different torques. The equation for shaft horsepower is simple:

$$\text{Horsepower} = \frac{2\pi\ \text{ST}}{33.000}$$

Where,

S = shaft speed in r.p.m.

T = shaft torque in lb- ft.

Notice how there are only two variable terms on the right-hand side of the equation, S and T. All the other terms on that side are constant: 2, pi, and 33,000 are all constants (they do not change in value). The horsepower varies only with changes in speed and torque, nothing else. We can re-write the equation to show this relationship:

$$\text{Horespower } \alpha \text{ S T}$$

α This symbol means "proportional to"

Because the unit of the "horsepower" doesn't coincide exactly with speed in revolutions per minute multiplied by torque in pound-feet, we can't say that horsepower *equals* ST. However, they are *proportional* to one another. As the mathematical product of ST changes, the value for horsepower will change by the same proportion.

In electric circuits, power is a function of both voltage and current. Not surprisingly, this relationship bears striking resemblance to the "proportional" horsepower formula above:

$$P = I\ E$$

In this case, however, power (P) is exactly equal to current (I) multiplied by voltage (E), rather than merely being proportional to IE. When using this formula, the unit of measurement for power is the *watt*, abbreviated with the letter "W."

It must be understood that neither voltage nor current by themselves constitute power. Rather, power is the combination of both voltage *and* current in a circuit. Remember that voltage is the specific work (or potential energy) per unit charge, while current is the rate at which electric charges move through a conductor. Voltage (specific work) is analogous to the work done in lifting a weight against the pull of gravity. Current (rate) is analogous to the speed at which that weight is lifted. Together as a product (multiplication), voltage (work) and current (rate) constitute power.

Just as in the case of the diesel tractor engine and the motorcycle engine, a circuit with high voltage and low current may be dissipating the same amount of power as a circuit with low voltage and high current. Neither the amount of voltage alone nor the amount of current alone indicates the amount of power in an electric circuit.

In an open circuit, where voltage is present between the terminals of the source and there is zero current, there is *zero* power dissipated, no matter how great that voltage may be. Since P=IE and I=0 and anything multiplied by zero is zero, the power dissipated in any open circuit must be zero.

Likewise, if we were to have a short circuit constructed of a loop of superconducting wire (absolutely zero resistance), we could have a condition of current in the loop with zero voltage, and likewise no power would be dissipated. Since P=IE and E=0 and anything multiplied by zero is zero, the power dissipated in a superconducting loop must be zero. (We'll be exploring the topic of superconductivity in a later chapter).

Whether we measure power in the unit of "horsepower" or the unit of "watt," we're still talking about the same thing: how much work can be done in a given amount of time. The two units are not numerically equal, but they express the same kind of thing. In fact, European automobile manufacturers typically advertise their engine power in terms of kilowatts (kW), or thousands of watts, instead of horsepower! These two units of power are related to each other by a simple conversion formula:

1 Horsepower = 745.7 Watts

So, our 100 horsepower diesel and motorcycle engines could also be rated as "74570 watt" engines, or more properly, as "74.57 kilowatt" engines. In European engineering specifications, this rating would be the norm rather than the exception.

- Power is the measure of how much work can be done in a given amount of time.
- Mechanical power is commonly measured (in America) in "horsepower."
- Electrical power is almost always measured in "watts," and it can be calculated by the formula P = IE.
- Electrical power is a product of both voltage *and* current, not either one separately.
- Horsepower and watts are merely two different units for describing the same kind of physical measurement, with 1 horsepower equaling 745.7 watts.

Calculating Electric Power

We've seen the formula for determining the power in an electric circuit: by multiplying the voltage in "volts" by the current in "amps" we arrive at an answer in "watts." Let's apply this to a circuit example:

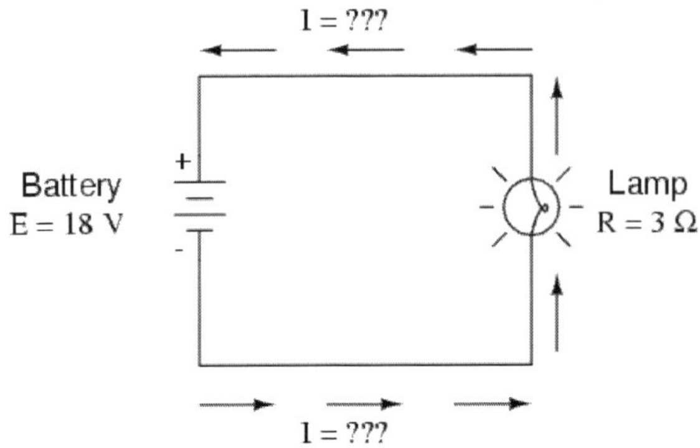

In the above circuit, we know we have a battery voltage of 18 volts and a lamp resistance of 3 Ω. Using Ohm's Law to determine current, we get:

$$I = \frac{E}{R} = \frac{18\,V}{3\Omega} = 6\,A$$

Now that we know the current, we can take that value and multiply it by the voltage to determine power:

$$P = IE = (6\,A)\,(18\,V) = 108\,W$$

Answer: the lamp is dissipating (releasing) 108 watts of power, most likely in the form of both light and heat.

Let's try taking that same circuit and increasing the battery voltage to see what happens. Intuition should tell us that the circuit current will increase as the voltage increases and the lamp resistance stays the same. Likewise, the power will increase as well:

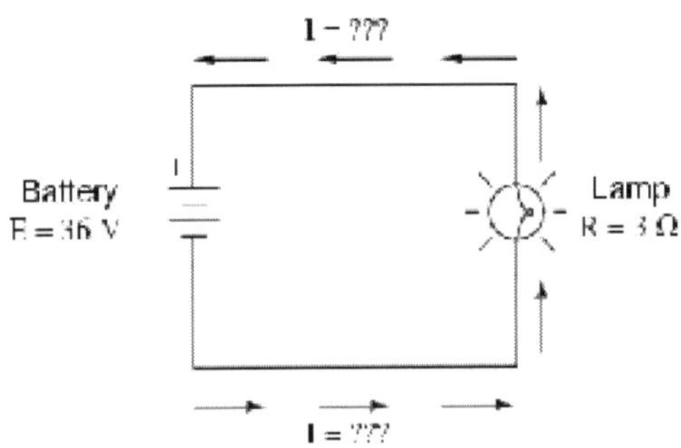

Now, the battery voltage is 36 volts instead of 18 volts. The lamp is still providing 3 Ω of electrical resistance to the flow of electrons. The current is now:

$$I = \frac{E}{R} = \frac{36\,V}{3\Omega} = 12\,A$$

This stands to reason: if I = E/R, and we double E while R stays the same, the current should double. Indeed, it has: we now have 12 amps of current instead of 6. Now, what about power?

$$P = IE = (12\,A)\,(36\,V) = 432\ W$$

Notice that the power has increased just as we might have suspected, but it increased quite a bit more than the current. Why is this? Because power is a function of voltage multiplied by current, and *both* voltage and current doubled from their previous values, the power will increase by a factor of 2 × 2, or 4. You can check this by dividing 432 watts by 108 watts and seeing that the ratio between them is indeed 4.

Using algebra again to manipulate the formulae, we can take our original power formula and modify it for applications where we don't know both voltage and current:

If we only know voltage (E) and resistance (R):

$$\text{If,}\quad I = \frac{E}{R} \ \text{ and } \ P = IE$$

$$\text{Then,}\quad P = \frac{E}{R}E \text{ or } P = \frac{E^2}{R}$$

If we only know current (I) and resistance (R):

$$\textit{If},\quad E = IR \ \textit{ and } \ P = IE$$

$$\textit{Then},\quad P = I\,(IR) \ \textit{or} \ P = I^2\,R$$

A historical note: it was James Prescott Joule, not Georg Simon Ohm, who first discovered the mathematical relationship between power dissipation and current through a resistance. This discovery, published in 1841, followed the form of the last equation ($P = I^2R$), and is properly known as Joule's Law. However, these power equations are so commonly associated with the Ohm's Law equations relating voltage, current, and resistance (E=IR ; I=E/R ; and R=E/I) that they are frequently credited to Ohm.

Power equations

$$P = IE \quad P = \frac{E^2}{R} \quad P = I^2\,R$$

- Power measured in *watts*, symbolized by the letter "W".
- Joule's Law: $P = I^2R$; $P = IE$; $P = E^2/R$

Resistors

Because the relationship between voltage, current, and resistance in any circuit is so regular, we can reliably control any variable in a circuit simply by controlling the other two. Perhaps the easiest variable in any circuit to control is its resistance. This can be done by changing the material, size, and shape of its conductive components (remember how the thin metal filament of a lamp created more electrical resistance than a thick wire?).

Special components called *resistors* are made for the express purpose of creating a precise quantity of resistance for insertion into a circuit. They are typically constructed of metal wire or carbon, and engineered to maintain a stable resistance value over a wide range of environmental conditions. Unlike lamps, they do not produce light, but they do produce heat as electric power is dissipated by them in a working circuit. Typically, though, the purpose of a resistor is not to produce usable heat, but simply to provide a precise quantity of electrical resistance.

The most common schematic symbol for a resistor is a zig-zag line:

Resistor values in ohms are usually shown as an adjacent number, and if several resistors are present in a circuit, they will be labelled with a unique identifier number such as R_1, R_2, R_3, etc. As you can see, resistor symbols can be shown either horizontally or vertically:

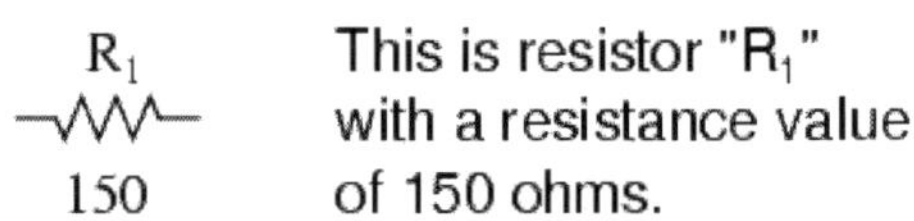

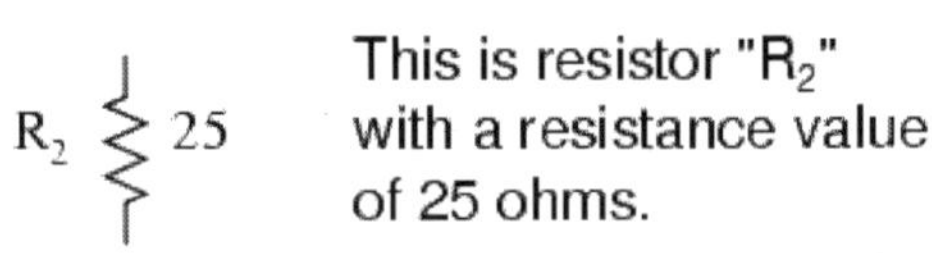

Real resistors look nothing like the zig-zag symbol. Instead, they look like small tubes or cylinders with two wires protruding for connection to a circuit. Here is a sampling of different kinds and sizes of resistors:

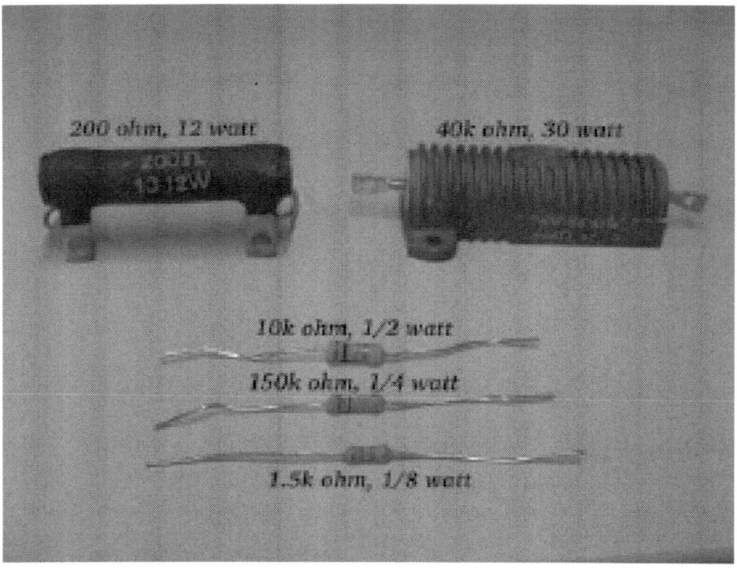

In keeping more with their physical appearance, an alternative schematic symbol for a resistor looks like a small, rectangular box:

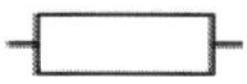

Resistors can also be shown to have varying rather than fixed resistances. This might be for the purpose of describing an actual physical device designed for the purpose of providing an adjustable resistance, or it could be to show some component that just happens to have an unstable resistance:

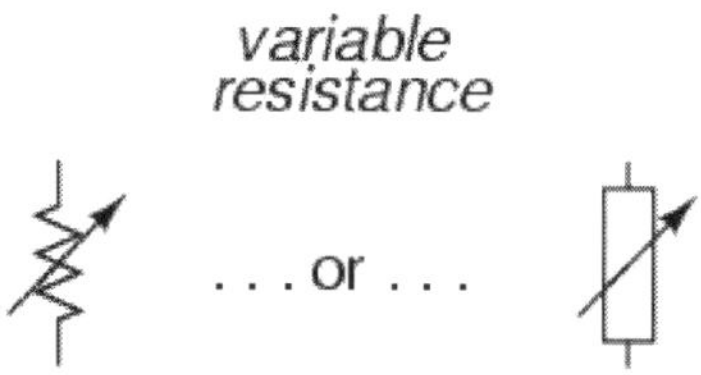

In fact, any time you see a component symbol drawn with a diagonal arrow through it, that component has a variable rather than a fixed value. This symbol "modifier" (the diagonal arrow) is standard electronic symbol convention.

Variable resistors must have some physical means of adjustment, either a rotating shaft or lever that can be moved to vary the amount of electrical resistance. Here is a photograph showing some devices called *potentiometers*, which can be used as variable resistors:

Because resistors dissipate heat energy as the electric currents through them overcome the "friction" of their resistance, resistors are also rated in terms of how much heat energy they can dissipate without overheating and sustaining damage. Naturally, this power rating is specified in the physical unit of "watts." Most resistors found in small electronic devices such as portable radios are rated at 1/4 (0.25) watt or less. The power rating of any resistor is roughly proportional to its physical size. Note in the first resistor photograph how the power ratings relate with size: the bigger the resistor, the higher its power dissipation rating. Also note how resistances (in ohms) have nothing to do with size!

Although it may seem pointless now to have a device doing nothing but resisting electric current, resistors are extremely useful devices in circuits. Because they are simple and so commonly used throughout the world of electricity and electronics, we'll spend a considerable amount of time analyzing circuits composed of nothing but resistors and batteries.

For a practical illustration of resistors' usefulness, examine the photograph below. It is a picture of a *printed circuit board*, or *PCB*: an assembly made of sandwiched layers of insulating phenolic fibre-board and conductive copper strips, into which components may be inserted and secured by a low-temperature welding process called "soldering."

The various components on this circuit board are identified by printed labels. Resistors are denoted by any label beginning with the letter "R".

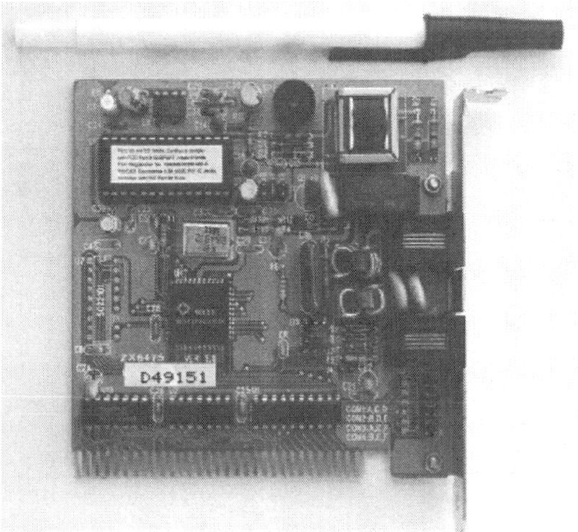

This particular circuit board is a computer accessory called a "modem," which allows digital information transfer over telephone lines. There are at least a dozen resistors (all rated at 1/4 watt power dissipation) that can be seen on this modem's board. Every one of the black rectangles (called "integrated circuits" or "chips") contain their own array of resistors for their internal functions, as well.

Another circuit board example shows resistors packaged in even smaller units, called "surface mount devices." This particular circuit board is the underside of a personal computer hard disk drive, and once again the resistors soldered onto it are designated with labels beginning with the letter "R":

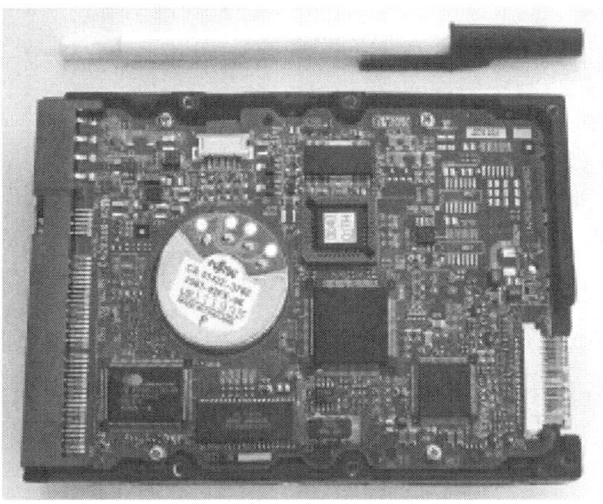

There are over one hundred surface-mount resistors on this circuit board, and this count of course does not include the number of resistors internal to the black "chips." These two photographs should convince anyone that resistors — devices that "merely" oppose the flow of electrons — are very important components in the realm of electronics!

In schematic diagrams, resistor symbols are sometimes used to illustrate any general type of device in a circuit doing something useful with electrical energy. Any non-specific electrical device is generally called a *load*, so if you see a schematic diagram showing a resistor symbol labelled "load," especially in a tutorial circuit diagram explaining some concept unrelated to the actual use of electrical power, that symbol may just be a kind of shorthand representation of something else more practical than a resistor.

To summarize what we've learned in this lesson, let's analyze the following circuit, determining all that we can from the information given:

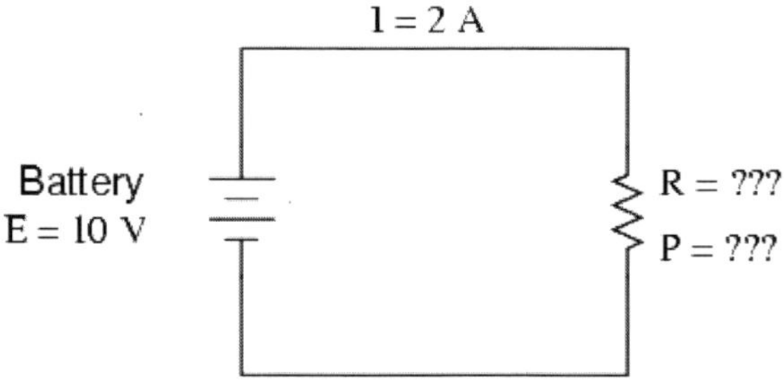

All we've been given here to start with is the battery voltage (10 volts) and the circuit current (2 amps). We don't know the resistor's resistance in ohms or the power dissipated by it in watts. Surveying our array of Ohm's Law equations, we find two equations that give us answers from known quantities of voltage and current:

$$R = \frac{E}{I} \quad \textit{and} \quad P = IE$$

Inserting the known quantities of voltage (E) and current (I) into these two equations, we can determine circuit resistance (R) and power dissipation (P):

$$R = \frac{10V}{2A} = 5\Omega$$

$$P = (2\text{ A})(10\text{ V}) = 20\text{ W}$$

For the circuit conditions of 10 volts and 2 amps, the resistor's resistance must be 5 Ω. If we were designing a circuit to operate at these values, we would have to specify a resistor with a minimum power rating of 20 watts, or else it would overheat and fail.

- REVIEW:
- Devices called *resistors* are built to provide precise amounts of resistance in electric circuits. Resistors are rated both in terms of their resistance (ohms) and their ability to dissipate heat energy (watts).
- Resistor resistance ratings cannot be determined from the physical size of the resistor(s) in question, although approximate power ratings can. The larger the resistor is, the more power it can safely dissipate without suffering damage.
- Any device that performs some useful task with electric power is generally known as a *load*. Sometimes resistor symbols are used in schematic diagrams to designate a non-specific load, rather than an actual resistor.

Nonlinear Conduction

"Advances are made by answering questions. Discoveries are made by questioning answers."

Bernhard Haisch, Astrophysicist

Ohm's Law is a simple and powerful mathematical tool for helping us analyze electric circuits, but it has limitations, and we must understand these limitations in order to properly apply it to real circuits. For most conductors, resistance is a rather stable property, largely unaffected by voltage or current. For this reason we can regard the resistance of many circuit components as a constant, with voltage and current being directly related to each other.

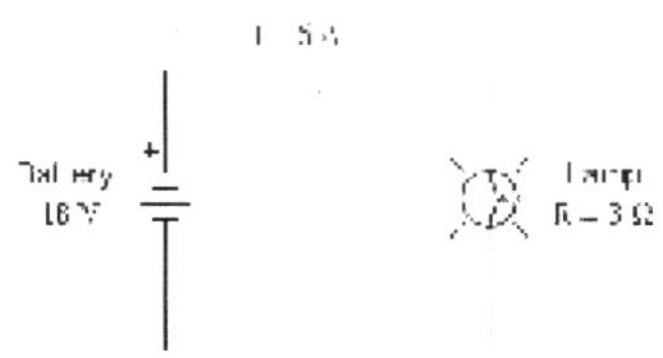

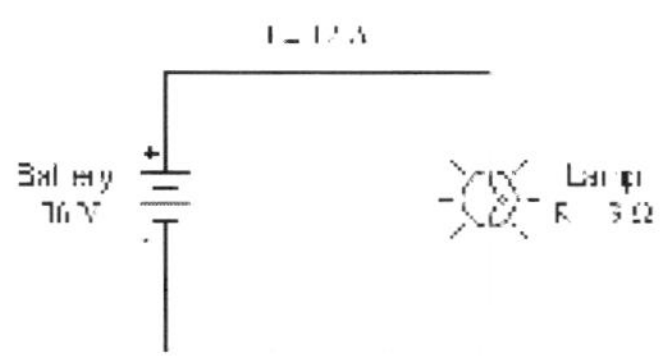

For instance, our previous circuit example with the 3 Ω lamp, we calculated current through the circuit by dividing voltage by resistance (I=E/R). With an 18 volt battery, our circuit current was 6 amps. Doubling the battery voltage to 36 volts resulted in a doubled current of 12 amps. All of this makes sense, of course, so long as the lamp continues to provide exactly the same amount of friction (resistance) to the flow of electrons through it: 3 Ω.

However, reality is not always this simple. One of the phenomena explored in a later chapter is that of conductor resistance *changing* with temperature. In an incandescent lamp (the kind employing the principle of electric current heating a thin filament of wire to the point that it glows white-hot), the resistance of the filament wire will increase dramatically as it warms from room temperature to operating temperature. If we were to increase the supply voltage in a real lamp circuit, the resulting increase in current would cause the filament to increase temperature, which would in turn increase its resistance, thus preventing further increases in current without further increases in battery voltage. Consequently, voltage and current do not follow the simple equation "I=E/R" (with R assumed to be equal to 3 Ω) because an incandescent lamp's filament resistance does not remain stable for different currents.

The phenomenon of resistance changing with variations in temperature is one shared by almost all metals, of which most wires are made. For most applications, these changes in resistance are small enough to be ignored. In the application of metal lamp filaments, the change happens to be quite large.

This is just one example of "nonlinearity" in electric circuits. It is by no means the only example. A "linear" function in mathematics is one that tracks a straight line when plotted on a graph. The simplified version of the lamp circuit with a constant filament resistance of 3 Ω generates a plot like this:

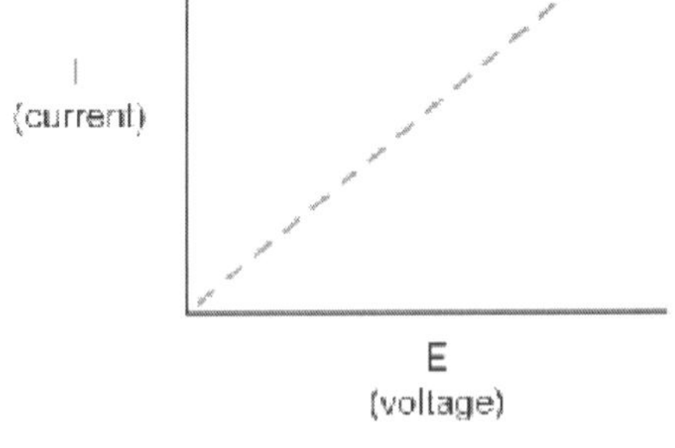

The straight-line plot of current over voltage indicates that resistance is a stable, unchanging value for a wide range of circuit voltages and currents. In an "ideal" situation, this is the case. Resistors, which are manufactured to provide a definite, stable value of resistance, behave very much like the plot of values seen above. A mathematician would call their behaviour "linear."

A more realistic analysis of a lamp circuit, however, over several different values of battery voltage would generate a plot of this shape:

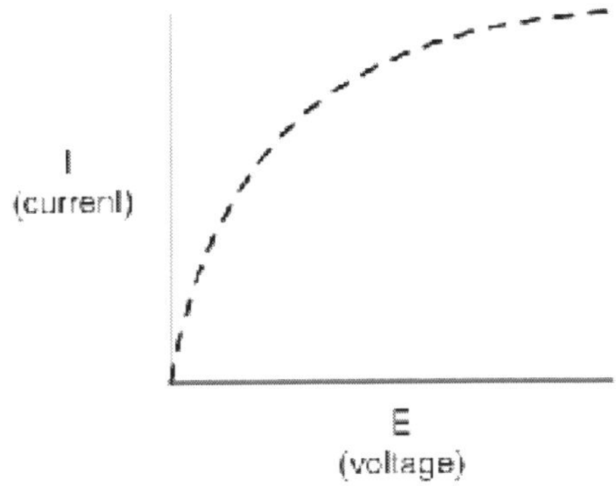

The plot is no longer a straight line. It rises sharply on the left, as voltage increases from zero to a low level. As it progresses to the right we see the line flattening out, the circuit requiring greater and greater increases in voltage to achieve equal increases in current.

If we try to apply Ohm's Law to find the resistance of this lamp circuit with the voltage and current values plotted above, we arrive at several different values. We could say that the resistance here is *nonlinear*, increasing with increasing current and voltage. The nonlinearity is caused by the effects of high temperature on the metal wire of the lamp filament.

Another example of nonlinear current conduction is through gases such as air. At standard temperatures and pressures, air is an effective insulator. However, if the voltage between two conductors separated by an air gap is increased greatly enough, the air molecules between the gap will become "ionized," having their electrons stripped off by the force of the high voltage between the wires. Once ionized, air (and other gases) become good conductors of electricity, allowing electron flow where none could exist prior to ionization. If we were to plot current over voltage on a graph as we did with the lamp circuit, the effect of ionization would be clearly seen as nonlinear:

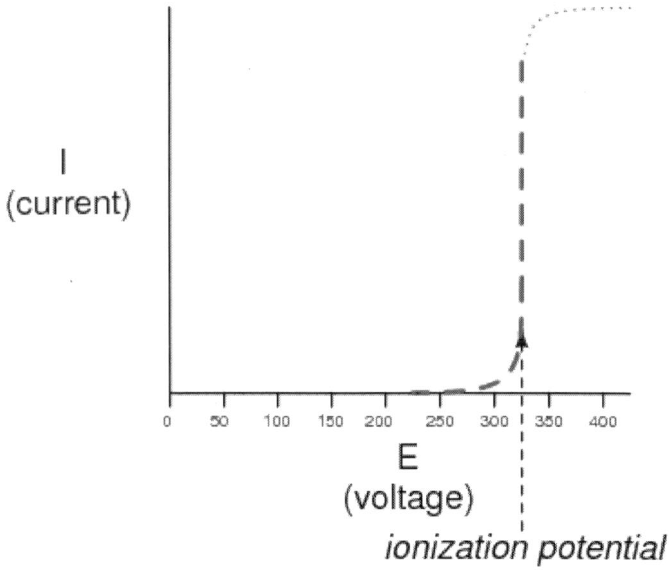

The graph shown is approximate for a small air gap (less than one inch). A larger air gap would yield a higher ionization potential, but the shape of the I/E curve would be very similar: practically no current until the ionization potential was reached, then substantial conduction after that.

Incidentally, this is the reason lightning bolts exist as momentary surges rather than continuous flows of electrons. The voltage built up between the earth and clouds (or between different sets of clouds) must increase to the point where it overcomes the ionization potential of the air gap before the air ionizes enough to support a substantial flow of electrons.

Once it does, the current will continue to conduct through the ionized air until the static charge between the two points depletes. Once the charge depletes enough so that the voltage falls below another threshold point, the air de-ionizes and returns to its normal state of extremely high resistance.

Many solid insulating materials exhibit similar resistance properties: extremely high resistance to electron flow below some critical threshold voltage, then a much lower resistance at voltages beyond that threshold.

Once a solid insulating material has been compromised by high-voltage *breakdown*, as it is called, it often does not return to its former insulating state, unlike most gases.

It may insulate once again at low voltages, but its breakdown threshold voltage will have been decreased to some lower level, which may allow breakdown to occur more easily in the future. This is a common mode of failure in high-voltage wiring: insulation damage due to breakdown. Such failures may be detected through the use of special resistance metres employing high voltage (1000 volts or more).

There are circuit components specifically engineered to provide nonlinear resistance curves, one of them being the *varistor*.

Commonly manufactured from compounds such as zinc oxide or silicon carbide, these devices maintain high resistance across their terminals until a certain "firing" or "breakdown" voltage (equivalent to the "ionization potential" of an air gap) is reached, at which point their resistance decreases dramatically.

Unlike the breakdown of an insulator, varistor breakdown is repeatable: that is, it is designed to withstand repeated breakdowns without failure. A picture of a varistor is shown here:

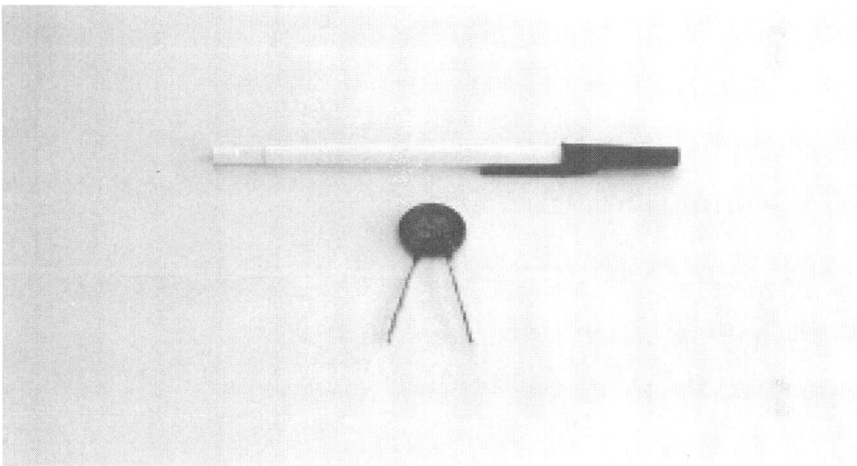

There are also special gas-filled tubes designed to do much the same thing, exploiting the very same principle at work in the ionization of air by a lightning bolt.

Other electrical components exhibit even stranger current/voltage curves than this. Some devices actually experience a *decrease* in current as the applied voltage *increases*. Because the slope of the current/voltage for this phenomenon is negative (angling down instead of up as it progresses from left to right), it is known as *negative resistance*.

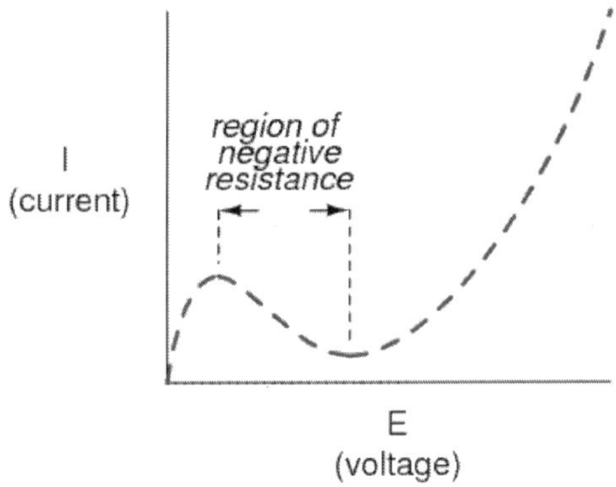

Most notably, high-vacuum electron tubes known as *tetrodes* and semiconductor diodes known as *Esaki* or *tunnel* diodes exhibit negative resistance for certain ranges of applied voltage.

Ohm's Law is not very useful for analyzing the behaviour of components like these where resistance varies with voltage and current. Some have even suggested that "Ohm's Law" should be demoted from the status of a "Law" because it is not universal. It might be more accurate to call the equation (R=E/I) a *definition of resistance*, befitting of a certain class of materials under a narrow range of conditions.

For the benefit of the student, however, we will assume that resistances specified in example circuits *are* stable over a wide range of conditions unless otherwise specified. I just wanted to expose you to a little bit of the complexity of the real world, lest I give you the false impression that the whole of electrical phenomena could be summarized in a few simple equations.

- The resistance of most conductive materials is stable over a wide range of conditions, but this is not true of all materials.
- Any function that can be plotted on a graph as a straight line is called a *linear* function. For circuits with stable resistances, the plot of current over voltage is linear (I=E/R).
- In circuits where resistance varies with changes in either voltage or current, the plot of current over voltage will be *nonlinear* (not a straight line).
- A *varistor* is a component that changes resistance with the amount of voltage impressed across it. With little voltage across it, its resistance is high. Then, at a certain "breakdown" or "firing" voltage, its resistance decreases dramatically.
- *Negative resistance* is where the current through a component actually decreases as the applied voltage across it is increased.

Some electron tubes and semiconductor diodes (most notably, the *tetrode* tube and the *Esaki*, or *tunnel* diode, respectively) exhibit negative resistance over a certain range of voltages.

Circuit Wiring

So far, we've been analyzing single-battery, single-resistor circuits with no regard for the connecting wires between the components, so long as a complete circuit is formed. Does the wire length or circuit "shape" matter to our calculations? Let's look at a couple of circuit configurations and find out:

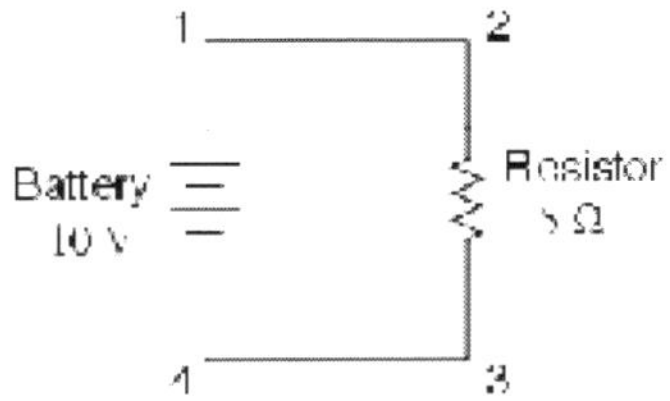

When we draw wires connecting points in a circuit, we usually assume those wires have negligible resistance. As such, they contribute no appreciable effect to the overall resistance of the circuit, and so the only resistance we have to contend with is the resistance in the components. In the above circuits, the only resistance comes from the 5 Ω resistors, so that is all we will consider in our calculations. In real life, metal wires actually *do* have resistance (and so do power sources!), but those resistances are generally so much smaller than the resistance present in the other circuit components that they can be safely ignored. Exceptions to this rule exist in power system wiring, where even very small amounts of conductor resistance can create significant voltage drops given normal (high) levels of current.

If connecting wire resistance is very little or none, we can regard the connected points in a circuit as being *electrically common*. That is, points 1 and 2 in the above circuits may be physically joined close together or far apart, and it doesn't matter for any voltage or resistance measurements relative to those points. The same goes for points 3 and

4. It is as if the ends of the resistor were attached directly across the terminals of the battery, so far as our Ohm's Law calculations and voltage measurements are concerned. This is useful to know, because it means you can re-draw a circuit diagram or re-wire a circuit, shortening or lengthening the wires as desired without appreciably impacting the circuit's function. All that matters is that the components attach to each other in the same sequence.

It also means that voltage measurements between sets of "electrically common" points will be the same. That is, the voltage between points 1 and 4 (directly across the battery) will be the same as the voltage between points 2 and 3 (directly across the resistor). Take a close look at the following circuit, and try to determine which points are common to each other:

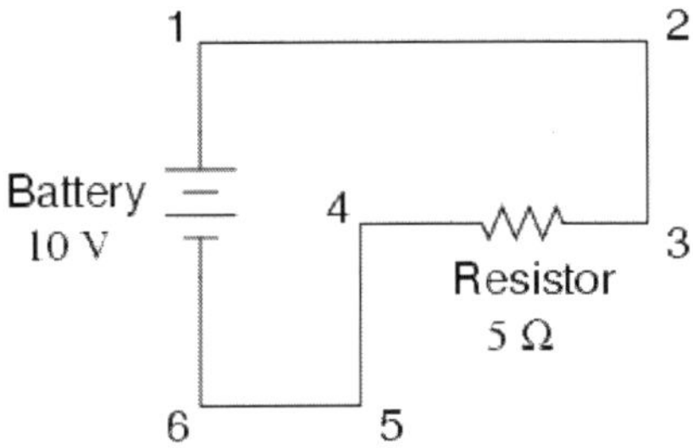

Here, we only have 2 components excluding the wires: the battery and the resistor. Though the connecting wires take a convoluted path in forming a complete circuit, there are several electrically common points in the electrons' path. Points 1, 2, and 3 are all common to each other, because they're directly connected together by wire. The same goes for points 4, 5, and 6.

The voltage between points 1 and 6 is 10 volts, coming straight from the battery. However, since points 5 and 4 are common to 6, and points 2 and 3 common to 1, that same 10 volts also exists between these other pairs of points:

Between points 1 and 4 = 10 volts
Between points 2 and 4 = 10 volts
Between points 3 and 4 = 10 volts (directly across the resistor)
Between points 1 and 5 = 10 volts
Between points 2 and 5 = 10 volts
Between points 3 and 5 = 10 volts
Between points 1 and 6 = 10 volts (directly across the battery)
Between points 2 and 6 = 10 volts
Between points 3 and 6 = 10 volts

Since electrically common points are connected together by (zero resistance) wire, there is no significant voltage drop between them regardless of the amount of current conducted from one to the next through that connecting wire. Thus, if we were to read voltages between common points, we should show (practically) zero:

```
Between points 1 and 2 = 0 volts     Points 1, 2, and 3 are
Between points 2 and 3 = 0 volts       electrically common
Between points 1 and 3 = 0 volts

Between points 4 and 5 = 0 volts     Points 4, 5, and 6 are
Between points 5 and 6 = 0 volts       electrically common
Between points 4 and 6 = 0 volts
```

This makes sense mathematically, too. With a 10 volt battery and a 5 Ω resistor, the circuit current will be 2 amps. With wire resistance being zero, the voltage drop across any continuous stretch of wire can be determined through Ohm's Law as such:

$$E = IR$$

$$E = (2\,A)\,(0\Omega)$$

$$E = 0\,V$$

It should be obvious that the calculated voltage drop across any uninterrupted length of wire in a circuit where wire is assumed to have zero resistance will always be zero, no matter what the magnitude of current, since zero multiplied by anything equals zero.

Because common points in a circuit will exhibit the same relative voltage and resistance measurements, wires connecting common points are often labelled with the same designation. This is not to say that the *terminal* connection points are labelled the same, just the connecting wires. Take this circuit as an example:

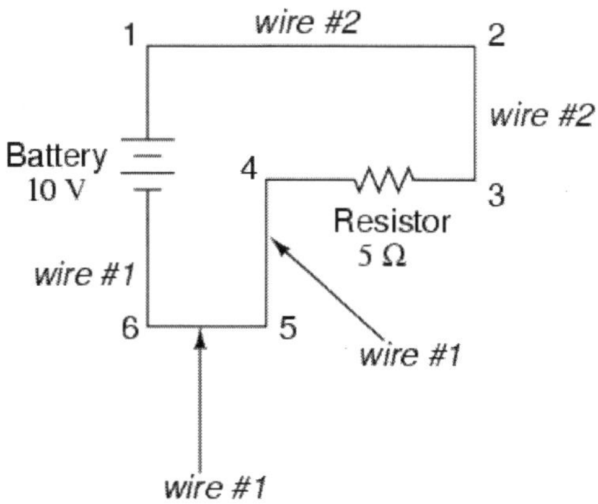

Points 1, 2, and 3 are all common to each other, so the wire connecting point 1 to 2 is labelled the same (wire 2) as the wire connecting point 2 to 3 (wire 2). In a real circuit, the wire stretching from point 1 to 2 may not even be the same colour or size as the wire connecting point 2 to 3, but they should bear the exact same label. The same goes for the wires connecting points 6, 5, and 4.

Knowing that electrically common points have zero voltage drop between them is a valuable troubleshooting principle. If I measure for voltage between points in a circuit that are supposed to be common to each other, I should read zero. If, however, I read substantial voltage between those two points, then I know with certainty that they cannot be directly connected together. If those points are *supposed* to be electrically common but they register otherwise, then I know that there is an "open failure" between those points.

One final note: for most practical purposes, wire conductors can be assumed to possess zero resistance from end to end. In reality, however, there will always be some small amount of resistance encountered along the length of a wire, unless its a superconducting wire. Knowing this, we need to bear in mind that the principles learned here about electrically common points are all valid to a large degree, but not to an *absolute* degree.

That is, the rule that electrically common points are guaranteed to have zero voltage between them is more accurately stated as such: electrically common points will have *very little* voltage dropped between them. That small, virtually unavoidable trace of resistance found in any piece of connecting wire is bound to create a small voltage across the length of it as current is conducted through. So long as you understand that these rules are based upon *ideal* conditions, you won't be perplexed when you come across some condition appearing to be an exception to the rule.

- Connecting wires in a circuit are assumed to have zero resistance unless otherwise stated.
- Wires in a circuit can be shortened or lengthened without impacting the circuit's function — all that matters is that the components are attached to one another in the same sequence.
- Points directly connected together in a circuit by zero resistance (wire) are considered to be *electrically common*.
- Electrically common points, with zero resistance between them, will have zero voltage dropped between them, regardless of the magnitude of current (ideally).

- The voltage or resistance readings referenced between sets of electrically common points will be the same.
- These rules apply to *ideal* conditions, where connecting wires are assumed to possess absolutely zero resistance. In real life this will probably not be the case, but wire resistances should be low enough so that the general principles stated here still hold.

Polarity of Voltage Drops

We can trace the direction that electrons will flow in the same circuit by starting at the negative (-) terminal and following through to the positive (+) terminal of the battery, the only source of voltage in the circuit. From this we can see that the electrons are moving counter-clockwise, from point 6 to 5 to 4 to 3 to 2 to 1 and back to 6 again.

As the current encounters the 5 Ω resistance, voltage is dropped across the resistor's ends. The polarity of this voltage drop is negative (-) at point 4 with respect to positive (+) at point 3. We can mark the polarity of the resistor's voltage drop with these negative and positive symbols, in accordance with the direction of current (whichever end of the resistor the current is *entering* is negative with respect to the end of the resistor it is *exiting*:

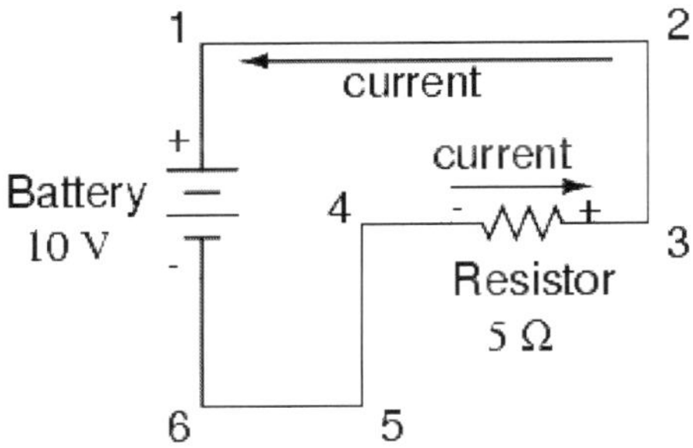

We could make our table of voltages a little more complete by marking the polarity of the voltage for each pair of points in this circuit:

```
Between points 1 (+) and 4 (-) = 10 volts
Between points 2 (+) and 4 (-) = 10 volts
Between points 3 (+) and 4 (-) = 10 volts
Between points 1 (+) and 5 (-) = 10 volts
Between points 2 (+) and 5 (-) = 10 volts
```

```
Between points 3 (+) and 5 (-) = 10 volts
Between points 1 (+) and 6 (-) = 10 volts
Between points 2 (+) and 6 (-) = 10 volts
Between points 3 (+) and 6 (-) = 10 volts
```

While it might seem a little silly to document polarity of voltage drop in this circuit, it is an important concept to master. It will be critically important in the analysis of more complex circuits involving multiple resistors and/or batteries.

It should be understood that polarity has nothing to do with Ohm's Law: there will never be negative voltages, currents, or resistance entered into any Ohm's Law equations! There are other mathematical principles of electricity that do take polarity into account through the use of signs (+ or -), but not Ohm's Law.

- The polarity of the voltage drop across any resistive component is determined by the direction of electron flow through it: *negative* entering, and *positive* exiting.

Computer Simulation of Electric Circuits

Computers can be powerful tools if used properly, especially in the realms of science and engineering. Software exists for the simulation of electric circuits by computer, and these programmes can be very useful in helping circuit designers test ideas before actually building real circuits, saving much time and money.

These same programmes can be fantastic aids to the beginning student of electronics, allowing the exploration of ideas quickly and easily with no assembly of real circuits required. Of course, there is no substitute for actually building and testing real circuits, but computer simulations certainly assist in the learning process by allowing the student to experiment with changes and see the effects they have on circuits. Throughout this book, I'll be incorporating computer printouts from circuit simulation frequently in order to illustrate important concepts. By observing the results of a computer simulation, a student can gain an intuitive grasp of circuit behaviour without the intimidation of abstract mathematical analysis.

To simulate circuits on computer, I make use of a particular programme called SPICE, which works by describing a circuit to the computer by means of a listing of text. In essence, this listing is a kind of computer programme in itself, and must adhere to the syntactical rules of the SPICE language. The computer is then used to process, or "run," the SPICE programme, which interprets the text listing describing the circuit and outputs the results of its detailed mathematical analysis, also in text form. Many details of using SPICE are described in volume 5 ("Reference") of this book series for those wanting more information. Here, I'll just introduce the basic concepts and then apply SPICE to the analysis of these simple circuits we've been reading about.

First, we need to have SPICE installed on our computer. As a free programme, it is commonly available on the internet for download, and in formats appropriate for many different operating systems. In this book, I use one of the earlier versions of SPICE: version 2G6, for its simplicity of use.

Next, we need a circuit for SPICE to analyze. Let's try one of the circuits illustrated earlier in the chapter. Here is its schematic diagram:

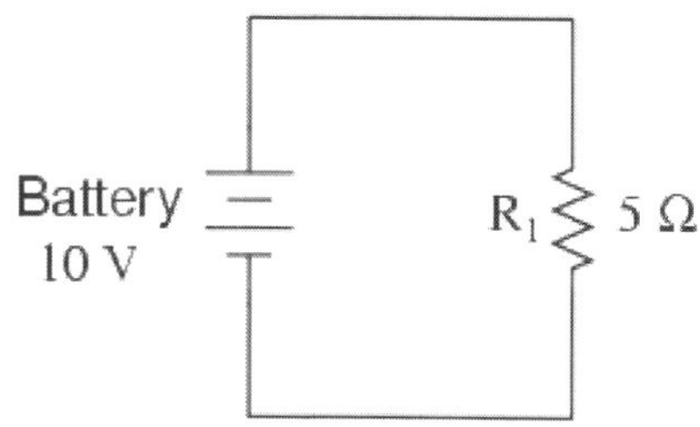

This simple circuit consists of a battery and a resistor connected directly together. We know the voltage of the battery (10 volts) and the resistance of the resistor (5 Ω), but nothing else about the circuit. If we describe this circuit to SPICE, it should be able to tell us (at the very least), how much current we have in the circuit by using Ohm's Law (I=E/R).

SPICE cannot directly understand a schematic diagram or any other form of graphical description. SPICE is a text-based computer programme, and demands that a circuit be described in terms of its constituent components and connection points. Each unique connection point in a circuit is described for SPICE by a "node" number. Points that are electrically common to each other in the circuit to be simulated are designated as such by sharing the same number. It might be helpful to think of these numbers as "wire" numbers rather than "node" numbers, following the definition given in the previous section. This is how the computer knows what's connected to what: by the sharing of common wire, or node, numbers. In our example circuit, we only have two "nodes," the top wire and the bottom wire. SPICE demands there be a node 0 somewhere in the circuit, so we'll label our wires 0 and 1:

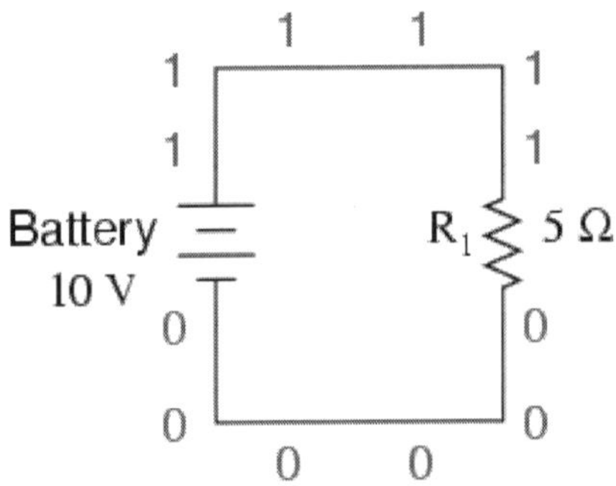

In the above illustration, I've shown multiple "1" and "0" labels around each respective wire to emphasize the concept of common points sharing common node numbers, but still this is a graphic image, not a text description. SPICE needs to have the component values and node numbers given to it in text form before any analysis may proceed.

Creating a text file in a computer involves the use of a programme called a *text editor*. Similar to a word processor, a text editor allows you to type text and record what you've typed in the form of a file stored on the computer's hard disk. Text editors lack the formatting ability of word processors (no *italic*, bold, or underlined characters), and this is a good thing, since programmes such as SPICE wouldn't know what to do with this extra information. If we want to create a plain-text file, with absolutely nothing recorded except the keyboard characters we select, a text editor is the tool to use.

If using a Microsoft operating system such as DOS or Windows, a couple of text editors are readily available with the system. In DOS, there is the old *Edit* text editing programme, which may be invoked by typing edit at the command prompt. In Windows (3.x/95/98/NT/Me/2k/XP), the *Notepad* text editor is your stock choice. Many other text editing programmes are available, and some are even free. I happen to use a free text editor called *Vim*, and run it under both Windows 95 and Linux operating systems. It matters little which editor you use, so don't worry if the screenshots in this section don't look like yours; the important information here is *what you type*, not *which editor* you happen to use.

To describe this simple, two-component circuit to SPICE, I will begin by invoking my text editor programme and typing in a "title" line for the circuit:

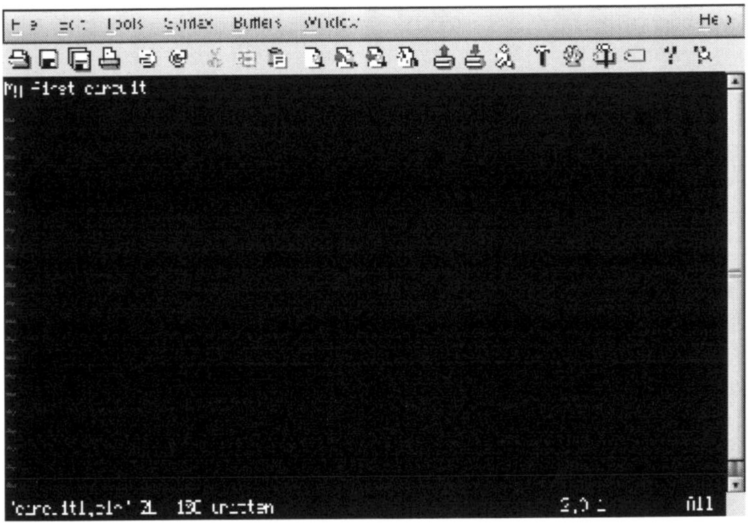

We can describe the battery to the computer by typing in a line of text starting with the letter "v" (for "Voltage source"), identifying which wire each terminal of the battery connects to (the node numbers), and the battery's voltage, like this:

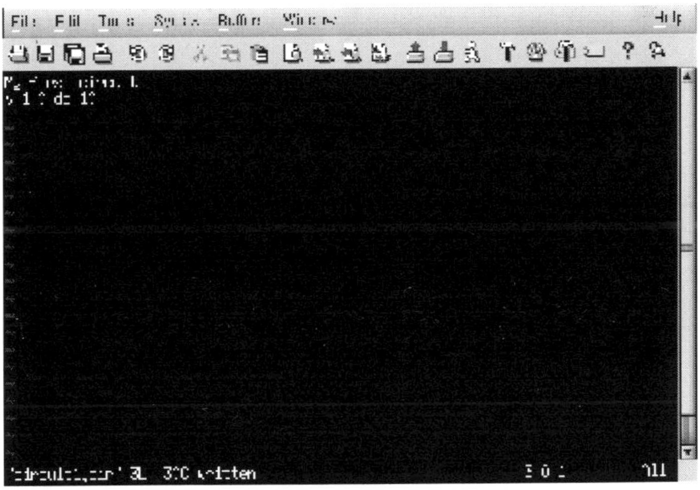

This line of text tells SPICE that we have a voltage source connected between nodes 1 and 0, direct current (DC), 10 volts. That's all the computer needs to know regarding the battery. Now we turn to the resistor: SPICE requires that resistors be described with a letter "r," the numbers of the two nodes (connection points), and the resistance in ohms. Since this is a computer simulation, there is no need to specify a power rating for the resistor. That's one nice thing about "virtual" components: they can't be harmed by excessive voltages or currents!

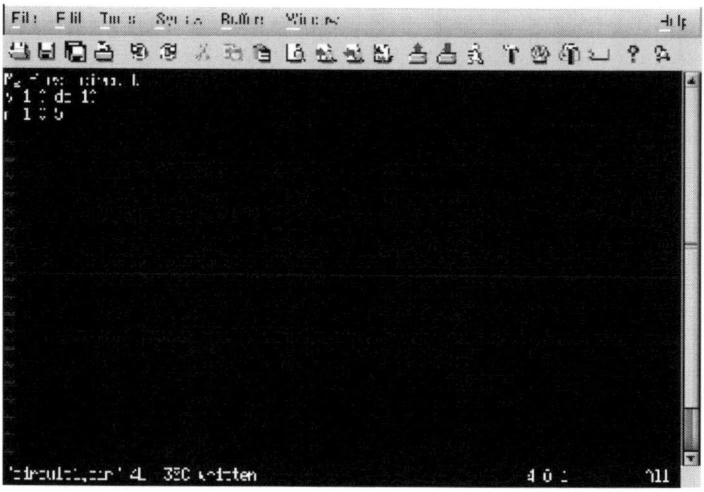

Now, SPICE will know there is a resistor connected between nodes 1 and 0 with a value of 5 Ω. This very brief line of text tells the computer we have a resistor ("r") connected between the same two nodes as the battery (1 and 0), with a resistance value of 5 Ω.

If we add an end statement to this collection of SPICE commands to indicate the end of the circuit description, we will have all the information SPICE needs, collected in one file and ready for processing. This circuit description, comprised of lines of text in a computer file, is technically known as a *netlist*, or *deck*:

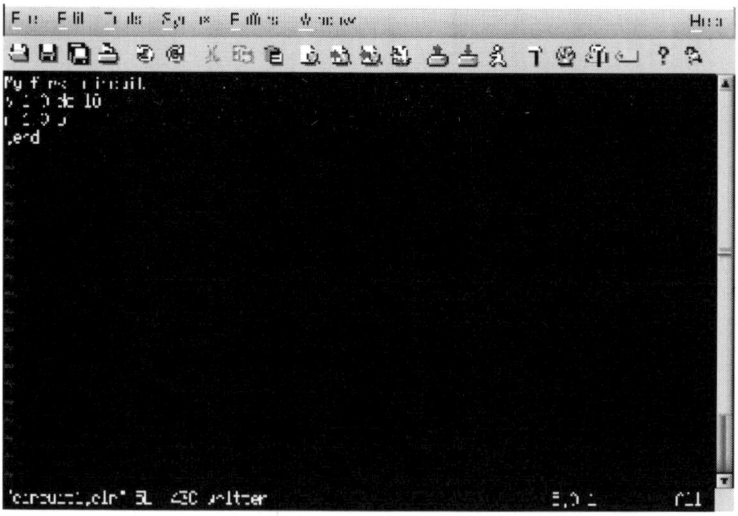

Once we have finished typing all the necessary SPICE commands, we need to "save" them to a file on the computer's hard disk so that SPICE has something to reference to when invoked. Since this is my first SPICE netlist, I'll save it under the filename "circuit1.cir" (the actual name being arbitrary).

You may elect to name your first SPICE netlist something completely different, just as long as you don't violate any filename rules for your operating system, such as using no more than 8+3 characters (eight characters in the name, and three characters in the extension: 12345678.123) in DOS. To invoke SPICE (tell it to process the contents of the circuit1.cir netlist file), we have to exit from the text editor and access a command prompt (the "DOS prompt" for Microsoft users) where we can enter text commands for the computer's operating system to obey. This "primitive" way of invoking a programme may seem archaic to computer users accustomed to a "point-and-click" graphical environment, but it is a very powerful and flexible way of doing things.

Remember, what you're doing here by using SPICE is a simple form of computer programming, and the more comfortable you become in giving the computer text-form commands to follow — as opposed to simply clicking on icon images using a mouse — the more mastery you will have over your computer. Once at a command prompt, type in this command, followed by an [Enter] keystroke (this example uses the filename circuit1.cir; if you have chosen a different filename for your netlist file, substitute it):

spice < circuit1.cir

Here is how this looks on my computer (running the Linux operating system), just before I press the [Enter] key:

As soon as you press the [Enter] key to issue this command, text from SPICE's output should scroll by on the computer screen.

Here is a screenshot showing what SPICE outputs on my computer (I've lengthened the "terminal" window to show you the full text.

With a normal-size terminal, the text easily exceeds one page length):

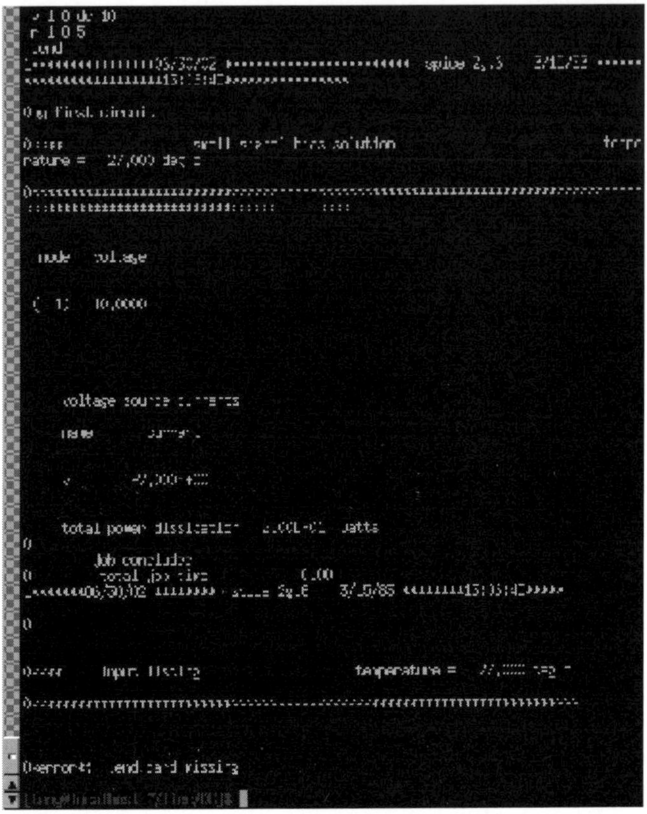

SPICE begins with a reiteration of the netlist, complete with title line and .end statement. About halfway through the simulation it displays the voltage at all nodes with reference to node 0. In this example, we only have one node other than node 0, so it displays the voltage there: 10.0000 volts. Then it displays the current through each voltage source. Since we only have one voltage source in the entire circuit, it only displays the current through that one. In this case, the source current is 2 amps. Due to a quirk in the way SPICE analyzes current, the value of 2 amps is output as a negative (-) 2 amps.

The last line of text in the computer's analysis report is "total power dissipation," which in this case is given as "2.00E+01" watts: 2.00×10^1, or 20 watts. SPICE outputs most figures in scientific notation rather than normal (fixed-point) notation. While this may seem to be more confusing at first, it is actually less confusing when very large or very small numbers are involved. The details of scientific notation will be covered in the next chapter of this book. One of the benefits of using a "primitive" text-based programme such as SPICE is that the text files dealt with are extremely small compared to other file formats, especially graphical formats used in other circuit simulation software. Also, the fact that SPICE's output is plain text means you can direct SPICE's output to another text file where it may be further manipulated. To do this, we re-issue a command to the computer's operating system to invoke SPICE, this time redirecting the output to a file I'll call "output.txt":

SPICE will run "silently" this time, without the stream of text output to the computer screen as before. A new file, output1.txt, will be created, which you may open and change using a text editor or word processor. For this illustration, I'll use the same text editor (*Vim*) to open this file:

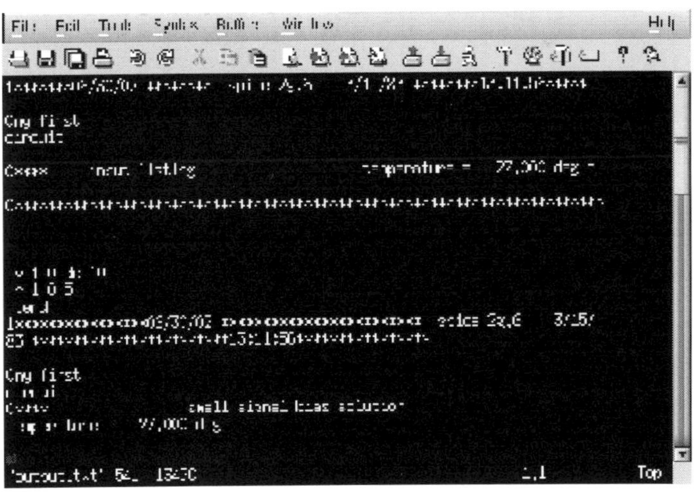

Now, I may freely edit this file, deleting any extraneous text (such as the "banners" showing date and time), leaving only the text that I feel to be pertinent to my circuit's analysis:

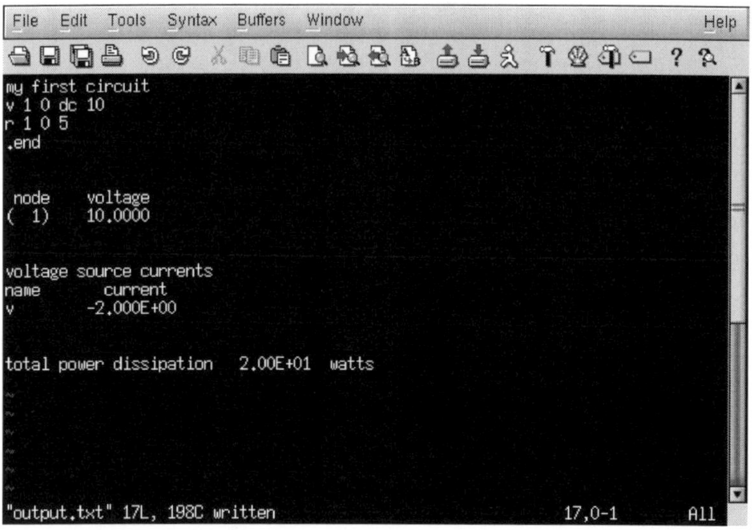

Once suitably edited and re-saved under the same filename (output.txt in this example), the text may be pasted into any kind of document, "plain text" being a universal file format for almost all computer systems. I can even include it directly in the text of this book — rather than as a "screenshot" graphic image — like this:

```
my first circuit
v 1 0 dc 10
r 1 0 5
.end


node     voltage
(1)     10.0000


voltage source currents
name        current
v         -2.000E+00
total power dissipation 2.00E+01 watts
```

Incidentally, this is the preferred format for text output from SPICE simulations in this book series: as real text, not as graphic screenshot images.

To alter a component value in the simulation, we need to open up the netlist file (circuit1.cir) and make the required modifications in the text description of the circuit, then save those changes to the same filename, and re-invoke SPICE at the command prompt. This process of editing and processing a text file is one familiar to every computer programmer. One of the reasons I like to teach SPICE is that it prepares the learner to think and work like a computer programmer, which is good because computer programming is a significant area of advanced electronics work.

Earlier we explored the consequences of changing one of the three variables in an electric circuit (voltage, current, or resistance) using Ohm's Law to mathematically predict what would happen. Now let's try the same thing using SPICE to do the math for us.

If we were to triple the voltage in our last example circuit from 10 to 30 volts and keep the circuit resistance unchanged, we would expect the current to triple as well. Let's try this, re-naming our netlist file so as to not over-write the first file. This way, we will have *both* versions of the circuit simulation stored on the hard drive of our computer for future use. The following text listing is the output of SPICE for this modified netlist, formatted as plain text rather than as a graphic image of my computer screen:

```
second example circuit
v 1 0 dc 30
r 1 0 5
.end

node     voltage
(1)     30.0000

voltage source currents
name        current
v         -6.000E+00
total power dissipation   1.80E+02 watts
```

Just as we expected, the current tripled with the voltage increase. Current used to be 2 amps, but now it has increased to 6 amps (-6.000 x 10^0). Note also how the total power dissipation in the circuit has increased. It was 20 watts before, but now is 180 watts (1.8 x 10^2). Recalling that power is related to the square of the voltage (Joule's Law: $P=E^2/R$), this makes sense. If we triple the circuit voltage, the power should increase by a factor of nine ($3^2 = 9$). Nine times 20 is indeed 180, so SPICE's output does indeed correlate with what we know about power in electric circuits.

If we want to see how this simple circuit would respond over a wide range of battery voltages, we can invoke some of the more advanced options within SPICE. Here, I'll use the ".dc" analysis option to vary the battery voltage from 0 to 100 volts in 5 volt increments, printing out the circuit voltage and current at every step. The lines in the SPICE netlist beginning with a star symbol ("*") are *comments*. That is, they don't tell the computer to do anything relating to circuit analysis, but merely serve as notes for any human being reading the netlist text.

```
third example circuit
v 1 0
r 1 0 5
*the ".dc" statement tells spice to sweep the "v"
supply
*voltage from 0 to 100 volts in 5 volt steps.
.dc v 0 100 5
.print dc v(1) i(v)
.end
```

The .print command in this SPICE netlist instructs SPICE to print columns of numbers corresponding to each step in the analysis:

```
v          i(v)
0.000E+00  0.000E+00
5.000E+00  -1.000E+00
1.000E+01  -2.000E+00
1.500E+01  -3.000E+00
2.000E+01  -4.000E+00
2.500E+01  -5.000E+00
3.000E+01  -6.000E+00
3.500E+01  -7.000E+00
4.000E+01  -8.000E+00
4.500E+01  -9.000E+00
5.000E+01  -1.000E+01
5.500E+01  -1.100E+01
6.000E+01  -1.200E+01
6.500E+01  -1.300E+01
7.000E+01  -1.400E+01
7.500E+01  -1.500E+01
8.000E+01  -1.600E+01
8.500E+01  -1.700E+01
9.000E+01  -1.800E+01
9.500E+01  -1.900E+01
1.000E+02  -2.000E+01
```

If I re-edit the netlist file, changing the .print command into a .plot command, SPICE will output a crude graph made up of text characters:

```
Legend:  + = v#branch
------------------------------------------------------------------------
sweep       v#branch-2.00e+01               -1.00e+01               0.00e+00
---------------------|-----------------------|-----------------------|
0.000e+00  0.000e+00 .                       .                       +
5.000e+00 -1.000e+00 .                       .                     + .
1.000e+01 -2.000e+00 .                       .                   +   .
1.500e+01 -3.000e+00 .                       .                +      .
2.000e+01 -4.000e+00 .                       .              +        .
2.500e+01 -5.000e+00 .                       .           +           .
3.000e+01 -6.000e+00 .                       .         +             .
3.500e+01 -7.000e+00 .                       .      +                .
4.000e+01 -8.000e+00 .                       .    +                  .
4.500e+01 -9.000e+00 .                       . +                     .
5.000e+01 -1.000e+01 .                       +                       .
5.500e+01 -1.100e+01 .                     + .                       .
6.000e+01 -1.200e+01 .                   +   .                       .
6.500e+01 -1.300e+01 .                +      .                       .
7.000e+01 -1.400e+01 .              +        .                       .
7.500e+01 -1.500e+01 .           +           .                       .
8.000e+01 -1.600e+01 .         +             .                       .
8.500e+01 -1.700e+01 .      +                .                       .
9.000e+01 -1.800e+01 .    +                  .                       .
9.500e+01 -1.900e+01 . +                     .                       .
1.000e+02 -2.000e+01 +                       .                       .
---------------------|-----------------------|-----------------------|
sweep       v#branch-2.00e+01               -1.00e+01               0.00e+00
```

In both output formats, the left-hand column of numbers represents the battery voltage at each interval, as it increases from 0 volts to 100 volts, 5 volts at a time. The numbers in the right-hand column indicate the circuit current for each of those voltages. Look closely at those numbers and you'll see the proportional relationship between each pair: Ohm's Law (I=E/R) holds true in each and every case, each current value being 1/5 the respective voltage value, because the circuit resistance is exactly 5 Ω. Again, the negative numbers for current in this SPICE analysis is more of a quirk than anything else. Just pay attention to the absolute value of each number unless otherwise specified.

There are even some computer programmes able to interpret and convert the non-graphical data output by SPICE into a graphical plot. One of these programmes is called *Nutmeg*, and its output looks something like this:

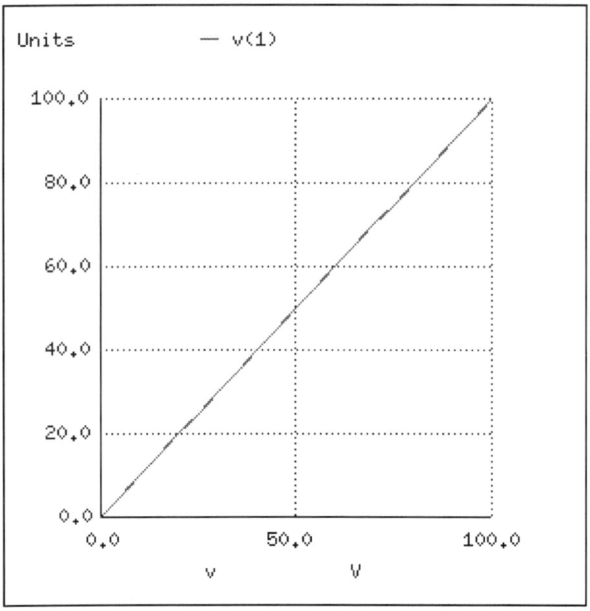

Note how Nutmeg plots the resistor voltage v(1) (voltage between node 1 and the implied reference point of node 0) as a line with a positive slope (from lower-left to upper-right).

Whether or not you ever become proficient at using SPICE is not relevant to its application in this book. All that matters is that you develop an understanding for what the numbers mean in a SPICE-generated report. In the examples to come, I'll do my best to annotate the numerical results of SPICE to eliminate any confusion, and unlock the power of this amazing tool to help you understand the behaviour of electric circuits.

Kirchhoffs Laws

Kirchhoff's circuit laws are two approximate equalities that deal with the current and voltage in electrical circuits. They were first described in 1845 by Gustav Kirchhoff.

This generalized the work of Georg Ohm and preceded the work of Maxwell. Widely used in electrical engineering, they are also called Kirchhoff's *rules* or simply Kirchhoff's *laws.*

Both of Kirchhoff's laws can be understood as corollaries of the Maxwell equations in the low-frequency limit — conventionally called "DC" circuits. They serve as first approximations for AC circuits.

Kirchhoff's Current Law (KCL)

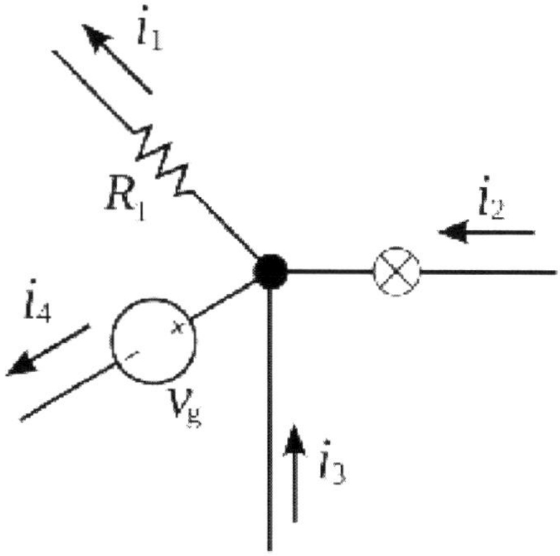

Figure: *The current entering any junction is equal to the current leaving that junction.* $i_2 + i_3 = i_1 + i_4$

This law is also called Kirchhoff's first law, Kirchhoff's point rule, or Kirchhoff's junction rule (or nodal rule).

The principle of conservation of electric charge implies that:

At any node (junction) in an electrical circuit, the sum of currents flowing into that node is equal to the sum of currents flowing out of that node, or:

The algebraic sum of currents in a network of conductors meeting at a point is zero.

Recalling that current is a signed (positive or negative) quantity reflecting direction towards or away from a node, this principle can be stated as:

$$\sum_{k=1}^{n} I_k = 0$$

n is the total number of branches with currents flowing towards or away from the node.

This formula is valid for complex currents:

$$\sum_{k=1}^{n} \tilde{I}_k = 0$$

The law is based on the conservation of charge whereby the charge (measured in coulombs) is the product of the current (in amperes) and the time (in seconds).

Limitations

KCL, in its usual form, is dependent on the assumption that current flows only in conductors, and that whenever current flows into one end of a conductor it immediately flows out the other end. This is not a safe assumption for AC circuits. It may be possible to salvage the form of KCL by considering "parasitic capacitances" distributed along the conductors. However, this greatly detracts from the simplicity of KCL and invalidates the notion of topological circuit diagram as discussed below. Significant violations of KCL can occur even at 60Hz, which is not a very high frequency.

As another way of saying almost the same thing, KCL is valid only if the total electric charge, Q, remains constant in the region being considered. In practical cases this is always so when KCL is applied at a geometric point. When investigating a finite region, however, it is possible that the charge density within the region may change. Since charge is conserved, this can only come about by a flow of charge across the region boundary. This flow represents a net current and KCL is violated.

Formally, from the volume integral of the current continuity equation,

$$\int_V \nabla\cdot\mathbf{J}\,dV = -\frac{d}{dt}Q,$$

where J is the current density vector and V is the volume of the region

Converting the volume integral to a surface integral using the divergence theorem

$$\int_V \nabla\cdot\mathbf{J}\,dV = \oiint_S S(\mathbf{J}\cdot\mathbf{n})\,dS$$

Hence,

$$\oiint_S (\mathbf{J}\cdot\mathbf{n})dS = -\frac{d}{dt}Q$$

The right-hand side vanishes if Q is independent of time. If practically all of J is contained within small regions, conducting wires for instance, then the left-hand side can be interpreted as a sum of discrete currents and KCL is recovered, providing that $dQ/dt = 0$.

A particular case where KCL does not hold is the current entering a single plate of a capacitor. If one imagines a closed surface around that single plate, current enters through the surface, but does not exit, thus violating KCL. Certainly, the currents through a closed surface around the entire capacitor will meet KCL since the current entering one plate is balanced by the current exiting the other plate, and that is usually all that is important in circuit analysis, but there is a problem when considering just one plate. Another common example is the current in an antenna where current enters the antenna from the transmitter feeder but no current exits from the other end (Johnson and Graham, pp. 36–37).

Maxwell introduced the concept of displacement currents to describe these situations. The current flowing into a capacitor plate is equal to the rate of accumulation of charge and hence is also equal to the rate of change of electric flux due to that charge (electric flux is measured in the same units, Coulombs, as electric charge in the SI system of units). This rate of change of flux, ψ , is what Maxwell called displacement current I_D;

$$I_{\mathrm{D}} = \frac{d\psi}{dt}$$

When the displacement currents are included, Kirchhoff's current law once again holds. Displacement currents are not real currents in that they do not consist of moving charges, they should be viewed more as a correction factor to make KCL true. In the case of the capacitor plate, the real current entering the plate is exactly cancelled by a displacement current leaving the plate and heading for the opposite plate.

This can also be expressed in terms of vector field quantities by taking the divergence of Ampère's law with Maxwell's correction and combining with Gauss's law, yielding:

$$\nabla\cdot\mathbf{J} = -\nabla\cdot\frac{\partial\mathbf{D}}{\partial t} = -\frac{\partial\rho}{\partial t}$$

This is simply the charge conservation equation (in integral form, it says that the current flowing out of a closed surface is equal to the rate of loss of charge within the enclosed volume (divergence theorem). Kirchhoff's current law is equivalent to the statement that the divergence of the current is zero, true for time-invariant ρ, or always true if the displacement current is included with J.

Uses

A matrix version of Kirchhoff's current law is the basis of most circuit simulation software, such as SPICE. Kirchhoff's current law combined with Ohm's Law is used in nodal analysis.

Kirchhoff's Voltage Law (KVL)

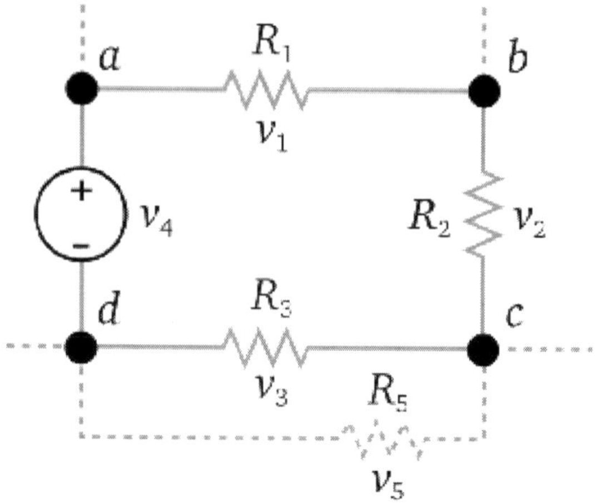

Figure: *The sum of all the voltages around the loop is equal to zero.* $v_1 + v_2 + v_3 - v_4 = 0$

This law is also called Kirchhoff's second law, Kirchhoff's loop (or mesh) rule, and Kirchhoff's second rule.

Similarly to KCL, it can be stated as:

$$\sum_{k=1}^{n} V_k = 0$$

Here, n is the total number of voltages measured. The voltages may also be complex:

$$\sum_{k=1}^{n} \tilde{V}_k = 0$$

This law is based on one of the Maxwell equations, namely the Maxwell-Faraday law of induction, which tells us that the voltage drop around any closed loop is equal to the rate-of-change of the flux threading the loop. The amount of flux depends on the area of the loop and on the magnetic field strength. KVL says the loop voltage is zero. The Maxwell equations tell us that the loop voltage will be *small* if the area of the loop is small, the magnetic field is weak, and/ or the magnetic field is slowly changing.

Routine engineering techniques — such as the use of coaxial cable and twisted pairs — can be used to minimize stray magnetic fields and minimize the area of vulnerable loops. In this way things can be *arranged* so that KVL becomes a good approximation, even in situations where it otherwise would not have been.

Limitations

KVL is based on the assumption that there is no fluctuating magnetic field linking the closed loop. This is not a safe assumption for AC circuits. In the presence of a changing magnetic field the electric field is not a conservative vector field. Therefore it cannot be the gradient of any potential. That is to say, the line integral of the electric field around the loop is not zero, which directly contradicts KVL.

It may be possible to salvage the form of KVL by considering "parasitic inductances" (including mutual inductances) distributed along the conductors. These are treated as imaginary circuit elements that produce a voltage drop equal to the rate-of-change of the flux. However, this greatly detracts from the simplicity of KVL and invalidates the notion of topological circuit diagram.

Generalization

In the DC limit, the voltage drop around any loop is zero. This includes imaginary loops arranged arbitrarily in space — not limited to the loops delineated by the circuit elements and conductors. In the low-frequency limit, this is a corollary of Faraday's law of induction (which is one of the Maxwell equations).

This has practical application in situations involving "static electricity".

Topological circuit diagrams

The approximations that lead to Kirchhoff's circuit laws are part of a package that also leads to *topological circuit diagrams*, i.e. the idea that the physical and geometrical layout of the circuit does not matter; the only thing that matters is the topology as determined by the conductors and circuit elements connected to the nodes. These can be treated as the arcs and nodes of formal graph theory. In other words, Kirchhoff's laws say it suffices to use a circuit diagram that is purely schematic. This is a very useful, powerful simplification.

This works fine in the DC limit, but it is only a first approximation for AC circuits. For high-power, high-precision, and/or high-frequency work, the deviations from Kirchhoff's laws cannot be neglected. The physical and geometrical layout of the circuit matters, because it determines the magnitude of the parasitic capacitances and inductances.

Example: Assume an electric network consisting of two voltage sources and three resistors:

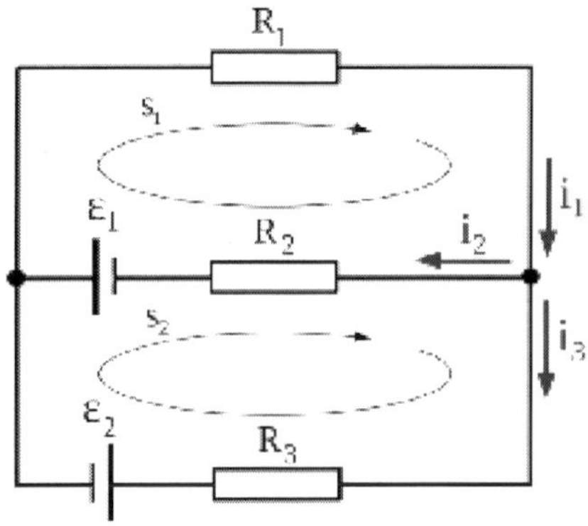

According to the first law we have

$$i_1 - i_2 - i_3 = 0$$

The second law applied to the closed circuit s_1 gives

$$-R_2 i_2 + \epsilon_1 - R_1 i_1 = 0$$

The second law applied to the closed circuit s_2 gives

$$-R_3 i_3 - \epsilon_2 - \epsilon_1 + R_2 i_2 = 0$$

Thus we get a linear system of equations in i_1, i_2, i_3:

$$\begin{cases} i_1 - i_2 - i_3 & = 0 \\ -R_2 i_2 + \epsilon_1 - R_1 i_1 & = 0 \\ -R_3 i_3 - \epsilon_2 - \epsilon_1 + R_2 i_2 & = 0 \end{cases}$$

Assuming

$$R_1 = 100,\ R_2 = 200,\ R_3 = 300,\ \epsilon_1 = 3,\ \epsilon_2 = 4$$

the solution is

$$\begin{cases} i_1 = \dfrac{1}{1100} \text{ or } 0.\overline{90}\text{mA} \\ i_2 = \dfrac{4}{275} \text{ or } 14.\overline{54}\text{mA} \\ i_3 = -\dfrac{3}{220} \text{ or } -13.\overline{63}\text{mA} \end{cases}$$

i_3 has a negative sign, which means that the direction of i_3 is opposite to the assumed direction (the direction defined in the picture).

4

Electronics Technology

Power electronics is the application of solid-state electronics for the control and conversion of electric power. It also refers to a subject of research in electri3cal engineering which deals with design, control, computation and integration of nonlinear, time varying energy processing electronic systems with fast dynamics.

Figure: *An HVDC thyristor valve tower* ***16.8*** *m tall in a hall at Baltic Cable AB in Sweden*

Power electronic converters can be found wherever there is a need to modify a form of electrical energy (i.e. change its voltage, current or frequency). The power range of these converters is from some milliwatts (as in a mobile phone) to hundreds of megawatts (e.g. in a High-voltage direct-current (HVDC) transmission system). With "classical" electronics, electrical currents and voltage are used to carry information, whereas with power electronics, they carry power. Thus, the main metric of power electronics becomes the efficiency.

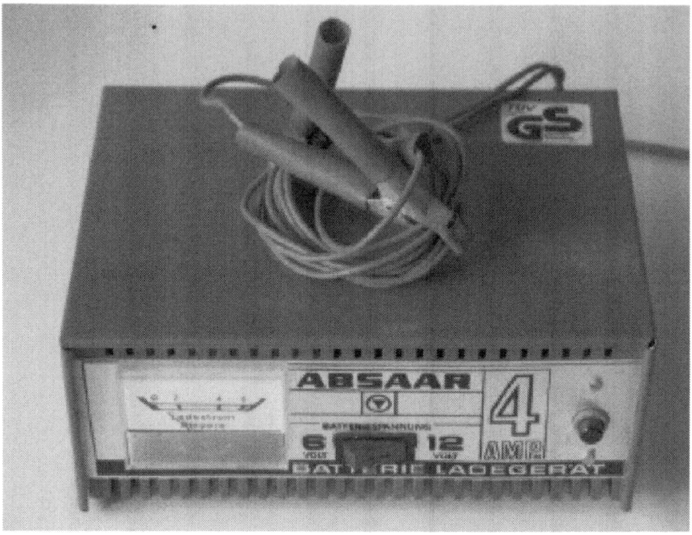

Figure: *A battery charger is an example of a piece of power electronics*

The first very high power electronic devices were mercury-arc valves. In modern systems the conversion is performed with semiconductor switching devices such as diodes, thyristors and transistors, as pioneered by R. D. Middlebrook and others beginning in the 1950s. In contrast to electronic systems concerned with transmission and processing of signals and data, in power electronics substantial amounts of electrical energy are processed. An AC/DC converter (rectifier) is the most typical power electronics device found in many consumer electronic devices, e.g. television sets, personal computers, battery chargers, etc. The power range is typically from tens of watts to several hundred watts. In industry the most common application is the variable speed drive (VSD) that is used to control an induction motor. The power range of VSDs start from a few hundred watts and end at tens of megawatts.

The power conversion systems can be classified according to the type of the input and output power

- AC to DC (rectifier)
- DC to AC (inverter)

- DC to DC (DC-to-DC converter)
- AC to AC (AC-to-AC converter)

Switching

As efficiency is at a premium in a power electronic converter, the losses that a power electronic device generates should be as low as possible. The instantaneous dissipated power of a device is equal to the product of the voltage across the device and the current through it.

The losses of a power device are at a minimum when the voltage across it is zero (the device is on) or when no current flows through it (off). Power electronic converters are built around one (or more) device operating in switching mode. Practical devices have non-zero voltage drop and dissipate power when on, and take some time to pass through an active region until they reach the "on" or "off" state. These losses are a significant part of the total lost power in a converter.

Devices

The capabilities and economy of power electronics system are determined by the active devices that are available. Their characteristics and limitations are a key element in the design of power electronics systems. Formerly, the mercury arc valve, the high-vacuum and gas-filled diode thermionic rectifiers, and triggered devices such as the thyratron and ignitron were widely used in power electronics. As the ratings of solid-state devices improved in both voltage and current-handling capacity, vacuum devices have been nearly entirely replaced by solid-state equivalents, or by solid state devices that have no thermionic equivalent.

Power electronic devices may be used as switches, or as amplifiers. An ideal switch is either open or closed and so dissipates no power; it withstands an applied voltage and passes no current, or passes any amount of current with no voltage drop. Semiconductor devices used as switches can approximate this ideal property and so most power electronic applications rely on switching devices on and off, which makes systems very efficient as no power is wasted in the switching devices. By contrast, in the case of the amplifier, the current through the device varies continuously according to a controlled input. The voltage and current at the device terminals follow a load line, and the power dissipation inside the device is large compared with the power delivered to the load.

Several attributes dictate how devices are used. Devices such as diodes conduct when a forward voltage is applied and have no external control of the start of conduction. Power devices such as silicon controlled rectifiers and thyristors (as well as the former mercury valve and thyratron) allow control of the start of conduction, but rely on periodic reversal of current flow to turn them off.

Devices such as gate turn-off thyristors, bipolar junction transistors (BJT), and MOSFET transistors provide full switching control and can be turned on or off without regard to the current flow through them. Transistor devices also allow proportional amplification, but this is rarely used for systems rated more than a few hundred watts. The control input characteristics of a device also greatly affect design; sometimes the control input is at a very high voltage with respect to ground and must be driven by an isolated source.

Devices vary in switching speed. Some diodes and thyristors are suited for relatively slow speed and are useful for power frequency switching and control; certain thyristors are useful at a few kilohertz. Devices such as MOSFETS and BJTs can switch at tens of kilohertz up to a few megahertz in power applications, but with decreasing power levels.

Very high power (hundreds of kilowatts) at very high frequency (hundreds or thousands of megahertz) is still the area where vacuum tube devices predominate. The use of faster switching devices minimises energy lost in the transitions from on to off and back, but may create problems with radiated electromagnetic interference. Gate drive (or equivalent) circuits must be designed to supply sufficient drive current to achieve the full switching speed possible with a device. A device that doesn't get sufficient drive to switch rapidly, may be destroyed by excess heating.

Power handling and dissipation of devices is also a critical factor in design. Power electronic devices may have to dissipate tens or hundreds of watts of waste heat, even switching as efficiently as possible between conducting and non-conducting states. In the switching mode, the power controlled is much larger than the power dissipated in the switch.

The forward voltage drop in the conducting state translates into heat that must be dissipated. High power semiconductors require specialised heat sinks or active cooling systems to keep their junction temperature from rising too high; exotic semiconductors such as silicon carbide have an advantage over straight silicon in this respect, and germanium, once the main-stay of solid-state electronics is now little used due to its unfavourable properties at high temperature.

Semiconductor devices exist with ratings up to a few kilovolts in a single device. Where very high voltage must be controlled, multiple devices must be used in series, with networks to equalize voltage across all devices. Again, switching speed is a critical factor since the slowest-switching device will have to withstand a disproportionate share of the overall voltage. The former mercury valves were available with ratings to 100 kV in a single unit, simplifying their application in HVDC systems.

The current rating of a semiconductor device is limited by the heat generated within the dies and the heat developed in the resistance of the interconnecting leads. Semiconductor devices must be designed so that current is evenly distributed within the device across its internal junctions (or channels); once a "hot spot" develops, breakdown effects can rapidly destroy the device. Certain SCRs are available with current ratings to 3000 amperes in a single unit.

Applications

Power electronic systems are found in virtually every electronic device. For example:

- DC/DC converters are used in most mobile devices (mobile phones, PDA etc.) to maintain the voltage at a fixed value whatever the voltage level of the battery is. These converters are also used for electronic isolation and power factor correction.
- AC/DC converters (rectifiers) are used every time an electronic device is connected to the mains (computer, television etc.). These may simply change AC to DC or can also change the voltage level as part of their operation.
- AC/AC converters are used to change either the voltage level or the frequency (international power adapters, light dimmer). In power distribution networks AC/AC converters may be used to exchange power between utility frequency 50 Hz and 60 Hz power grids.
- DC/AC converters (inverters) are used primarily in UPS or renewable energy systems or emergency lighting systems. When mains power is available, it will charge the DC battery. If the mains fails, an inverter will be used to produce AC electricity at mains voltage from the DC battery.

Power Electronics Technology

Power electronics is the application of electronics for the control and conversion of electric power. Applications of power electronics range in power from a switched mode power supply in an AC adapter, battery chargers, fluorescent lamp ballasts, through variable frequency drives and DC motor drives used to operate pumps, fans, and manufacturing machinery, up to gigawatt-scale High voltage direct current power transmission systems used to interconnect electrical grids.

Power electronic converters can be found wherever there is a need to modify a form of electrical energy (i.e. change its voltage, current or frequency). The power range of these converters is from some milliwatts (as in a mobile phone) to hundreds of megawatts in an HVDC transmission system. With "classical" electronics, electrical currents and voltage are used to carry information, whereas with power electronics, they carry power. Thus, the main metric of power electronics becomes the efficiency.

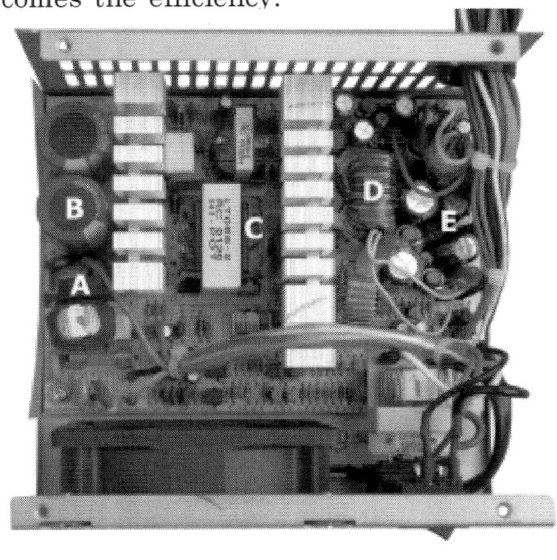

Figure: *A PCs power supply is an example of a piece of power electronics, whether inside or outside of the cabinet*

The first very high power electronic devices were mercury-arc valves. In modern systems the conversion is performed with semiconductor switching devices such as diodes, thyristors and transistors, beginning in the 1950s. In contrast to electronic systems concerned with transmission and processing of signals and data, in power electronics substantial amounts of electrical energy are processed. An AC/DC converter (rectifier) is the most typical power electronics device found in many consumer electronic devices, e.g. television sets, personal computers, battery chargers, etc. The power range is typically from tens of watts to several hundred watts. In industry the most common application is the variable speed drive (VSD) that is used to control an induction motor. The power range of VSDs start from a few hundred watts and end at tens of megawatts. The power conversion systems can be classified according to the type of the input and output power

- AC to DC (rectifier)
- DC to AC (inverter)
- DC to DC (DC to DC converter)
- AC to AC (AC to AC converter)

DC/AC Converters

The main objective of DC to AC converters is to produce an AC output waveform from a DC source. This type of conversion is required for applications such as adjustable speed drives (ASD), uninterruptable power supplies (UPS), static VAR compensators, active filters, flexible AC transmission systems (FACT), voltage compensators, and photovoltaic generators. Topologies for these converters can be separated into two distinct categories: voltage source inverters and current source inverters. Voltage source inverters (VSIs) are named so because the independently controlled output is a voltage waveform. Similarly, current source inverters (CSIs) are distinct in that the controlled AC output is a current waveform. Being static power converters, the DC to AC power conversion is the result of power switching devices, which are commonly fully controllable semiconductor power switches. The output waveforms are therefore made up of discrete values, producing fast transitions rather than smooth ones. The ability to produce near sinusoidal waveforms around the fundamental frequency is dictated by the modulation technique controlling when, and for how long, the power valves are on and off. Common modulation techniques include the carrier-based technique, or pulse width modulation, space-vector technique, and the selective-harmonic technique.

Voltage source inverters have practical uses in both single-phase and three-phase applications. Single-phase VSIs utilise half-bridge and full-bridge configurations, and are widely used for power supplies, single-phase UPSs, and elaborate high-power topologies when used in multicell configurations. Three-phase VSIs are used in applications that require sinusoidal voltage waveforms, such as ASDs, UPSs, FACTs, and VAR compensators. They are also used in applications where arbitrary voltages are required as in the case of active filters and voltage compensators. Current source inverters are used to produce an AC output current from a DC current supply. This type of inverter is practical for three-phase applications in which high-quality voltage waveforms are required.

A relatively new class of inverters, called multilevel inverters, has gained widespread interest. Normal operation of CSIs and VSIs can be classified as two-level inverters, due to the fact that power switches connect to either the positive or to the negative DC bus. If more than two voltage levels were available to the inverter output terminals, the AC output could better approximate a sine wave. It is for this reason that multilevel inverters, although more complex and costly, offer higher performance. Each inverter type differs in the DC links used, and in whether or not they require freewheeling diodes. Either can be made to operate in square-wave or pulse-width modulation (PWM) mode, depending on its intended usage. Square-wave mode offers simplicity, while PWM can be implemented several different ways and produces higher quality waveforms.

Voltage Source Inverters (VSI) feed the output inverter section from an approximately constant-voltage source..

The desired quality of the current output waveform determines which modulation technique needs to be selected for a given application. The output of a VSI is composed of discrete values. In order to obtain a smooth current waveform, the loads need to be inductive at the select harmonic frequencies. Without some sort of inductive filtering between the source and load, a capacitive load will cause the load to receive a choppy current waveform, with large and frequent current spikes.

There are three main types of VSIs:

1. Single-phase half-bridge inverter
2. Single-phase full-bridge inverter
3. Three-phase voltage source inverter

Single-phase Half-bridge Inverter

The single-phase voltage source half-bridge inverters, are meant for lower voltage applications and are commonly used in power supplies.

Low-order current harmonics get injected back to the source voltage by the operation of the inverter. This means that two large capacitors are needed for filtering purposes in this design. Only one switch can be on at time in each leg of the inverter. If both switches in a leg were on at the same time, the DC source will be shorted out.

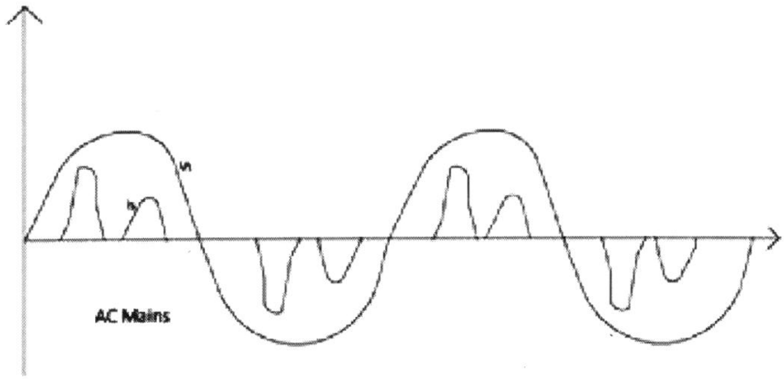

Figure: *The AC input for an ASD.*

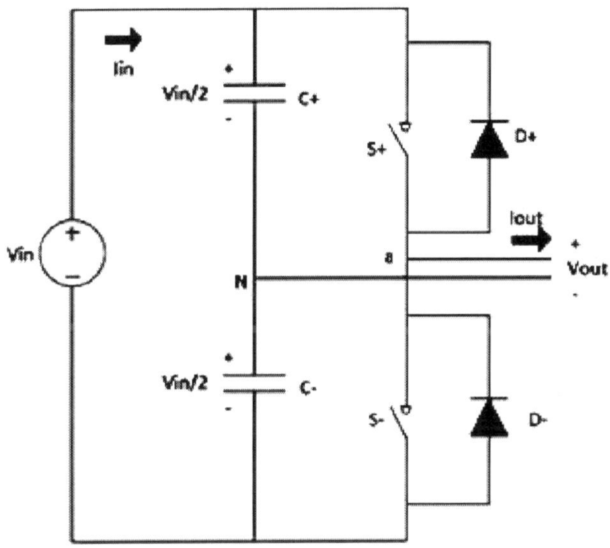

Figure: *Single-Phase Half-Bridge Voltage Source Inverter*

Inverters can use several modulation techniques to control their switching schemes. The carrier-based PWM technique compares the the AC output waveform, v_c, to a carrier voltage signal, v_Δ. When v_c is greater than v_Δ, S+ is on, and when v_c is less than v_Δ, S- is on. When the AC output is at frequency fc with its amplitude at v_c, and the triangular carrier signal is at frequency f_Δ with its amplitude at v_Δ, the PWM becomes a special sinusoidal case of the carrier based PWM.

This case is dubbed sinusoidal pulse-width modulation (SPWM).For this, the modulation index, or amplitude-modulation ratio, is defined as $m_a = v_c / v_-$.

The normalized carrier frequency, or frequency-modulation ratio, is calculated using the equation $m_f = f_- / f_c$.

If the over-modulation region, ma, exceeds one, a higher fundamental AC output voltage will be observed, but at the cost of saturation. For SPWM, the harmonics of the output waveform are at well-defined frequencies and amplitudes. This simplifies the design of the filtering components needed for the low-order current harmonic injection from the operation of the inverter. The maximum output amplitude in this mode of operation is half of the source voltage. If the maximum output amplitude, m_a, exceeds 3.24, the output waveform of the inverter becomes a square wave.

As was true for PWM, both switches in a leg for square wave modulation cannot be turned on at the same time, as this would cause a short across the voltage source. The switching scheme requires that both S+ and S- be on for a half cycle of the AC output period. The fundamental AC output amplitude is equal to $v_{o1} = v_{aN1} = (4 \cdot v_i) / (2 \cdot \pi)$.

Its harmonics have an amplitude of$v_{oh} = v_{o1} / h$.

Therefore, the AC output voltage is not controlled by the inverter, but rather by the magnitude of the DC input voltage of the inverter.

Using selctive harmonic elimination (SHE) as a modulation technique allows the switching of the inverter to selectively eliminate intrinsic harmonics. The fundamental component of the AC output voltage can also be adjusted within a desirable range. Since the AC output voltage obtained from this modulation technique has odd half and odd quarter wave symmetry, even harmonics do not exist. Any undesirable odd (N-1) intrinsic harmonics from the output waveform can be eliminated.

Single-phase Full-bridge Inverter

The full-bridge inverter is similar to the half bridge-inverter, but it has an additional leg to connect the neutral point to the load. To avoid shorting out the voltage source, S1+ and S1- cannot be on at the same time, and S2+ and S2- also cannot be on at the same time. Any modulating technique used for the full-bridge configuration should have either the top or the bottom switch of each leg on at any given time. Due to the extra leg, the maximum amplitude of the output waveform is Vi, and is twice as large as the maximum achievable output amplitude for the half-bridge configuration.

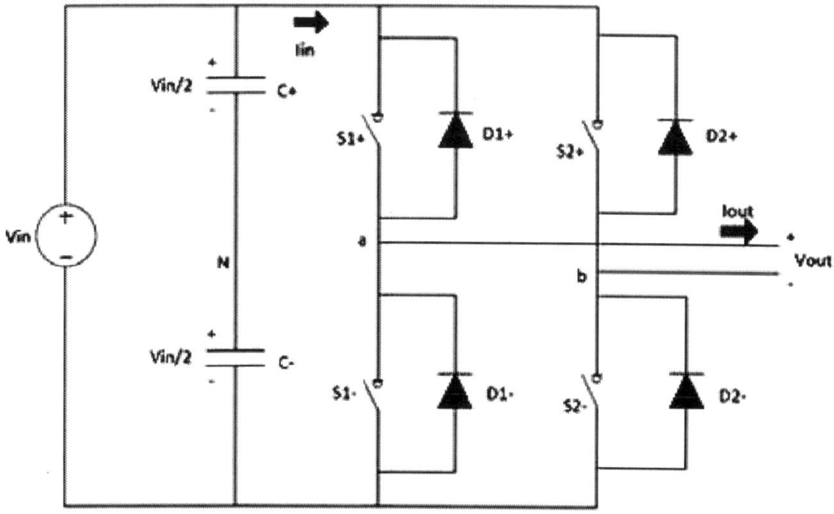

Figure: *Single-Phase Voltage Source Full-Bridge Inverter*

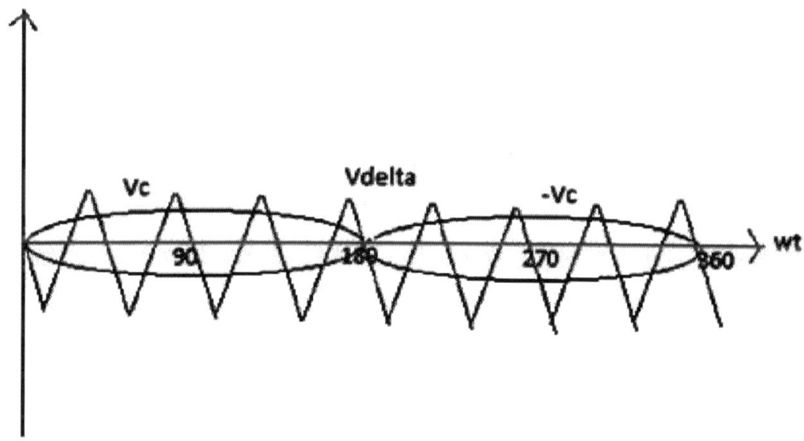

Figure: *Carrier and Modulating Signals for the Bipolar Pulsewidth Modulation Technique*

States 1 and 2 are used to generate the AC output voltage with bipolar SPWM. The AC output voltage can take on only two values, either Vi or –Vi. To generate these same states using a half-bridge configuration, a carrier based technique can be used. S+ being on for the half-bridge corresponds to S1+ and S2- being on for the full-bridge. Similarly, S- being on for the half-bridge corresponds to S1- and S2+ being on for the full bridge. The output voltage for this modulation technique is more or less sinusoidal, with a fundamental component that has an amplitude in the linear region of ma less than or equal to one $v_{o1} = v_{ab1} = v_i \cdot m_a$.

Unlike the bipolar PWM technique, the unipolar approach uses states 1, 2, 3 and 4 from Table 2 to generate its AC output voltage. Therefore, the AC output voltage can take on the values Vi, 0 or –V [1]i. To generate these states, two sinusoidal modulating signals, Vc and –Vc, are needed. Vc is used to generate VaN, while –Vc is used to generate VbN. The following relationship is called unipolar carrier-based SPWM $v_{o1} = 2 \cdot v_{aN1} = v_i \cdot m_a$.

The phase voltages VaN and VbN are identical, but 180 degrees out of phase with each other. The output voltage is equal to the difference of the two phase voltages, and do not contain any even harmonics. Therefore, if mf is taken, even the AC output voltage harmonics will appear at normalized odd frequencies, fh. These frequencies are centred on double the value of the normalized carrier frequency. This particular feature allows for smaller filtering components when trying to obtain a higher quality output waveform. As was the case for the half-bridge SHE, the AC output voltage contains no even harmonics due to its odd half and odd quarter wave symmetry.

Three-phase voltage source inverter

Single-phase VSIs are used primarily for low power range applications, while three-phase VSIs cover both medium and high power range applications.

Switches in any of the three legs of the inverter cannot be switched off simultaneously due to this reulting in the voltages being dependent on the respective line current's polarity. States 7 and 8 produce zero AC line voltages, which result in AC line currents freewheeling through either the upper or the lower components. However, the line voltages for states 1 through 6 produce an AC line voltage consisting of the discrete values of Vi, 0 or –Vi. For three-phase SPWM, three modulating signals that are 120 degrees out of phase with one another are used in order to produce out of phase load voltages. In order to preserve the PWM features with a single carrier signal, the normalized carrier frequency, mf, needs to be a multiple of three. This keeps the magnitude of the phase voltages identical, but out of phase with each other by 120 degrees. The maximum achievable phase voltage amplitude in the linear region, ma less than or equal to one, is $v_{phase} = v_i / 2$. The maximum achievable line voltage amplitude is $V_{ab1} = v_{ab} \cdot \sqrt{3}/2$.

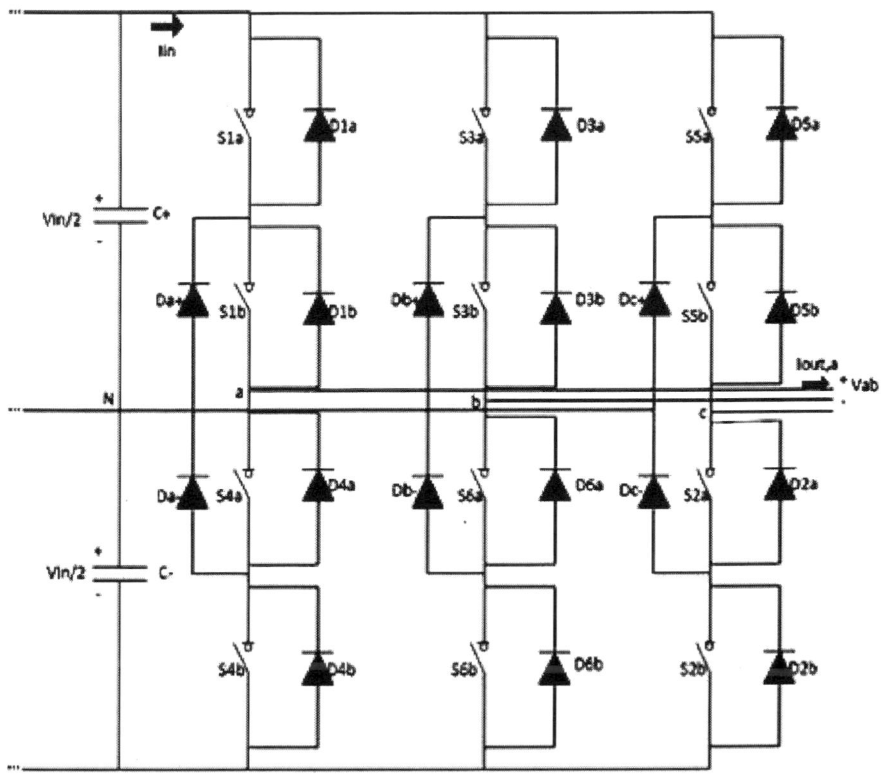

Figure: *Three-Phase Voltage Source Inverter Circuit Schematic*

Therefore, to increase the amplitude of the load voltage, the amplitude of the modulating signal Vc can simply be increased. Using this idea, you can create over-modulation by making the amplitude of Vc higher than the amplitude of the carrier signal. The only way to control the load voltage is by changing the input DC voltage. Current source inverters convert DC current into an AC current waveform. In applications requiring sinusoidal AC waveforms, magnitude, frequency, and phase should all be controlled. CSIs have high changes in current overtime, so capacitors are commonly employed on the AC side, while inductors are commonly employed on the DC side. Due to the absence of freewheeling diodes, the power circuit is reduced in size and weight, and tends to be more reliable than VSIs. Although single-phase topologies are possible, three-phase CSIs are more practical. In its most generalised form, a three-phase CSI employs the same conduction sequence as a six-pulse rectifier. At any time, only one common-cathode switch and one common-anode switch are on.

As a result, line currents take discrete values of –ii, 0 and ii. States are chosen such that a desired waveform is outputted and only valid states are used.

This selection is based on modulating techniques, which include carrier-based PWM, selective harmonic elimination, and space-vector techniques.

Carrier-based techniques used for VSIs can also be implemented for CSIs, resulting in CSI line currents that behave in the same way as VSI line voltages.

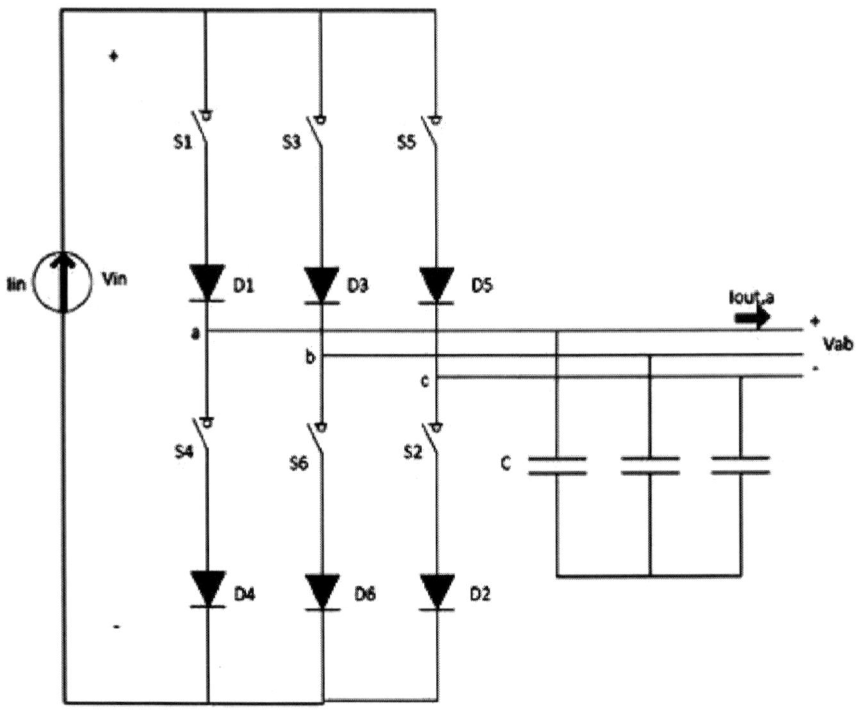

Figure: *Three-Phase Current Source Inverter*

The digital circuit utilised for modulating signals contains a switching pulse generator, a shorting pulse generator, a shorting pulse distributor, and a switching and shorting pulse combiner.

A gating signal is produced based on a carrier current and three modulating signals. A shorting pulse is added to this signal when no top switches and no bottom switches are gated, causing the RMS currents to be equal in all legs. The same methods are utilised for each phase, however, switching variables are 120 degrees out of phase relative to one another, and the current pulses are shifted by a half-cycle with respect to output currents.

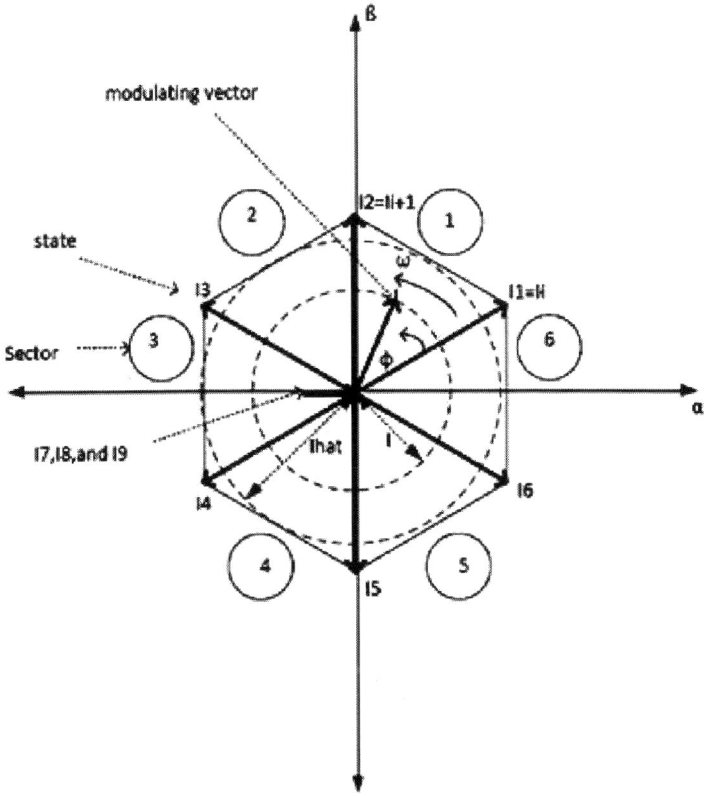

Figure: *Space-Vector Representation in Current Source Inverters*

If a triangular carrier is used with sinusoidal modulating signals, the CSI is said to be utilising synchronized-pulse-width-modulation (SPWM). If full over-modulation is used in conjunction with SPWM the inverter is said to be in square-wave operation. The second CSI modulation category, SHE is also similar to its VSI counterpart. Utilising the gating signals developed for a VSI and a set of synchronizing sinusoidal current signals, results in symmetrically distributed shorting pulses and, therefore, symmetrical gating patterns. This allows any arbitrary number of harmonics to be eliminated.

It also allows control of the fundamental line current through the proper selection of primary switching angles. Optimal switching patterns must have quarter-wave and half-wave symmetry, as well as symmetry about 30 degrees and 150 degrees. Switching patterns are never allowed between 60 degrees and 120 degrees. The current ripple can be further reduced with the use of larger output capacitors, or by increasing the number of switching pulses.

The third category, space-vector-based modulation, generates PWM load line currents that equal load line currents, on average. Valid switching states and time selections are made digitally based on space vector transformation. Modulating signals are represented as a complex vector using a transformation equation. For balanced three-phase sinusoidal signals, this vector becomes a fixed module, which rotates at a frequency, ω. These space vectors are then used to approximate the modulating signal. If the signal is between arbitrary vectors, the vectors are combined with the zero vectors I7, I8, or I9. The following equations are used to ensure that the generated currents and the current vectors are on average equivalent.

Multilevel Inverters

A relatively new class called multilevel inverters has gained widespread interest. Normal operation of CSIs and VSIs can be classified as two-level inverters because the power switches connect to either the positive or the negative DC bus. If more than two voltage levels were available to the inverter output terminals, the AC output could better approximate a sine wave. For this reason multilevel inverters, although more complex and costly, offer higher performance. Control methods for a three-level inverter only allow two switches of the four switches in each leg to simultaneously change conduction states.

This allows smooth commutation and avoids shoot through by only selecting valid states. It may also be noted that since the DC bus voltage is shared by at least two power valves, their voltage ratings can be less than a two-level counterpart. Carrier-based and space-vector modulation techniques are used for multilevel topologies. The methods for these techniques follow those of classic inverters, but with added complexity. Space-vector modulation offers a greater number of fixed voltage vectors to be used in approximating the modulation signal, and therefore allows more effective space vector PWM strategies to be accomplished at the cost of more elaborate algorithms. Due to added complexity and number of semiconductor devices, multilevel inverters are currently more suitable for high-power high-voltage applications.

Inverter Applications: In general, inverters are utilised in applications requiring direct conversion of electrical energy from DC to AC or indirect conversion from AC to AC. Dc to AC conversion is useful for many fields, including power conditioning, harmonic compensation, motor drives, and renewable energy grid-integration.

In power systems it is often desired to eliminate harmonic content found in line currents. VSIs can be used as active power filters to provide this compensation. Based on measured line currents and voltages, a control system determines reference current signals for each phase. This is fed back through an outer loop and subtracted from actual current signals to create current signals for an inner loop to the inverter. These signals then cause the inverter to generate output currents that compensate for the harmonic content. This configuration requires no real power consumption, as it is fully fed by the line; the DC link is simply a capacitor that is kept at a constant voltage by the control system. In this configuration, output currents are in phase with line voltages to produce a unity power factor. Conversely, VAR compensation is possible in a similar configuration where output currents lead line voltages to improve the overall power factor. In facilities that require energy at all times, such as hospitals and airports, UPS systems are utilised.

In a standby system, an inverter is brought online when the normally supplying grid is interrupted. Power is instantaneously drawn from onsite batteries and converted into usable AC voltage by the VSI, until grid power is restored, or until backup generators are brought online. In an online UPS system, a rectifier-DC-link-inverter is used to protect the load from transients and harmonic content. A battery in parallel with the DC-link is kept fully charged by the output in case the grid power is interrupted, while the output of the inverter is fed through a low pass filter to the load. High power quality and independence from disturbances is achieved. Various AC motor drives have been developed for speed, torque, and position control of AC motors. These drives can be categorized as low-performance or as high-performance, based on whether they are scalar-controlled or vector-controlled, respectively.

In scalar-controlled drives, fundamental stator current, or voltage frequency and amplitude, are the only controllable quantities. Therefore, these drives are employed in applications where high quality control is not required, such as fans and compressors. On the other hand, vector-controlled drives allow for instantaneous current and voltage values to be controlled continuously. This high performance is necessary for applications such as elevators and electric cars. Inverters are also vital to many renewable energy applications.

In photovoltaic purposes, the inverter, which is usually a PWM VSI, gets fed by the DC electrical energy output of a photovoltaic module or array. The inverter then converts this into an AC voltage to be interfaced with either a load or the utility grid. Inverters may also be employed in other renewable systems, such as wind turbines. In these applications, the turbine speed usually varies causing changes in voltage frequency and sometimes in the magnitude. In this case, the generated voltage can be rectified and then inverted to stabilise frequency and magnitude.

AC/AC Converters

Power electronics is the application of electronics for power conversion. A subcategory of power conversion is the AC to AC conversion. Converting an AC waveform to another AC waveform allows one to control the voltage, frequency, and phase of the waveform applied to a load from a supplied AC waveform. The two main categories that can be used to separate the types of converters are whether the frequency of the waveform is changed. AC/AC converter that don't allow the user to modify the frequencies are known as AC Voltage Controllers, or AC Regulators. AC converters that allow the user to change the frequency are simply referred to as frequency converters for AC to AC conversion. Under frequency converters there are three different types of converters that are typically used: cycloconverter, matrix converter, DC link converter (aka AC/DC/AC converter).

AC Voltage Controller: The purpose of an AC Voltage Controller, or AC Regulator, is to vary the RMS voltage across the load while at a constant frequency. Three control methods that are generally accepted are ON/OFF Control, Phase-Angle Control, and Pulse Width Modulation AC Chopper Control (PWM AC Chopper Control). All three of these methods can be implemented not only in single-phase circuits, but three-phase circuits as well.

- *ON/OFF Control:* Typically used for heating loads or speed control of motors, this control method involves turning the switch on for n integral cycles and turning the switch off for m integral cycles. Because turning the switches on and off cause's undesirable harmonics to be created, the switches are turned on and off during zero-voltage and zero-current conditions (zero-crossing), effectively reducing the distortion.
- *Phase-Angle Control:* Various circuits exist to implement a phase-angle control on different waveforms, such as half-wave or full-wave voltage control. The power electronic components that are typically used are diodes, SCR's, and Triac's. With the use of these components, the user can delay the firing angle in a wave which will only cause part of the wave to be outputted.

- *PWM AC Chopper Control:* The other two control methods often have poor harmonics, output current quality, and input power factor. In order to improve these values PWM can be used instead of the other methods. What PWM AC Chopper does is have switches that turn on and off several times within alternate half-cycles of input voltage.

Matrix Converters and Cycloconverters: Cycloconverters are widely used in industry for ac to ac conversion, because they are able to be used in high-power applications. They are commutated direct frequency converters that are synchronized by a supply line. The cycloconverters output voltage waveforms have complex harmonics with the higher order harmonics being filtered by the machine inductance.

Causing the machine current to have fewer harmonics, while the remaining harmonics causes losses and torque pulsations. Note that in a cycloconverter, unlike other converters, there are no inductors or capacitors, i.e. no storage devices. For this reason, the instantaneous input power and the output power are equal.

- *Single-Phase to Single-Phase Cycloconverters:* Single-Phase to Single-Phase Cycloconverters started drawing more interest recently because of the decrease in both size and price of the power electronics switches. The single-phase high frequency ac voltage can be either sinusoidal or trapezoidal. These might be zero voltage intervals for control purpose or zero voltage commutation.
- *Three-Phase to Single-Phase Cycloconverters:* There are two kinds of three-phase to single-phase cycloconverters: 3φ to 1φ half wave cycloconverters and 3φ to 1φ bridge cycloconverters. Both positive and negative converters can generate voltage at either polarity, resulting in the positive converter only supplying positive current, and the negative converter only supplying negative current.

With recent device advances, newer forms of cycloconverters are being developed, such as matrix converters. The first change that is first noticed is that matrix converters utilise bi-directional, bipolar switches. A single phase to a single phase matrix converter consists of a matrix of 9 switches connecting the three input phases to the tree output phase.

Any input phase and output phase can be connected together at any time without connecting any two switches from the same phase at the same time; otherwise this will cause a short circuit of the input phases. Matrix converters are lighter, more compact and versatile than other converter solutions. As a result, they are able to achieve higher levels of integration, higher temperature operation, broad output frequency and natural bi-directional power flow suitable to regenerate energy back to the utility.

The matrix converters are subdivided into two types: direct and indirect converters. A direct matrix converter with three-phase input and three-phase output, the switches in a matrix converter must be bi-directional, that is, they must be able to block voltages of either polarity and to conduct current in either direction. This switching strategy permits the highest possible output voltage and reduces the reactive line-side current.

Therefore the power flow through the converter is reversible. Because of its commutation problem and complex control keep it from being broadly utilised in industry. Unlike the direct matrix converters, the indirect matrix converters has the same functionality, but uses separate input and output sections that are connected through a dc link without storage elements. The design includes a four-quadrant current source rectifier and a voltage source inverter. The input section consists of bi-directional bipolar switches.

The commutation strategy can be applied by changing the switching state of the input section while the output section is in a freewheeling mode. This commutation algorithm is significantly less complexity and higher reliability as compared to a conventional direct matrix converter. *DC Link Converters:* DC Link Converters, also referred to as AC/DC/AC converters, convert an AC input to an AC output with the use of a DC link in the middle. Meaning that the power in the converter is converted to DC from AC with the use of a rectifier, and then it is converted back to AC from DC with the use of an inverter.

The end result is an output with a lower voltage and variable (higher or lower) frequency. Due to their wide area of application, the AC/DC/AC converters are the most common contemporary solution. Other advantages to AC/DC/AC converters is that they are stable in overload and no-load conditions, as well as they can be disengaged from a load without damage. Applications: Understanding how each of the converters work is all good and well, but it is useless in a practical sense if one does not understand where each converter is applied in the real world. Below is a list of common applications that each converter is used in.

- AC Voltage Controller: Lighting Control; Domestic and Industrial Heating; Speed Control of Fan,Pump or Hoist Drives, Soft Starting of Induction Motors, Static AC Switches (Temperature Control, Transformer Tap Changing, etc)
- Cycloconverter: High-Power Low-Speed Reversible AC Motor Drives; Constant Frequency Power Supply with Variable Input Frequency; Controllable VAR Generators for Power Factor Correction; AC System Interties Linking Two Independent Power Systems.
- DC Link: Can be used for individual or multiple load applications of machine building and construction.

New Technology, Hybrid Matrix Converter: Hybrid matrix converters are relatively new for AC/AC converters. These converters combine the AC/DC/AC design with the matrix converter design. Multiple types of hybrid converters have been developed in this new category, an example being a converter that uses uni-directional switches and two converter stages without the dc-link; without the capacitors or inductors needed for a dc-link, the weight and size of the converter is reduced. Two sub-categories exist from the hybrid converters, named hybrid direct matrix converter (HDMC) and hybrid indirect matrix converter (HIMC). HDMC convert the voltage and current in one stage, while the HIMC utilises separate stages, like the AC/DC/AC converter, but without the use of an intermediate storage element.Simulations of power electronic systems

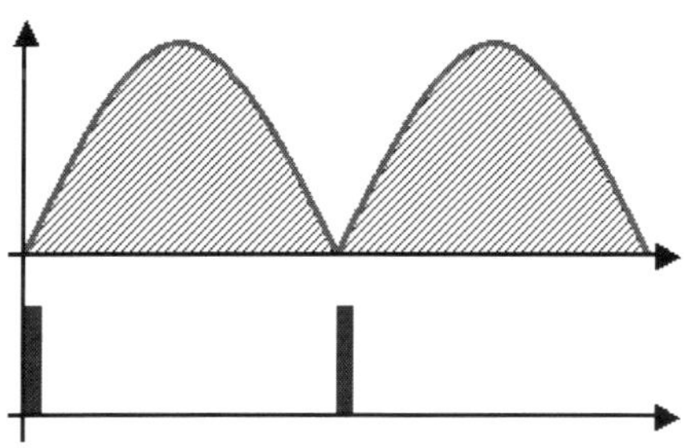

Figure: *Output voltage of a full-wave rectifier with controlled thyristors*

Power electronic circuits are simulated using computer simulation programs such as PSIM and MATLAB/simulink. Circuits are simulated before they are produced to test how the circuits respond under certain conditions. Also, creating a simulation is both cheaper and faster than creating a prototype to use for testing.

5

Analog Signal

An analog or analogue signal is any continuous signal for which the time varying feature (variable) of the signal is a representation of some other time varying quantity, i.e., analogous to another time varying signal. It differs from a digital signal in terms of small fluctuations in the signal which are meaningful. Analog is usually thought of in an electrical context; however, mechanical, pneumatic, hydraulic, and other systems may also convey analog signals.

An analog signal uses some property of the medium to convey the signal's information. For example, an aneroid barometre uses rotary position as the signal to convey pressure information. Electrically, the property most commonly used is voltage followed closely by frequency, current, and charge.

Any information may be conveyed by an analog signal; often such a signal is a measured response to changes in physical phenomena, such as sound, light, temperature, position, or pressure, and is achieved using a transducer. An analog signal is one where at each point in time the value of the signal is significant, whereas a digital signal is one where at each point in time, the value of the signal must be above or below some discrete threshold.

For example, in sound recording, fluctuations in air pressure (that is to say, sound) strike the diaphragm of a microphone which induces corresponding fluctuations in the current produced by a coil in an electromagnetic microphone, or the voltage produced by a condensor microphone. The voltage or the current is said to be an "analog" of the sound. An analog signal has a theoretically infinite resolution. In practice an analog signal is subject to electronic noise and a finite slew rate. Therefore, both analog and digital systems are subject to limitations in resolution and bandwidth.

As analog systems become more complex, effects such as non-linearity and noise ultimately degrade analog resolution to such an extent that the performance of digital systems may surpass it. Similarly, as digital systems become more complex, errors can occur in the digital data stream. A comparable performing digital system is more complex and requires more bandwidth than its analog counterpart. In analog systems, it is difficult to detect when such degradation occurs. However, in digital systems, degradation can not only be detected but corrected as well.

Disadvantages

The primary disadvantage of analog signaling is that any system has noise – i.e., random unwanted variation. As the signal is copied and re-copied, or transmitted over long distances, these apparently random variations become dominant.

Electrically, these losses can be diminished by shielding, good connections, and several cable types such as coaxial or twisted pair. The effects of noise create signal loss and distortion.

This is impossible to recover, since amplifying the signal to recover attenuated parts of the signal amplifies the noise (distortion/interference) as well. Even if the resolution of an analog signal is higher than a comparable digital signal, the difference can be overshadowed by the noise in the signal. Most of the analog systems also suffer from generation loss.

Modulation

Another method of conveying an analog signal is to use modulation. In this, some base signal (e.g., a sinusoidal carrier wave) has one of its properties modulated: amplitude modulation involves altering the amplitude of a sinusoidal voltage waveform by the source information, frequency modulation changes the frequency. Other techniques, such as changing the phase of the base signal also work.

Analog circuits do not involve quantisation of information into digital format. The concept being measured over the circuit, whether sound, light, pressure, temperature, or an exceeded limit, remains from end to end.

Sources: Parts of an earlier version of this article were originally taken from Federal Standard 1037C in support of MIL-STD-188.

Inherent Noise

Analogue systems invariably include noise; that is, random disturbances or variations, some caused by the random thermal vibrations of atomic particles. Since all variations of an analogue signal are significant, any disturbance is equivalent to a change in the original signal and so appears as noise. As the signal is copied and re-copied, or transmitted over long distances, these random variations become more significant and lead to signal degradation. Other sources of noise may include external electrical signals or poorly designed components. These disturbances are reduced by shielding, and using low-noise amplifiers (LNA).

Noise

Because of the way information is encoded in analogue circuits, they are much more susceptible to noise than digital circuits, since a small change in the signal can represent a significant change in the information present in the signal and can cause the information present to be lost. Since digital signals take on one of only two different values, a disturbance would have to be about one-half the magnitude of the digital signal to cause an error; this property of digital circuits can be exploited to make signal processing noise-resistant. In digital electronics, because the information is quantized, as long as the signal stays inside a range of values, it represents the same information. Digital circuits use this principle to regenerate the signal at each logic gate, lessening or removing noise.

Precision

A number of factors affect how precise a signal is, mainly the noise present in the original signal and the noise added by processing. See signal-to-noise ratio. Fundamental physical limits such as the shot noise in components limits the resolution of analogue signals. In digital electronics additional precision is obtained by using additional digits to represent the signal; the practical limit in the number of digits is determined by the performance of the analogue-to-digital converter (ADC), since digital operations can usually be performed without loss of precision. The ADC takes an analogue signal and changes into a series of binary numbers. The ADC may be used in simple digital display devices e. g. thermometres, light metres but it may also be used in digital sound recording and in data acquisition. However, a digital-to-analogue converter (DAC) is used to change a digital signal to an analogue signal. A DAC takes a series of binary numbers and converts it to an analogue signal. It is common to find a DAC in the gain-control system of an op-amp which in turn may be used to control digital amplifiers and filters.

Design Difficulty

Analogue circuits are harder to design, requiring more skill, than comparable digital systems. This is one of the main reasons why digital systems have become more common than analogue devices. An analogue circuit must be designed by hand, and the process is much less automated than for digital systems. However, if a digital electronic device is to interact with the real world, it will always need an analogue interface. For example, every digital radio receiver has an analogue preamplifier as the first stage in the receive chain.

Electronic Circuit

An electronic circuit is composed of individual electronic components, such as resistors, transistors, capacitors, inductors and diodes, connected by conductive wires or traces through which electric current can flow.

The combination of components and wires allows various simple and complex operations to be performed: signals can be amplified, computations can be performed, and data can be moved from one place to another.

Figure: *The die from an Intel 8742, an 8-bit microcontroller that includes a CPU, 128 bytes of RAM, 2048 bytes of EPROM, and I/O in the same chip.*

Circuits can be constructed of discrete components connected by individual pieces of wire, but today it is much more common to create interconnections by photolithographic techniques on a laminated substrate (a printed circuit board or PCB) and solder the components to these interconnections to create a finished circuit.

In an Integrated Circuit or IC, the components and interconnections are formed on the same substrate, typically a semiconductor such as silicon or (less commonly) gallium arsenide. Breadboards, perfboards or stripboards are common for testing new designs. They allow the designer to make quick changes to the circuit during development.

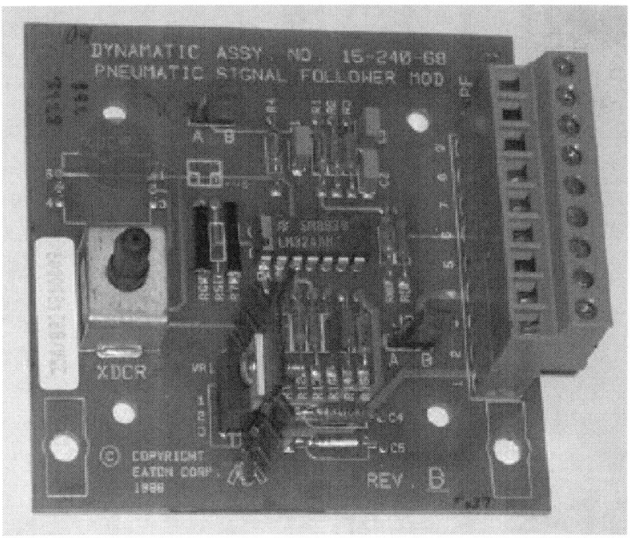

Figure: *A circuit built on a printed circuit board (PCB).*

An electronic circuit can usually be categorized as an analog circuit, a digital circuit or a mixed-signal circuit (a combination of analog circuits and digital circuits).

Analog Circuits

Analog electronic circuits are those in which current or voltage may vary continuously with time to correspond to the information being represented. Analog circuitry is constructed from two fundamental building blocks: series and parallel circuits. In a series circuit, the same current passes through a series of components. A string of Christmas lights is a good example of a series circuit: if one goes out, they all do. In a parallel circuit, all the components are connected to the same voltage, and the current divides between the various components according to their resistance.

The basic components of analog circuits are wires, resistors, capacitors, inductors, diodes, and transistors. (Recently, memristors have been added to the list of available components.) Analog circuits are very commonly represented in schematic diagrams, in which wires are shown as lines, and each component has a unique symbol. Analog circuit analysis employs Kirchhoff's circuit laws: all the currents at a node (a place where wires meet) must add to 0, and the voltage around a closed loop of wires is 0. Wires are usually treated as ideal zero-voltage interconnections; any resistance or reactance is captured by explicitly adding a parasitic element, such as a discrete resistor or inductor. Active components such as transistors are often treated as controlled current or voltage sources: for example, a field-effect transistor can be modelled as a current source from the source to the drain, with the current controlled by the gate-source voltage.

When the circuit size is comparable to a wavelength of the relevant signal frequency, a more sophisticated approach must be used. Wires are treated as transmission lines, with (hopefully) constant characteristic impedance, and the impedances at the start and end determine transmitted and reflected waves on the line. Such considerations typically become important for circuit boards at frequencies above a GHz; integrated circuits are smaller and can be treated as lumped elements for frequencies less than 10 GHz or so. An alternative model is to take independent power sources and induction as basic electronic units; this allows modelling frequency dependent negative resistors, gyrators, negative impedance converters, and dependent sources as secondary electronic components.

Digital Circuits

In digital electronic circuits, electric signals take on discrete values, to represent logical and numeric values. These values represent the information that is being processed. In the vast majority of cases, binary encoding is used: one voltage (typically the more positive value) represents a binary '1' and another voltage (usually a value near the ground potential, 0 V) represents a binary '0'. Digital circuits make extensive use of transistors, interconnected to create logic gates that provide the functions of Boolean logic: AND, NAND, OR, NOR, XOR and all possible combinations thereof. Transistors interconnected so as to provide positive feedback are used as latches and flip flops, circuits that have two or more metastable states, and remain in one of these states until changed by an external input. Digital circuits therefore can provide both logic and memory, enabling them to perform arbitrary computational functions. (Memory based on flip-flops is known as Static random-access memory(SRAM). Memory based on the storage of charge in a capacitor, dynamic random-access memory(DRAM) is also widely used.)

The design process for digital circuits is fundamentally different than the process for analog circuits. Each logic gate regenerates the binary signal, so the designer need not account for distortion, gain control, offset voltages, and other concerns faced in an analog design. As a consequence, extremely complex digital circuits, with billions of logic elements integrated on a single silicon chip, can be fabricated at low cost. Such digital integrated circuits are ubiquitous in modern electronic devices, such as calculators, mobile phone handsets, and computers. As digital circuits become more complex, issues of time delay, logic races, power dissipation, non-ideal switching, on-chip and inter-chip loading, and leakage currents, become limitations to the density, speed and performance.

Digital circuitry is used to create general purpose computing chips, such as microprocessors, and custom-designed logic circuits, known as Application Specific Integrated Circuits (ASICs). Field Programmable Gate Arrays (FPGAs), chips with logic circuitry whose configuration can be modified after fabrication, are also widely used in prototyping and development.

Mixed-Signal Circuits

Mixed-signal or hybrid circuits contain elements of both analog and digital circuits. Examples include comparators, timers, PLLs, ADCs (analog-to-digital converters), and DACs (digital-to-analog converters). Most modern radio and communications circuitry uses mixed signal circuits. For example, in a receiver, analog circuitry is used to amplify and frequency-convert signals so that they reach a suitable state to be converted into digital values, after which further signal processing can be performed in the digital domain.

Digital Electronics

Three Digital Circuits

Digital electronics represent signals by discrete bands of analog levels, rather than by a continuous range. All levels within a band represent the same signal state. Relatively small changes to the analog signal levels due to manufacturing tolerance, signal attenuation or parasitic noise do not leave the discrete envelope, and as a result are ignored by signal state sensing circuitry.

Figure: *An industrial digital controller*

In most cases the number of these states is two, and they are represented by two voltage bands: one near a reference value (typically termed as "ground" or zero volts) and a value near the supply voltage, corresponding to the "false" ("0") and "true" ("1") values of the Boolean domain respectively. Digital techniques are useful because it is easier to get an electronic device to switch into one of a number of known states than to accurately reproduce a continuous range of values. Digital electronic circuits are usually made from large assemblies of logic gates, simple electronic representations of Boolean logic functions.

Advantages

An advantage of digital circuits when compared to analog circuits is that signals represented digitally can be transmitted without degradation due to noise. For example, a continuous audio signal transmitted as a sequence of 1s and 0s, can be reconstructed without error, provided the noise picked up in transmission is not enough to prevent identification of the 1s and 0s. An hour of music can be stored on a compact disc using about 6 billion binary digits.

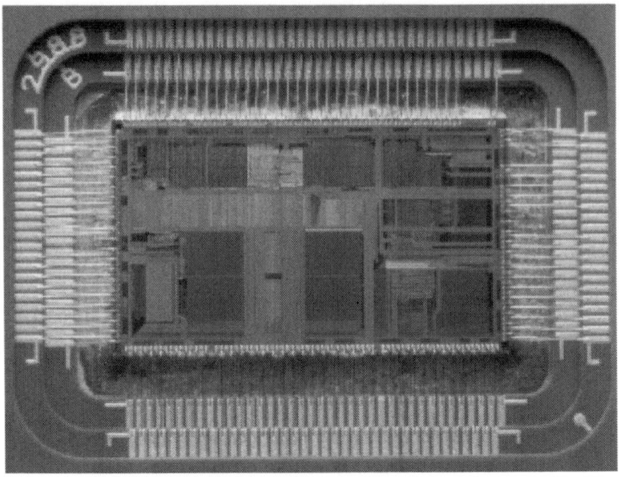

Figure: *Intel 80486DX2 microprocessor*

In a digital system, a more precise representation of a signal can be obtained by using more binary digits to represent it. While this requires more digital circuits to process the signals, each digit is handled by the same kind of hardware. In an analog system, additional resolution requires fundamental improvements in the linearity and noise characteristics of each step of the signal chain.

Computer-controlled digital systems can be controlled by software, allowing new functions to be added without changing hardware. Often this can be done outside of the factory by updating the product's software. So, the product's design errors can be corrected after the product is in a customer's hands.

Information storage can be easier in digital systems than in analog ones. The noise-immunity of digital systems permits data to be stored and retrieved without degradation. In an analog system, noise from aging and wear degrade the information stored. In a digital system, as long as the total noise is below a certain level, the information can be recovered perfectly.

Disadvantages

In some cases, digital circuits use more energy than analog circuits to accomplish the same tasks, thus producing more heat which increases the complexity of the circuits such as the inclusion of heat sinks. In portable or battery-powered systems this can limit use of digital systems. For example, battery-powered cellular telephones often use a low-power analog front-end to amplify and tune in the radio signals from the base station. However, a base station has grid power and can use power-hungry, but very flexible software radios. Such base stations can be easily reprogrammed to process the signals used in new cellular standards.

Digital circuits are sometimes more expensive, especially in small quantities. Most useful digital systems must translate from continuous analog signals to discrete digital signals. This causes quantization errors. Quantization error can be reduced if the system stores enough digital data to represent the signal to the desired degree of fidelity. The Nyquist-Shannon sampling theorem provides an important guideline as to how much digital data is needed to accurately portray a given analog signal.

In some systems, if a single piece of digital data is lost or misinterpreted, the meaning of large blocks of related data can completely change. Because of the cliff effect, it can be difficult for users to tell if a particular system is right on the edge of failure, or if it can tolerate much more noise before failing. Digital fragility can be reduced by designing a digital system for robustness. For example, a parity bit or other error management method can be inserted into the signal path. These schemes help the system detect errors, and then either correct the errors, or at least ask for a new copy of the data. In a state-machine, the state transition logic can be designed to catch unused states and trigger a reset sequence or other error recovery routine.

Digital memory and transmission systems can use techniques such as error detection and correction to use additional data to correct any errors in transmission and storage. On the other hand, some techniques used in digital systems make those systems more vulnerable to single-bit errors. These techniques are acceptable when the underlying bits are reliable enough that such errors are highly unlikely. A single-bit error in audio data stored directly as linear pulse code modulation (such as on a CD-ROM) causes, at worst. Instead, many people use audio compression to save storage space and download time, even though a single-bit error may corrupt the entire song.

Design Issues in Digital Circuits

Digital circuits are made from analog components. The design must assure that the analog nature of the components doesn't dominate the desired digital behaviour. Digital systems must manage noise and timing margins, parasitic inductances and capacitances, and filter power connections. Bad designs have intermittent problems such as "glitches", vanishingly-fast pulses that may trigger some logic but not others, "runt pulses" that do not reach valid "threshold" voltages, or unexpected ("undecoded") combinations of logic states. Additionally, where clocked digital systems interface to analogue systems or systems that are driven from a different clock, the digital system can be subject to metastability where a change to the input violates the set-up time for a digital input latch. This situation will self-resolve, but will take a random time, and while it persists can result in invalid signals being propagated within the digital system for a short time. Since digital circuits are made from analog components, digital circuits calculate more slowly than low-precision analog circuits that use a similar amount of space and power. However, the digital circuit will calculate more repeatably, because of its high noise immunity. On the other hand, in the high-precision domain (for example, where 14 or more bits of precision are needed), analog circuits require much more power and area than digital equivalents.

Construction

A digital circuit is often constructed from small electronic circuits called logic gates that can be used to create combinational logic. Each logic gate represents a function of boolean logic. A logic gate is an arrangement of electrically controlled switches, better known as transistors. Each logic symbol is represented by a different shape. The actual set of shapes was introduced in 1984 under IEEE\ANSI standard 91-1984. "The logic symbol given under this standard are being increasingly used now and have even started appearing in the literature published by manufacturers of digital integrated circuits."

The output of a logic gate is an electrical flow or voltage, that can, in turn, control more logic gates. Logic gates often use the fewest number of transistors in order to reduce their size, power consumption and cost, and increase their reliability. Integrated circuits are the least expensive way to make logic gates in large volumes. Integrated circuits are usually designed by engineers using electronic design automation software.

Another form of digital circuit is constructed from lookup tables, (many sold as "programmable logic devices", though other kinds of PLDs exist). Lookup tables can perform the same functions as machines based on logic gates, but can be easily reprogrammed without changing the wiring. This means that a designer can often repair design errors without changing the arrangement of wires. Therefore, in small volume products, programmable logic devices are often the preferred solution. They are usually designed by engineers using electronic design automation software. When the volumes are medium to large, and the logic can be slow, or involves complex algorithms or sequences, often a small microcontroller is programmed to make an embedded system. These are usually programmed by software engineers. When only one digital circuit is needed, and its design is totally customized, as for a factory production line controller, the conventional solution is a programmable logic controller, or PLC. These are usually programmed by electricians, using ladder logic.

Structure of Digital Systems

Engineers use many methods to minimise logic functions, in order to reduce the circuit's complexity. When the complexity is less, the circuit also has fewer errors and less electronics, and is therefore less expensive. The most widely used simplification is a minimisation algorithm like the Espresso heuristic logic minimiser within a CAD system, although historically, binary decision diagrams, an automated Quine–McCluskey algorithm, truth tables, Karnaugh maps, and Boolean algebra have been used.

Representations are crucial to an engineer's design of digital circuits. Some analysis methods only work with particular representations. The classical way to represent a digital circuit is with an equivalent set of logic gates. Another way, often with the least electronics, is to construct an equivalent system of electronic switches (usually transistors). One of the easiest ways is to simply have a memory containing a truth table. The inputs are fed into the address of the memory, and the data outputs of the memory become the outputs.

For automated analysis, these representations have digital file formats that can be processed by computer programs. Most digital engineers are very careful to select computer programs ("tools") with compatible file formats. To choose representations, engineers consider types of digital systems. Most digital systems divide into "combinational systems" and "sequential systems." A combinational system always presents the same output when given the same inputs. It is basically a representation of a set of logic functions, as already discussed. A sequential system is a combinational system with some of the outputs fed back as inputs. This makes the digital machine perform a "sequence" of operations. The simplest sequential system is probably a flip flop, a mechanism that represents a binary digit or "bit". Sequential systems are often designed as state machines. In this way, engineers can design a system's gross behaviour, and even test it in a simulation, without considering all the details of the logic functions. Sequential systems divide into two further subcategories. "Synchronous" sequential systems change state all at once, when a "clock" signal changes state. "Asynchronous" sequential systems propagate changes whenever inputs change. Synchronous sequential systems are made of well-characterised asynchronous circuits such as flip-flops, that change only when the clock changes, and which have carefully designed timing margins.

The usual way to implement a synchronous sequential state machine is to divide it into a piece of combinational logic and a set of flip flops called a "state register." Each time a clock signal ticks, the state register captures the feedback generated from the previous state of the combinational logic, and feeds it back as an unchanging input to the combinational part of the state machine. The fastest rate of the clock is set by the most time-consuming logic calculation in the combinational logic. The state register is just a representation of a binary number. If the states in the state machine are numbered (easy to arrange), the logic function is some combinational logic that produces the number of the next state.

In comparison, asynchronous systems are very hard to design because all possible states, in all possible timings must be considered. The usual method is to construct a table of the minimum and maximum time that each such state can exist, and then adjust the circuit to minimise the number of such states, and force the circuit to periodically wait for all of its parts to enter a compatible state (this is called "self-resynchronization"). Without such careful design, it is easy to accidentally produce asynchronous logic that is "unstable", that is, real electronics will have unpredictable results because of the cumulative delays caused by small variations in the values of the electronic components. Certain circuits (such as the synchronizer flip-flops, switch debouncers, arbiters, and the like which allow external unsynchronized signals to enter synchronous logic circuits) are inherently asynchronous in their design and must be analyzed as such.

As of 2005, almost all digital machines are synchronous designs because it is much easier to create and verify a synchronous design—the software currently used to simulate digital machines does not yet handle asynchronous designs. However, asynchronous logic is thought to be superior, if it can be made to work, because its speed is not constrained by an arbitrary clock; instead, it runs at the maximum speed of its logic gates. Building an asynchronous circuit using faster parts makes the circuit faster. Many digital systems are data flow machines. These are usually designed using synchronous register transfer logic, using hardware description languages such as VHDL or Verilog.

In register transfer logic, binary numbers are stored in groups of flip flops called registers. The outputs of each register are a bundle of wires called a "bus" that carries that number to other calculations. A calculation is simply a piece of combinational logic. Each calculation also has an output bus, and these may be connected to the inputs of several registers. Sometimes a register will have a multiplexer on its input, so that it can store a number from any one of several buses. Alternatively, the outputs of several items may be connected to a bus through buffers that can turn off the output of all of the devices except one. A sequential state machine controls when each register accepts new data from its input. In the 1980s, some researchers discovered that almost all synchronous register-transfer machines could be converted to asynchronous designs by using first-in-first-out synchronization logic. In this scheme, the digital machine is characterised as a set of data flows. In each step of the flow, an asynchronous "synchronization circuit" determines when the outputs of that step are valid, and presents a signal that says, "grab the data" to the stages that use that stage's inputs. It turns out that just a few relatively simple synchronization circuits are needed.

The most general-purpose register-transfer logic machine is a computer. This is basically an automatic binary abacus. The control unit of a computer is usually designed as a microprogram run by a microsequencer. A microprogram is much like a player-piano roll. Each table entry or "word" of the microprogram commands the state of every bit that controls the computer. The sequencer then counts, and the count addresses the memory or combinational logic machine that contains the microprogram. The bits from the microprogram control the arithmetic logic unit, memory and other parts of the computer, including the microsequencer itself. In this way, the complex task of designing the controls of a computer is reduced to a simpler task of programming a collection of much simpler logic machines.

Computer architecture is a specialised engineering activity that tries to arrange the registers, calculation logic, buses and other parts of the computer in the best way for some purpose. Computer architects have applied large amounts of ingenuity to computer design to reduce the cost and increase the speed and immunity to programming errors of computers. An increasingly common goal is to reduce the power used in a battery-powered computer system, such as a cell-phone. Many computer architects serve an extended apprenticeship as microprogrammers. "Specialised computers" are usually a conventional computer with a special-purpose microprogram.

Automated Design Tools

To save costly engineering effort, much of the effort of designing large logic machines has been automated. The computer programs are called "electronic design automation tools" or just "EDA." Simple truth table-style descriptions of logic are often optimized with EDA that automatically produces reduced systems of logic gates or smaller lookup tables that still produce the desired outputs. The most common example of this kind of software is the Espresso heuristic logic minimiser. Most practical algorithms for optimizing large logic systems use algebraic manipulations or binary decision diagrams, and there are promising experiments with genetic algorithms and annealing optimizations.

To automate costly engineering processes, some EDA can take state tables that describe state machines and automatically produce a truth table or a function table for the combinational logic of a state machine. The state table is a piece of text that lists each state, together with the conditions controlling the transitions between them and the belonging output signals. It is common for the function tables of such computer-generated state-machines to be optimized with logic-minimisation software such as Minilog.Often, real logic systems are designed as a series of sub-projects, which are combined using a "tool flow." The tool flow is usually a "script," a simplified computer language that can invoke the software design tools in the right order. Tool flows for large logic systems such as microprocessors can be thousands of commands long, and combine the work of hundreds of engineers.

Writing and debugging tool flows is an established engineering speciality in companies that produce digital designs. The tool flow usually terminates in a detailed computer file or set of files that describe how to physically construct the logic. Often it consists of instructions to draw the transistors and wires on an integrated circuit or a printed circuit board. Parts of tool flows are "debugged" by verifying the outputs of simulated logic against expected inputs. The test tools take computer files with sets of inputs and outputs, and highlight discrepancies between the simulated behaviour and the expected behaviour.

Once the input data is believed correct, the design itself must still be verified for correctness. Some tool flows verify designs by first producing a design, and then scanning the design to produce compatible input data for the tool flow. If the scanned data matches the input data, then the tool flow has probably not introduced errors. The functional verification data are usually called "test vectors." The functional test vectors may be preserved and used in the factory to test that newly constructed logic works correctly. However, functional test patterns don't discover common fabrication faults. Production tests are often designed by software tools called "test pattern generators". These generate test vectors by examining the structure of the logic and systematically generating tests for particular faults. This way the fault coverage can closely approach 100%, provided the design is properly made testable.

Once a design exists, and is verified and testable, it often needs to be processed to be manufacturable as well. Modern integrated circuits have features smaller than the wavelength of the light used to expose the photoresist. Manufacturability software adds interference patterns to the exposure masks to eliminate open-circuits, and enhance the masks' contrast.

Design for Testability

There are several reasons for testing a logic circuit. When the circuit is first developed, it is necessary to verify that the design circuit meets the required functional and timing specifications. When multiple copies of a correctly designed circuit are being manufactured, it is essential to test each copy to ensure that the manufacturing process has not introduced any flaws. A large logic machine (say, with more than a hundred logical variables) can have an astronomical number of possible states. Obviously, in the factory, testing every state is impractical if testing each state takes a microsecond, and there are more states than the number of microseconds since the universe began. Unfortunately, this ridiculous-sounding case is typical.

Fortunately, large logic machines are almost always designed as assemblies of smaller logic machines. To save time, the smaller sub-machines are isolated by permanently-installed "design for test" circuitry, and are tested independently. One common test scheme known as "scan design" moves test bits serially (one after another) from external test equipment through one or more serial shift registers known as "scan chains". Serial scans have only one or two wires to carry the data, and minimise the physical size and expense of the infrequently-used test logic. After all the test data bits are in place, the design is reconfigured to be in "normal mode" and one or more clock pulses are applied, to test for faults (e.g. stuck-at low or stuck-at high) and capture the test result into flip-flops and/or latches in the scan shift register(s). Finally, the result of the test is shifted out to the block boundary and compared against the predicted "good machine" result.

In a board-test environment, serial to parallel testing has been formalized with a standard called "JTAG" (named after the "Joint Test Action Group" that proposed it). Another common testing scheme provides a test mode that forces some part of the logic machine to enter a "test cycle." The test cycle usually exercises large independent parts of the machine.

Trade-offs

Several numbers determine the practicality of a system of digital logic. Engineers explored numerous electronic devices to get an ideal combination of fanout, speed, low cost and reliability. The cost of a logic gate is crucial. In the 1930s, the earliest digital logic systems were constructed from telephone relays because these were inexpensive and relatively reliable. After that, engineers always used the cheapest available electronic switches that could still fulfill the requirements.

The earliest integrated circuits were a happy accident. They were constructed not to save money, but to save weight, and permit the Apollo Guidance Computer to control an inertial guidance system for a spacecraft. The first integrated circuit logic gates cost nearly $50 (in 1960 dollars, when an engineer earned $10,000/year). To everyone's surprise, by the time the circuits were mass-produced, they had become the least-expensive method of constructing digital logic. Improvements in this technology have driven all subsequent improvements in cost.

With the rise of integrated circuits, reducing the absolute number of chips used represented another way to save costs. The goal of a designer is not just to make the simplest circuit, but to keep the component count down. Sometimes this results in slightly more complicated designs with respect to the underlying digital logic but nevertheless reduces the number of components, board size, and even power consumption.

For example, in some logic families, NAND gates are the simplest digital gate to build. All other logical operations can be implemented by NAND gates. If a circuit already required a single NAND gate, and a single chip normally carried four NAND gates, then the remaining gates could be used to implement other logical operations like logical and. This could eliminate the need for a separate chip containing those different types of gates. The "reliability" of a logic gate describes its mean time between failure (MTBF). Digital machines often have millions of logic gates. Also, most digital machines are "optimized" to reduce their cost. The result is that often, the failure of a single logic gate will cause a digital machine to stop working.

Digital machines first became useful when the MTBF for a switch got above a few hundred hours. Even so, many of these machines had complex, well-rehearsed repair procedures, and would be nonfunctional for hours because a tube burned-out, or a moth got stuck in a relay. Modern transistorized integrated circuit logic gates have MTBFs greater than 82 billion hours (8.2×10^{10}) hours, and need them because they have so many logic gates. Fanout describes how many logic inputs can be controlled by a single logic output without exceeding the current ratings of the gate. The minimum practical fanout is about five. Modern electronic logic using CMOS transistors for switches have fanouts near fifty, and can sometimes go much higher.

The "switching speed" describes how many times per second an inverter (an electronic representation of a "logical not" function) can change from true to false and back. Faster logic can accomplish more operations in less time. Digital logic first became useful when switching speeds got above fifty hertz, because that was faster than a team of humans operating mechanical calculators. Modern electronic digital logic routinely switches at five gigahertz (5×10^{9} hertz), and some laboratory systems switch at more than a terahertz (1×10^{12} hertz).

Logic Families

Design started with relays. Relay logic was relatively inexpensive and reliable, but slow. Occasionally a mechanical failure would occur. Fanouts were typically about ten, limited by the resistance of the coils and arcing on the contacts from high voltages.

Later, vacuum tubes were used. These were very fast, but generated heat, and were unreliable because the filaments would burn out. Fanouts were typically five to seven, limited by the heating from the tubes' current. In the 1950s, special "computer tubes" were developed with filaments that omitted volatile elements like silicon. These ran for hundreds of thousands of hours. The first semiconductor logic family was resistor-transistor logic. This was a thousand times more reliable than tubes, ran cooler, and used less power, but had a very low fan-in of three. Diode-transistor logic improved the fanout up to about seven, and reduced the power. Some DTL designs used two power-supplies with alternating layers of NPN and PNP transistors to increase the fanout.

Transistor transistor logic (TTL) was a great improvement over these. In early devices, fanout improved to ten, and later variations reliably achieved twenty. TTL was also fast, with some variations achieving switching times as low as twenty nanoseconds. TTL is still used in some designs. Emitter coupled logic is very fast but uses a lot of power. It was extensively used for high-performance computers made up of many medium-scale components (such as the Illiac IV). By far, the most common digital integrated circuits built today use CMOS logic, which is fast, offers high circuit density and low-power per gate. This is used even in large, fast computers, such as the IBM System z.

Recent Developments

In 2009, researchers discovered that memristors can implement a boolean state storage (similar to a flip flop, implication and logical inversion, providing a complete logic family with very small amounts of space and power, using familiar CMOS semiconductor processes. The discovery of superconductivity has enabled the development of rapid single flux quantum (RSFQ) circuit technology, which uses Josephson junctions instead of transistors. Most recently, attempts are being made to construct purely optical computing systems capable of processing digital information using nonlinear optical elements.

Thermal Management of Electronic Devices and Systems

Heat generated by electronic devices and circuitry must be dissipated to improve reliability and prevent premature failure. Techniques for heat dissipation can include heatsinks and fans for air cooling, and other forms of computer cooling such as liquid cooling. In cases of extreme low environmental temperatures, it may actually be necessary to heat the electronic components to achieve satisfactory operation.

Thermal Time Constants

A heatsink's thermal mass can be considered as a capacitor (storing heat instead of charge) and the thermal resistance as an electrical resistance (giving a measure of how fast stored heat can be dissipated). Together, these two components form a thermal RC circuit with an associated time constant given by the product of R and C. This quantity can be used to calculate the dynamic heat dissipation capability of a device, in an analogous way to the electrical case.

A specific type of thermal interface material is put between the heat sink and the heat source to increase thermal throughput, such as a microprocessor chip or other power handling semiconductor to stabilise its temperature through increased thermal mass and heat dissipation (primarily by conduction and convection and to a lesser extent by radiation).Thermal interface material A Thermal Interface Material or Mastic (aka TIM) is used to fill the gaps between thermal transfer surfaces, such as between microprocessors and heatsinks, in order to increase thermal transfer efficiency. These gaps are normally filled with air which is a very poor conductor.

Heat Sink

In electronic systems, a heat sink is a passive component that cools a device by dissipating heat into the surrounding air. Heat sinks are used to cool electronic components such as high-power semiconductor devices, and optoelectronic devices such as higher-power lasers and light emitting diodes (LEDs).

Figure: *A fan-cooled heat sink on the processor of a personal computer. To the right is a smaller heat sink cooling another integrated circuit of the motherboard.*

Heat sinks are heat exchangers such as those used in refrigeration and air conditioning systems, or the radiator in an automobile. A heat sink is designed to increase the surface area in contact with the cooling medium surrounding it, such as the air.

Figure: *A heat sink is an essential component for cooling high-power integrated circuits. This heat sink is a combination of aluminum fins and copper heat pipes for cooling high-heat-dissipation processors (As shown is Freezer Xtreme from Arctic).*

Approach air velocity, choice of material, fin (or other protrusion) design and surface treatment are some of the factors which affect the thermal performance of a heat sink. Heat sinks are used to cool computer central processing units or graphics processors. Heat sink attachment methods and thermal interface materials also affect the eventual die temperature of the integrated circuit. Thermal adhesive or thermal grease fills the air gap between the heat sink and device to improve its thermal performance. Theoretical, experimental and numerical methods can be used to determine a heat sink's thermal performance.

Basic Heat Sink Heat Transfer Principle

A heat sink is an object that transfers thermal energy from a higher temperature to a lower temperature fluid medium. The fluid medium is frequently air, but can also be water or in the case of heat exchangers, refrigerants and oil. If the fluid medium is water, the 'heat sink' is frequently called a cold plate. In thermodynamics a heat sink is a heat reservoir that can absorb an arbitrary amount of heat without significantly changing temperature.

Practical heat sinks for electronic devices must have a temperature higher than the surroundings to transfer heat by convection, radiation, and conduction. To understand the principle of a heat sink, consider Fourier's law of heat conduction. Joseph Fourier was a French mathematician who made important contributions to the analytical treatment of heat conduction. Fourier's law of heat conduction, simplified to a one-dimensional form in the x-direction, shows that when there is a temperature gradient in a body, heat will be transferred from the higher temperature region to the lower temperature region. The rate at which heat is transferred by conduction, q_k, is proportional to the product of the temperature gradient and the cross-sectional area through which heat is transferred.

$$q_k = -kA\frac{dT}{dx}$$

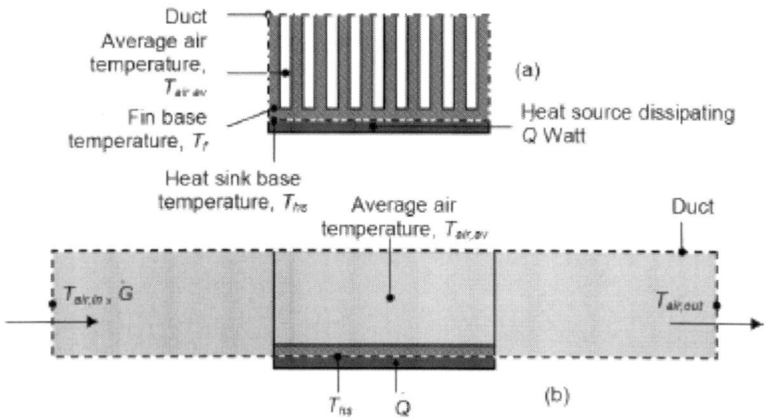

Figure: *Sketch of a heat sink in a duct used to calculate the governing equations from conservation of energy and Newton's law of cooling.*

Consider a heat sink in a duct, where air flows through the duct. It is assumed that the heat sink base is higher in temperature than the air. Applying the conservation of energy, for steady-state conditions, and Newton's law of cooling to the temperature nodes gives the following set of equations.

$$\dot{Q} = \dot{m}c_{p,in}(T_{air,out} - T_{air,in}) \tag{1}$$

$$\dot{Q} = \frac{T_{hs} - T_{air,av}}{R_{hs}} \tag{2}$$

where

$$T_{air,av} = \frac{T_{air,out} + T_{air,in}}{2} \tag{3}$$

Using the mean air temperature is an assumption that is valid for relatively short heat sinks. When compact heat exchangers are calculated, the logarithmic mean air temperature is used. m is the air mass flow rate in kg/s.

The above equations show that

- When the air flow through the heat sink decreases, this results in an increase in the average air temperature. This in turn increases the heat sink base temperature. And additionally, the thermal resistance of the heat sink will also increase. The net result is a higher heat sink base temperature.
    - o The increase in heat sink thermal resistance with decrease in flow rate will be shown in later in this article.
- The inlet air temperature relates strongly with the heat sink base temperature. For example, if there is recirculation of air in a product, the inlet air temperature is not the ambient air temperature. The inlet air temperature of the heat sink is therefore higher, which also results in a higher heat sink base temperature.
- If there is no air flow around the heat sink, energy cannot be transferred.
- A heat sink is not a device with the "magical ability to absorb heat like a sponge and send it off to a parallel universe".

Natural convection requires free flow of air over the heat sink. If fins are not aligned vertically, or if pins are too close together to allow sufficient air flow between them, the efficiency of the heat sink will decline.

Design Factors Which Influence the Thermal Performance of a Heat Sink

Thermal Resistance

For semiconductor devices used in a variety of consumer and industrial electronics, the idea of *thermal resistance* simplifies the selection of heat sinks. The heat flow between the semiconductor die and ambient air is modelled as a series of resistances to heat flow; there is a resistance from the die to the device case, from the case to the heat sink, and from the heat sink to the ambient. The sum of these resistances is the total thermal resistance from the die to the ambient. Thermal resistance is defined as temperature rise per unit of power, analogous to electrical resistance, and is expressed in units of degrees Celsius per watt (C/W). If the device dissipation in watts is known, and the total thermal resistance is calculated, the temperature rise of the die over ambient can be calculated.

The idea of thermal resistance of a semiconductor heat sink is an approximation. It does not take into account non-uniform distribution of heat over a device or heat sink. It only models a system in thermal equilibrium, and does not take into account the change in temperatures with time. Nor does it reflect the non-linearity of radiation and convection with respect to temperature rise. However, manufacturers tabulate typical values of thermal resistance for heat sinks and semiconductor devices, which allows selection of commercially manufactured heat sinks to be simplified.

Commercial extruded aluminium heat sinks have a thermal resistance (heat sink to ambient air) ranging from 0.4 C/W for a large sink meant for TO3 devices, up to as high as 85 C/W for a clip-on heat sink for a TO92 small plastic case. The famous, popular, historic and notable 2N3055 power transistor in a TO3 case has an internal thermal resistance from junction to case of 1.52 C/W. The contact between the device case and heat sink may have a thermal resistance of between 0.5 up to 1.7 C/W, depending on the case size, and use of grease or insulating mica washer.

Material

The most common heat sink materials are aluminium alloys. Aluminium alloy 1050A has one of the higher thermal conductivity values at 229 W/m•K but is mechanically soft. Aluminium alloys 6061 and 6063 are commonly used, with thermal conductivity values of 166 and 201 W/m•K, respectively. The values depend on the temper of the alloy. Copper has around twice the conductivity of aluminium, but is three times as dense and, depending on the market, around four to six times more expensive than aluminium. Aluminium can be extruded, but copper can not. Copper heat sinks are machined and skived. Another method of manufacture is to solder the fins into the heat sink base.

Diamond is another heat sink material, and its thermal conductivity of 2000 W/m•K exceeds copper five-fold. In contrast to metals, where heat is conducted by delocalized electrons, lattice vibrations are responsible for diamond's very high thermal conductivity. For thermal management applications, the outstanding thermal conductivity and diffusivity of diamond is an essential. Nowadays synthetic diamond is used as submounts for high-power integrated circuits and laser diodes. Composite materials can be used. Examples are a copper-tungsten pseudoalloy, AlSiC (silicon carbide in aluminium matrix), Dymalloy (diamond in copper-silver alloy matrix), and E-Material (beryllium oxide in beryllium matrix). Such materials are often used as substrates for chips, as their thermal expansion coefficient can be matched to ceramics and semiconductors.

Fin Efficiency

Fin efficiency is one of the parameters which makes a higher thermal conductivity material important. A fin of a heat sink may be considered to be a flat plate with heat flowing in one end and being dissipated into the surrounding fluid as it travels to the other. As heat flows through the fin, the combination of the thermal resistance of the heat sink impeding the flow and the heat lost due to convection, the temperature of the fin and, therefore, the heat transfer to the fluid, will decrease from the base to the end of the fin. Fin efficiency is defined as the actual heat transferred by the fin, divided by the heat transfer were the fin to be isothermal (hypothetically the fin having infinite thermal conductivity). Equations 6 and 7 are applicable for straight fins.

$$\eta_f = \frac{\tanh(mL_c)}{mL_c} \tag{6}$$

$$mL_c = \sqrt{\frac{2h_f}{kt_f}}L_f \tag{7}$$

Where:

- h_f is the convection coefficient of the fin
  - o Air: 10 to 100 W/(m^{2}K)
  - o Water: 500 to 10,000 W/(m^{2}K)
- k is the thermal conductivity of the fin material
  - o Aluminium: 120 to 240 W/(m·K)
- L_f is the fin height (m)
- t_f is the fin thickness (m)

Fin efficiency is increased by decreasing the fin aspect ratio (making them thicker or shorter), or by using more conductive material (copper instead of aluminium, for example).

Spreading Resistance

Another parameter that concerns the thermal conductivity of the heat sink material is spreading resistance. Spreading resistance occurs when thermal energy is transferred from a small area to a larger area in a substance with finite thermal conductivity. In a heat sink, this means that heat does not distribute uniformly through the heat sink base. The spreading resistance phenomenon is shown by how the heat travels from the heat source location and causes a large temperature gradient between the heat source and the edges of the heat sink. This means that some fins are at a lower temperature than if the heat source were uniform across the base of the heat sink. This nonuniformity increases the heat sink's effective thermal resistance.

To decrease the spreading resistance in the base of a heat sink:

- Increase the base thickness
- Choose a different material with better thermal conductivity
- Use a vapour chamber or heat pipe in the heat sink base.

6

Electrical Connector

An electrical connector is an electro-mechanical device for joining electrical circuits as an interface using a mechanical assembly. The connection may be temporary, as for portable equipment, require a tool for assembly and removal, or serve as a permanent electrical joint between two wires or devices. There are hundreds of types of electrical connectors. Connectors may join two lengths of flexible copper wire or cable, or connect a wire or cable or optical interface to an electrical terminal.

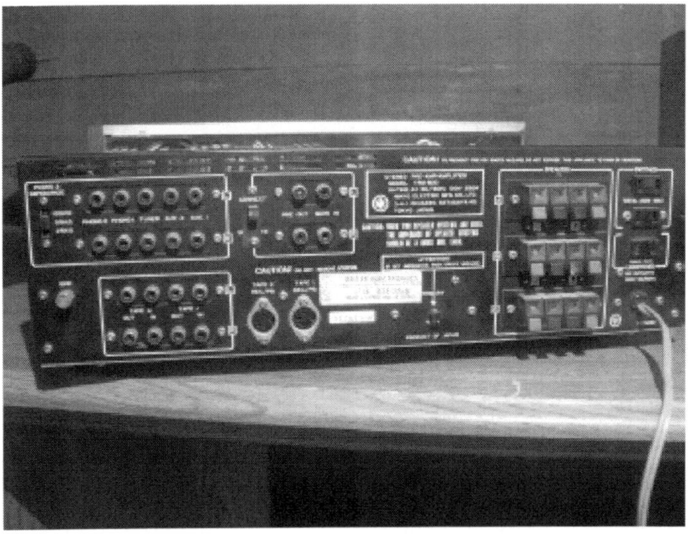

Figure: *Back of an audio amplifier features a variety of electrical connectors*

In computing, an electrical connector can also be known as a physical interface (compare Physical Layer in OSI model of networking).

Cable glands, known as *cable connectors* in the U.S., connect wires to devices mechanically rather than electrically and are distinct from quick-disconnects performing the latter.

Properties of Electrical Connectors

Electrical connectors are characterised by their pinout and physical construction, size, contact resistance, insulation between pins, ruggedness and resistance to vibration, resistance to entry of water or other contaminants, resistance to pressure, reliability, lifetime (number of connect/disconnect operations before failure), and ease of connecting and disconnecting.

They may be keyed to prevent insertion in the wrong orientation, connecting the wrong pins to each other, and have locking mechanisms to ensure that they are fully inserted and cannot work loose or fall out. Some connectors are designed such that certain pins make contact before others when inserted, and break first on disconnection; this protects circuits typically in connectors that apply power, e.g. connecting safety ground first, and sequencing connections properly in hot swapping applications.

It is usually desirable for a connector to be easy to identify visually, rapid to assemble, require only simple tooling, and be inexpensive. In some cases an equipment manufacturer might choose a connector specifically because it is *not* compatible with those from other sources, allowing control of what may be connected. No single connector has all the ideal properties; the proliferation of types is a reflection of differing requirements.

Keying

Many connectors are keyed, with some mechanical component which prevents mating except with a correctly-oriented matching connector.

This can be used to prevent incorrect or damaging interconnections, either preventing pins from being damaged by being jammed in at the wrong angle or fitting into imperfectly fitting plugs, or to prevent damaging connections, such as plugging an audio cable into a power outlet.

For instance, XLR connectors have a notch to ensure proper orientation, while Mini-DIN plugs have a plastic projection, which fits into a corresponding hole in the socket and prevent different connectors from being pushed together (they also have a notched metal skirt to provide secondary keying).

Locking Mechanisms

Some connector housings are designed with locking mechanisms to prevent inadvertent disconnection or poor environmental sealing. Locking mechanism designs include locking levers of various sorts, screw locking, and toggle or bayonet locking. Depending on application requirements, housings with locking mechanisms may be tested under various environmental simulations that include physical shock and vibration, water spray, dust, etc. to ensure the integrity of the electrical connection and housing seals.

Terminal Blocks

Terminal blocks (also called terminal *boards* or *strips*) provide a convenient means of connecting individual electrical wires without a splice or physically joining the ends. They are usually used to connect wiring among various items of equipment within an enclosure or to make connections among individually enclosed items. Since terminal blocks are readily available for a wide range of wire sizes and terminal quantity, they are one of the most flexible types of electrical connector available. Some disadvantages are that connecting wires is more difficult than simply plugging in a cable and the terminals are generally not very well protected from contact with persons or foreign conducting materials.

Figure: *Terminal blocks of various types.*

One type of terminal block accepts wires that are prepared only by removing (*stripping*) a short length of insulation from the end. Another type accepts wires that have ring or spade terminal *lugs* crimped onto the wires. Printed circuit board (PCB) mounted terminal blocks allow individual wires to be connected to the circuit board. PCB mounted terminal blocks are soldered to the board, but they are available in a pull-apart version that allows the wire-connecting half of the block to be unplugged from the part that is soldered to the PCB.

Posts

Figure: *A binding post (red and black) adaptor.*

A general type of connector that simply screws or clamps bare wire to a post; such connectors are frequently used in electronic test equipment and audio. Many, but not all binding posts will also accept a banana connector plug.

Insulation Displacement Connectors

Since stripping the insulation from wires is time-consuming, many connectors intended for rapid assembly use insulation-displacement connectors so that insulation need not be removed from the wire. These generally take the form of a fork-shaped opening in the terminal, into which the insulated wire is pressed and which cut through the insulation to contact the conductor within. To make these connections reliably on a production line, special tools are used which accurately control the forces applied during assembly. If properly assembled, the resulting terminations are gas-tight and will last the life of the product.

A common example is the multi-conductor flat ribbon cable used in computer disk drives; to terminate each of the many (approximately 40) wires individually would be slow and error-prone, but an insulation displacement connector can terminate all the wires in (literally) one stroke. Another very common use is so-called punch down blocks used for terminating telephone wiring. Insulation displacement connectors are usually used with small conductors for signal purposes and at low voltage. Power conductors carrying more than a few amperes are more reliably terminated with other means, though "hot tap" press-on connectors find some use in automotive applications for additions to existing wiring.

Plug and Socket Connectors

Plug and socket connectors are usually made up of a male plug (typically pin contacts) and a female receptacle (typically socket contacts), although *hermaphroditic* connectors exist, such as the original IBM token ring LAN connector. Plugs generally have one or more pins or prongs that are inserted into openings in the mating socket. The connection between the mating metal parts must be sufficiently tight to make a good electrical connection and complete the circuit. When working with multi-pin connectors, it is helpful to have a pinout diagram to identify the wire or circuit node connected to each pin.

A male plug made by Amphenol.

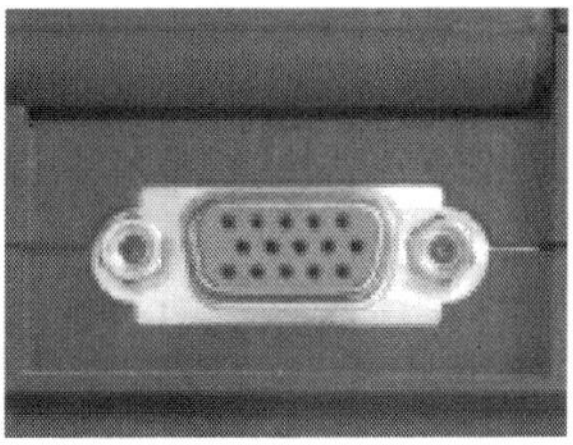

A female VGA connector.

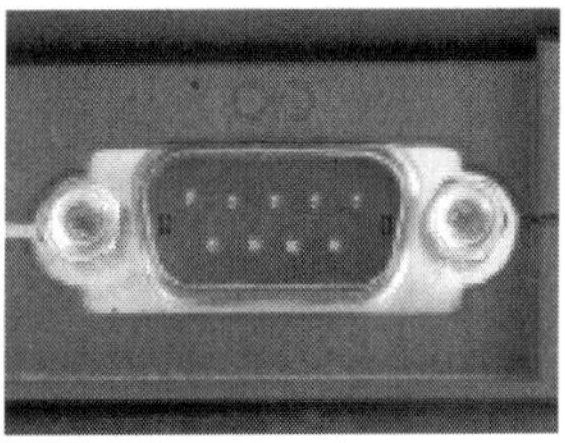

A male serial port connector

Jack commonly refers to a connector often with the female electrical contact or socket, and is the "more fixed" connector of a connector pair. *Plug* commonly refers to a movable connector, often (but not always) with the male electrical contact or pin, and is the movable (less fixed) connector of a connector pair.

Some connector styles may contain both pin and socket connection types. A jack is properly described as a connector that is designed to be fixed on the surface of a bulkhead or enclosure; "The stationary (more fixed) connector of a mating pair shall be designated J or X" where J means jack. Its counterpart, the "plug," is designed to attach to a wire, cable or removable electrical assembly; "The movable (less fixed) connector of a mating pair shall be designated P– where P means plug. This convention is currently defined in ASME Y14.44-2008 which is the current actively maintained follow on to the withdrawn IEEE 200-1975; IEEE 200-1975 was derived from the long withdrawn MIL-STD-16 which dates back at least to the 1950s which highlights the heritage of this connector naming convention. IEEE 315-1975 works alongside ASME Y14.44-2008 to define J, P and X references.

A plug is properly described as a connector that is designed to be attached to a wire, cable or removable electrical assembly: "The movable (less fixed) connector of a mating pair shall be designated P– where P means plug.

The term *jack* occurs in several related terms:

- The "registered jack" in RJ11, RJ45 and similar connectors, and includes the modular jacks used in modern telephone systems and computer network interfaces (for example, "Ethernet jack").
- The telephone jack of manual telephone switchboards, which is the socket fitting the original 1/4– telephone plug. This open-frame, open-circuit accepts 1/4– mono phone plugs.
- The 1/4– phone jack common to many electronic applications, either in a 2-conductor tip-sleeve (TS) or 3-conductor tip-ring-sleeve (TRS) configuration.
- The RCA jack, also known as a "phono jack", common to consumer electronics.
- The EIAJ jack designed for consumer appliances requiring less than an 18.0 volt power supply.

When the description includes a diametre, the term refers to the jack that matches the corresponding diametre of plug. For example:

- 6.35 mm or 1/4– jack
- 3.5 mm (1/8–) miniature jack
- 2.5 mm (3/32–) subminiature

A headphone (or earphone) jack is commonly one of the three standard sizes of 3-conductor TRS jacks, but the term could refer to any socket used for this purpose.

Component and Device Connectors

Electrical and electronic components and devices sometimes have plug and socket connectors or terminal blocks, but individual screw terminals and fast-on or quick-disconnect terminals are more common. Small components have bare lead wires for soldering. They are manufactured using casting.

Figure: *High-power transistor switch module with large screw connectors and small crimped-on "Fast-on" connectors*

Blade Connector

A blade connector is a type of single wire connection using a flat conductive blade which is inserted into a blade receptacle. Usually both blade connector and blade receptacle have wires attached to them either through soldering of the wire to the blade or crimping of the blade to the wire. In some cases the blade is an integral manufactured part of a component (such as a switch or a speaker unit), and a blade receptacle is pushed onto the blade to form a connection.

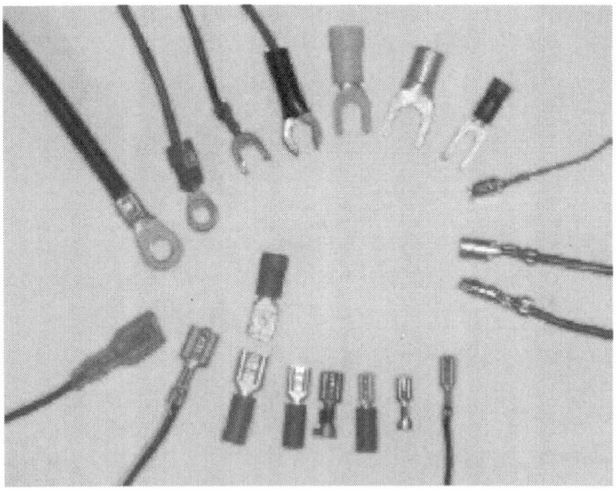

Figure: *Blade connectors (lower half of photo). Ring and spade terminals (upper half).*

A common type of blade connector is the "Faston". While Faston is a trademark of TE Connectivity (formerly Tyco Electronics), it has come into common usage. Faston connectors come in male and female types. They have been commonly used since the 1970s.

Ring and Spade Terminals

The connectors in the top row of the image are known as ring terminals and spade terminals (sometimes called split ring terminals). Electrical contact is made by passing a screw or bolt through them.

Figure: *Ring style wire end blade connectors are normally sold in lots.*

The spade terminal form factor facilitates connections since the screw or bolt can be left partially screwed in as the spade terminal is removed or attached. Their sizes can be determined by the size of the conducting wire AWG and the screw/bolt diametre size designation.

Commonly Used Connectors

8P8C Connector

Figure: *8P8C Connector crimped to cable*

8P8C is short for "eight positions, eight conductors", and so an 8P8C modular connector (plug or jack) is a modular connector with eight positions, all containing conductors. The connector is probably most famous for its use in Ethernet and widely used on CAT5 cables.

The 8P8C modular plugs and jacks look very similar to the plugs and jacks used for FCC's registered jack RJ45 variants, although the specified RJ45 socket is not compatible with 8P8C modular plug connectors. It neither uses all eight conductors (but only two of them for wires plus two for connecting a programming resistor) nor does it fit into 8P8C because the true RJ45 is "keyed".

D-Subminiature Connectors

Figure: *A male DE-9 plug.*

The D-subminiature electrical connector is commonly used for the RS-232 serial port on modems and IBM compatible computers. The D-subminiature connector is used in many different applications, for computers, telecommunications, and test and measurement instruments. A few examples are monitors (MGA, CGA, EGA), the Commodore 64, MSX, Apple II, Amiga, and Atari joysticks and mice, and game consoles such as Atari and Sega.

USB Connectors

The Universal Serial Bus is a serial bus standard to interface devices, founded in 1996. It is currently widely used among PCs, Apple Macintosh and many other devices. There are several types of USB connectors, and some have been added as the specification has progressed.

The most commonly used is the (male) series "A" plug on peripherals, when the cable is fixed to the peripheral. If there is no cable fixed to the peripheral, the peripheral always needs to have a

USB "B" socket. In this case a USB "A" plug to a USB "B" plug cable would be needed.

Figure: *A male USB series A plug*

USB "A" sockets are always used on the host PC and the USB "B" sockets on the peripherals. It is a 4-pin connector, surrounded by a shield. There are several other connectors in use, the mini-A, mini-B and mini-AB plug and socket (added in the On-The-Go Supplement to the USB 2.0 Specification).

Power Connectors

Power connectors must protect people from accidental contact with energized conductors. Power connectors often include a safety ground connection as well as the power conductors.

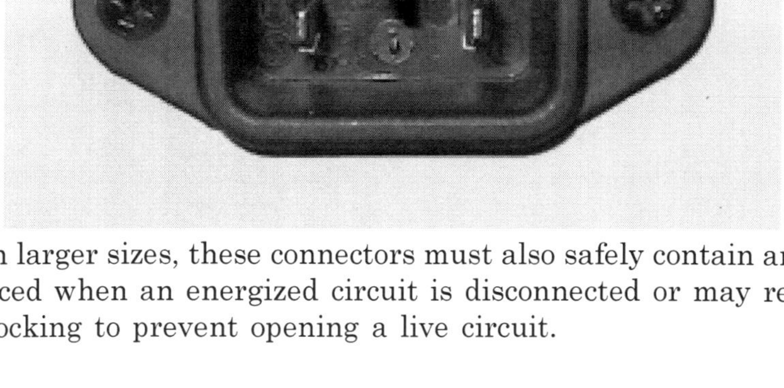

In larger sizes, these connectors must also safely contain any arc produced when an energized circuit is disconnected or may require interlocking to prevent opening a live circuit.

Radio Frequency Connectors

For more details on this topic, see Impedance matching and Signal reflection. Connectors used at radio frequencies must not change the impedance of the transmission line of which they are part, otherwise signal reflection and losses will result. A radio-frequency connector must not allow external signals into the circuit, and must prevent leakage of energy out of the circuit. At lower radio frequencies simple connectors can be used with success, but as the radio frequency increases, transmission line effects become more important, with small impedance variations from connectors causing the signal to reflect from the connector, rather than to pass through.

At UHF and above, silver-plating of connectors is common to reduce losses. For Wi-Fi antennas the R-TNC connectors are used. A BNC connector is common for radio and test equipment used up to about 1 GHz.

DC Connectors

A DC connector is an electrical connector for supplying direct current (DC) power. For portable consumer electronic devices, the coaxial power connector is frequently used, but many other types of connectors also exist.

Hybrid Connectors

Hybrid connectors have housings with inserts that allow the intermixing of many connector types, such as those mentioned above. These housings may also allow intermixing of electrical and non-electrical interfaces, examples of the latter being pneumatic line connectors, and optical fibre connectors. Because hybrid connectors are modular in nature, they tend to simplify assembly, repair, and future modifications. They also allow the creation of composite cable assemblies that can reduce equipment installation time by reducing the number of individual cable and connector assemblies.

Electrical Cables

Termination and Gender

When used to terminate cables, in some applications both ends of the cable are terminated using identical connectors (generally male), as in registered jack telephone cables or Ethernet over twisted pair network cables, while in other applications the two ends are terminated differently, either with male and female of the same connector (as in an extension cord), which ends can be connected to each other in a loop, or with incompatible connectors, in an adapter cable.

Wiring and Pinouts

When a cable is terminated by a connector, the various wires in the cable are connected to contacts (pins) in the connector. The most common methods of connecting pins to individual wires are soldering, insulation displacement, insulation piercing, screw clamping, axial screw termination, cage clamping, crimping, press-in termination, and wire wrapping. Some of these wiring methods can be accomplished without specialised tools. Other methods, while requiring a special tool, can assemble connectors to a cable much faster and more reliably, and make repairs easier. If one has specified wires within a cable (for instance, the coloured Ethernet cable wires in TIA/EIA-568-B), then the order in which different colour wires are attached to different connector pins defines the wiring scheme. Different ways of wiring numbered connector pins at the two ends of a cable creates different assemblies, which may appear identical but behave differently.

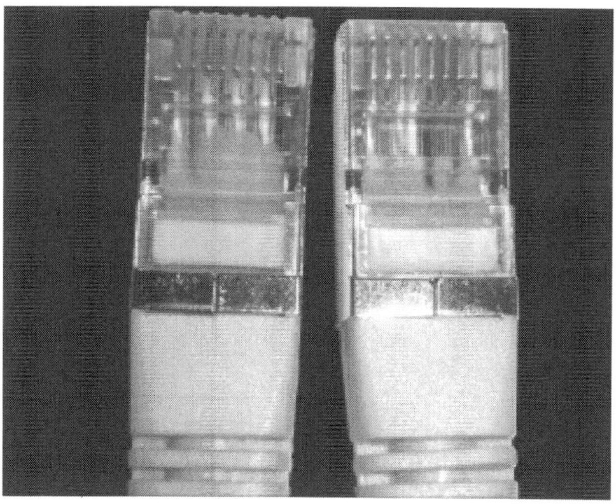

If both ends of a cable have the same connector, or male and female versions of a connector, or even similar connectors (such as RJ11 and BS 6312, both of which often have 6P4C (6 positions and 4 contacts)), there is a notion of straight through cable and crossover cable:

- in a straight through cable, pins on one end correspond exactly to the corresponding pins on the other end (pin 1 to pin 1, pin 2 to pin 2, etc.).

Using the same wiring (a given colour wire connects to a given number pin, the same at both ends) at each end yields a straight through cable.

- in a crossover cable, pins do not so correspond; most often in crossover cables some cables are swapped, meaning that if pin 1 on one end goes to pin 2 on the other end, then pin 2 on the first end goes to pin 1 on the second end, and not to pin 3 or some other: such crossover cables are symmetric, meaning that they work identically regardless of which way you plug them in (if you turn the cable around, it still connects the same pins as before).

Using different wiring (a given colour wire connects to one number pin at one end, and a different number pin at the other) at each end yields a crossover cable. A well-known crossover cable is the Ethernet crossover cable, which converts between T568A and T568B termination.

What matters specifically is not "which contact corresponds to which wire", but rather "which contact on one connector corresponds to which contact on the other connector": to illustrate the distinction, T568A straight through cables and T568B straight through cables are electrically identical: pin 1 on one end corresponds to pin 1 on the other end, though in the T568A it is a green/white striped wire that connects them, while in T568B it is an orange/white striped wire that connects them.

However, a cable wired with T568A at one end and T568B at the other is a crossover cable. The name "straight through" is suggestive but slightly misleading: if one has a ribbon cable, such that all wires are in fact straight and in a line, the pinouts at the two ends are the *mirror* of each other: the left-most wire on one end is the right-most wire on the other.

Screw Terminal

A screw terminal is a type of electrical connector where a wire is clamped down to metal by a screw. The wire is sometimes just stripped of electrical insulation at the end, and is bent in a U or J shape to fit around the shaft of the screw. Alternatively, a lug can be crimped onto the end of the wire to protect it. Setscrews are also used, as in a luster terminal or lustre terminal, but lugs will not fit into them. For both lugs and bare wire, the screw is tightened for a secure connection.

Description and Usage

Screw terminals are commonly used to connect a chassis ground, such as on a record player or surge protector. Most public address systems in buildings also use them for speakers, and sometimes for other outputs and inputs. They are also used extensively in wiring for electricity, for connecting electrical outlets and switches to the mains, and for connecting major appliances like clothes dryers and ovens to the particular plug installed in a home, or directly hard-wiring to the house, as required by local electrical codes in the US. For reliability reasons, screw terminals for earth ground connections are preferred on most USA-style outlets, even for those that otherwise have "rear-wire" push-in connections, despite the difficulty of bending heavy-gauge solid copper around a screw with pliers. Grounding screws are often marked green, and when used on consumer electronics often have a washer with gripping "teeth".

Multiway Version

Figure: *Two paired luster/lustre terminals (centimeter scale)*

Multiple screw terminals can be arranged as a barrier strip, with each short metal strip having a pair of screws. This is used for connecting two different components, one on each side of the pairs. This arrangement is common in luster terminals, as pictured at left. These are known as connector strips or chocolate blocks in the UK. Conversely, terminals can also be arranged as a terminal strip or terminal block, with several screws along (typically) two long strips. This creates a bus bar for power distribution, and so may also include a master input connector, usually binding posts or banana connectors.

Advantages and Disadvantages

Screw terminals are low in cost compared to other types of connectors, and can be readily designed into products for circuits carrying currents of a fraction of an ampere up to several hundred amperes at low to moderate frequencies. The terminals can be easily re-used in the field, allowing for replacement of wires or equipment, generally with standard hand tools. Screw terminals avoid the requirement for a specialized mating connector to be applied to the wire ends.

When properly tightened, the connections are physically and electrically secure because they firmly contact a large section of wire. The terminals are relatively low cost compared with other types of connector, and a screw terminal can easily be integrated into the design of a building wiring device (such as a socket, switch, or lamp holder).

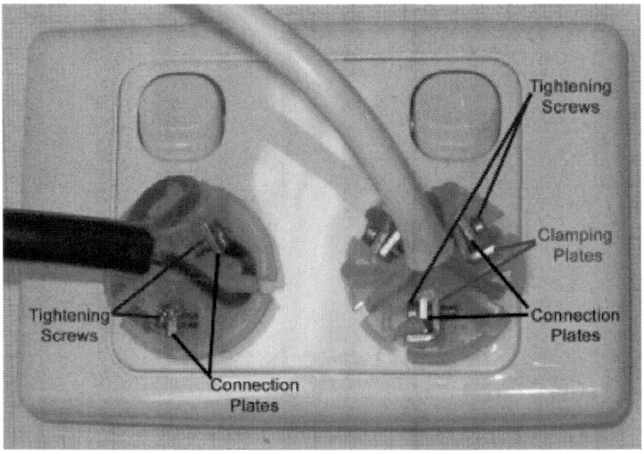

Figure: *Two types of screw terminals showing a significant development in design. Basic, with the wires held between the screws and the terminals (left) and with the wires held, reversely, between the metal (clamping) plates and the rear of the terminals (right).*

Disadvantages include the time taken to strip a wire and properly wrap it around the screw head, in type 1 terminals. This procedure is slower than a plug-in connector, making screw connections uncommon for portable equipment where wires are repeatedly connected and disconnected.

Assembly of a screw connection requires some care in workmanship to ensure adequate tightening of the screw, proper removal of insulation, and containment of all wire strands. If the wire is too small, it can be cut through by an overtightened screw head, in both type 1 and type 3 terminals. Wire strands may not be contained by the screw head in type 1 terminals, so sometimes stranded wires are crimped into a ferrule to prevent bridging of terminals; this partly offsets the economy of a "bare" wire termination.

Wires must never be tinned with solder prior to installation in a screw terminal, since the soft metal will cold flow, resulting in a loose connection and possible fire hazard.

In addition, the screw mechanism limits the minimum physical size of a terminal, making screw terminals less useful where very many connections are required. It is difficult to automate multiple terminations with screw connections. Vibration or corrosion can cause a screw connection to deteriorate over time.

Screw connectors sometimes come loose if not done up tightly enough at fitting time. Verifying adequate tightening torque requires calibrated installation tools and proper training. In the UK, all screw connectors on fixed mains installations are required to be accessible for servicing, for this reason.

Pin Header

A pin header (or simply header) is a form of electrical connector, often associated with ribbon cable connectors. It consists of one or more rows of pins typically spaced 0.1 inches (2.54 mm) apart, but sometimes 2 millimetres (0.079 in) or 0.05 inches (1.27 mm) is used as well.

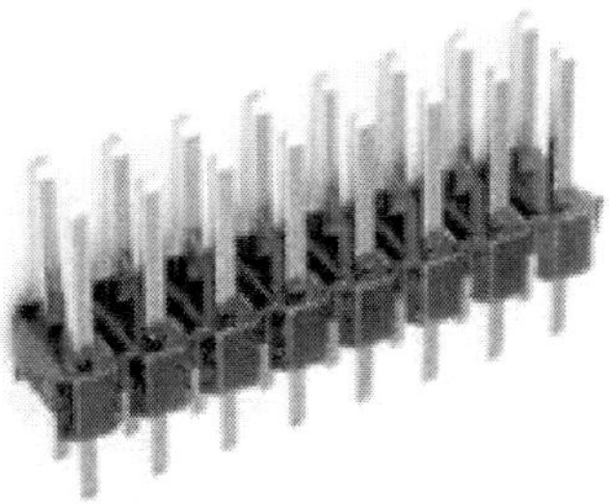

Figure: *8x2 male pin header*

In addition to being used to connect to a ribbon cable connector, pin headers often also function as recipients for jumpers. The most common jumper spacing is 0.1 inches (2.54 mm) spacing, though 2 millimetres (0.079 in) is sometimes used in smaller products. Pin header connectors are thus "male" connectors (female counterparts do exist, but these are normally just called "header connectors", without "pin") and are mostly used inside equipment, rather than being used as a connector on the outside of the device.

Normally pin headers are pin through hole (PTH) devices, but surface-mount technology (SMT) versions of one and two row pin headers also exist.

In the latter case the solder sides of the pins are simply bent on a 90 degree angle so as to be soldered to a solder plane. On single row pin headers the pins are bent alternating to one side or the other, on dual row pin headers the pins are simply bent outwards. If pin headers are optional, the PTH variant is often chosen for ease of manual assembly. Pin headers can be either straight or angled. The latter form is often used to connect two boards together.

Pin headers are cost-effective due to their simplicity. Headers are often sold as long strips (typically 40 pins for the dual row versions) which can easily be broken off to the right number of pins. Pin headers with a plastic guide box around them are known as "box headers" or "shrouded headers" and are normally only used in combination with a ribbon cable connector.

A notch (key) in the guide box normally prevents placing the connector the wrong way around. In absence of a pin one designation on the header, one or more pins in the header may be removed or clipped to indicate a key for correct orientation. If a designation is missing from the header, then examine the PCB for markings, (often the solder pad around the hole of pin-1, of a PTH header, is square rather than round) otherwise consult the user manual.

Analogue Electronics

Analogue electronics (or analog in American English) are electronic systems with a continuously variable signal, in contrast to digital electronics where signals usually take only two different levels. The term "analogue" describes the proportional relationship between a signal and a voltage or current that represents the signal. The word analogue is derived from the Greek word αíÜëïãïò (analogos) meaning "proportional".

7

Single Phase A.C. Circuits

Introduction

Figure: *Single phase power system schematic diagram shows little about the wiring of a practical power circuit.*

Depicted above (Figure above) is a very simple AC circuit. If the load resistor's power dissipation were substantial, we might call this a "power circuit" or "power system" instead of regarding it as just a regular circuit. The distinction between a "power circuit" and a "regular circuit" may seem arbitrary, but the practical concerns are definitely not.

One such concern is the size and cost of wiring necessary to deliver power from the AC source to the load. Normally, we do not give much thought to this type of concern if we're merely analyzing a circuit for the sake of learning about the laws of electricity. However, in the real world it can be a major concern. If we give the source in the above circuit a voltage value and also give power dissipation values to the two load resistors, we can determine the wiring needs for this particular circuit: (Figure below)

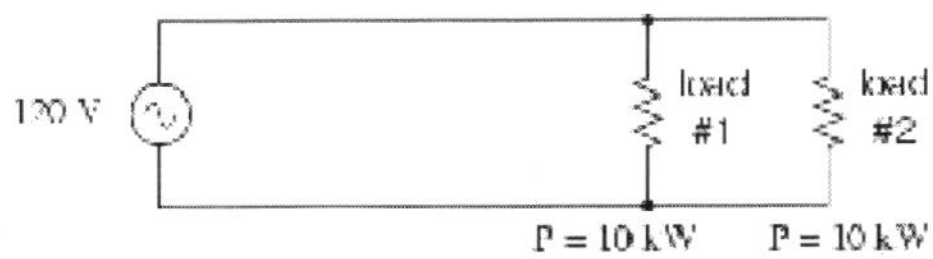

Figure: *As a practical matter, the wiring for the 20 kW loads at 120 Vac is rather substantial (167 A).*

$$I = \frac{P}{E}$$

$$I = \frac{10\,\text{kw}}{120\,\text{V}}$$

$$I = 83.33\,\text{A} \quad (\textit{for each load resistor})$$

$$1_{total} = 1_{load\#1} + 1_{load\#2} \qquad P_{total} = (10\text{kw}) + (10\text{kw})$$

$$1_{total} = (83.33\text{A}) + (83.33\text{A}) \qquad P_{total} = 20\text{kw}$$

$$1_{total} = 166.67\text{A}$$

83.33 amps for each load resistor in Figure above adds up to 166.66 amps total circuit current. This is no small amount of current, and would necessitate copper wire conductors of at least 1/0 gage. Such wire is well over 1/4 inch (6 mm) in diameter, weighing over 300 pounds per thousand feet. Bear in mind that copper is not cheap either! It would be in our best interest to find ways to minimize such costs if we were designing a power system with long conductor lengths.

One way to do this would be to increase the voltage of the power source and use loads built to dissipate 10 kW each at this higher voltage. The loads, of course, would have to have greater resistance values to dissipate the same power as before (10 kW each) at a greater voltage than before. The advantage would be less current required, permitting the use of smaller, lighter, and cheaper wire: (Figure below)

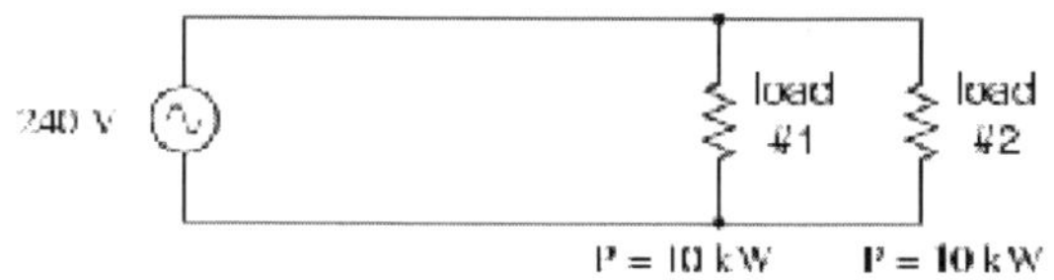

Same 10 kW loads at 240 Vac requires less substantial wiring than at 120 Vac (83 A).

$$I = \frac{P}{E}$$

$$I = \frac{10\,\text{kw}}{120\,\text{V}}$$

$$I = 41.67\,\text{A} \quad (\textit{for each load resistor})$$

$$I_{total} = I_{load\#1} + I_{load\#2} \qquad P_{total} = (10\,\text{kW}) + (10\,\text{kW})$$

$$I_{total} = (41.67\,\text{A}) + (41.67\,\text{A}) \quad P_{total} = 20\,\text{kW}$$

$$I_{total} = 83.33\,\text{A}$$

Now our *total* circuit current is 83.33 amps, half of what it was before. We can now use number 4 gage wire, which weighs less than half of what 1/0 gage wire does per unit length. This is a considerable reduction in system cost with no degradation in performance. This is why power distribution system designers elect to transmit electric power using very high voltages (many thousands of volts): to capitalize on the savings realized by the use of smaller, lighter, cheaper wire.

However, this solution is not without disadvantages. Another practical concern with power circuits is the danger of electric shock from high voltages. Again, this is not usually the sort of thing we concentrate on while learning about the laws of electricity, but it is a very valid concern in the real world, especially when large amounts of power are being dealt with. The gain in efficiency realized by stepping up the circuit voltage presents us with increased danger of electric shock. Power distribution companies tackle this problem by stringing their power lines along high poles or towers, and insulating the lines from the supporting structures with large, porcelain insulators.

At the point of use (the electric power customer), there is still the issue of what voltage to use for powering loads. High voltage gives greater system efficiency by means of reduced conductor current, but it might not always be practical to keep power wiring out of reach at the point of use the way it can be elevated out of reach in distribution systems. This tradeoff between efficiency and danger is one that European power system designers have decided to risk, all their households and appliances operating at a nominal voltage of 240 volts instead of 120 volts as it is in North America. That is why tourists from America visiting Europe must carry small step-down transformers for their portable appliances, to step the 240 VAC (volts AC) power down to a more suitable 120 VAC.

Is there any way to realize the advantages of both increased efficiency and reduced safety hazard at the same time? One solution would be to install step-down transformers at the end-point of power use, just as the American tourist must do while in Europe. However, this would be expensive and inconvenient for anything but very small loads (where the transformers can be built cheaply) or very large loads (where the expense of thick copper wires would exceed the expense of a transformer).

An alternative solution would be to use a higher voltage supply to provide power to two lower voltage loads in series. This approach combines the efficiency of a high-voltage system with the safety of a low-voltage system: (Figure below)

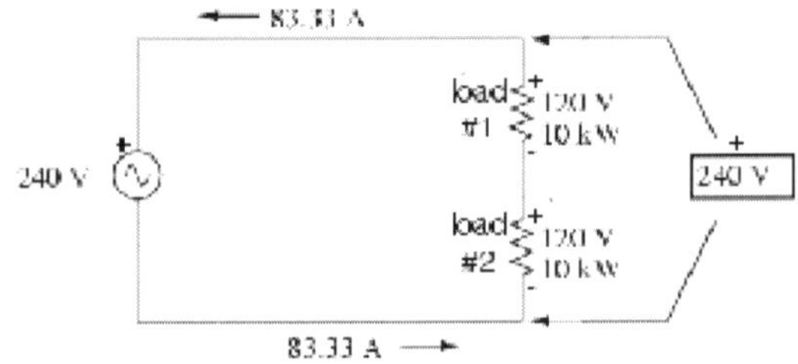

Figure: *Series connected 120 Vac loads, driven by 240 Vac source at 83.3 A total current.*

Notice the polarity markings (+ and -) for each voltage shown, as well as the unidirectional arrows for current. For the most part, I've avoided labelling "polarities" in the AC circuits we've been analyzing, even though the notation is valid to provide a frame of reference for phase. In later sections of this chapter, phase relationships will become very important, so I'm introducing this notation early on in the chapter for your familiarity.

The current through each load is the same as it was in the simple 120 volt circuit, but the currents are not additive because the loads are in series rather than parallel. The voltage across each load is only 120 volts, not 240, so the safety factor is better. Mind you, we still have a full 240 volts across the power system wires, but *each load* is operating at a reduced voltage. If anyone is going to get shocked, the odds are that it will be from coming into contact with the conductors of a particular load rather than from contact across the main wires of a power system.

There's only one disadvantage to this design: the consequences of one load failing open, or being turned off (assuming each load has a series on/off switch to interrupt current) are not good. Being a series circuit, if either load were to open, current would stop in the other load as well. For this reason, we need to modify the design a bit: (Figure below)

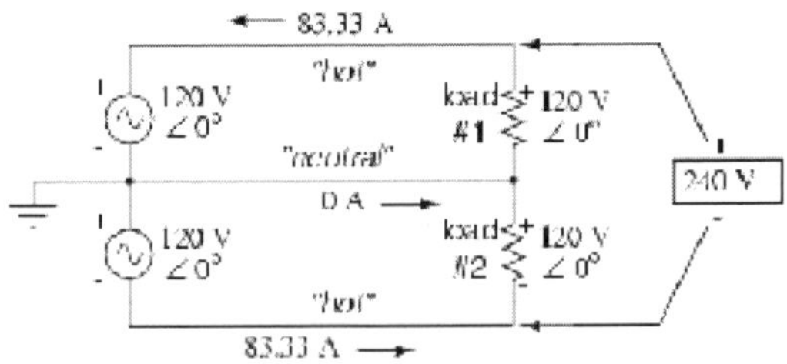

Figure: *Addition of neutral conductor allows loads to be individually driven.*

$$E_{total} = (120\,V \angle 0°) + (120\,V \angle 0°)$$
$$E_{total} = 240\,V \angle 0°$$

$$I = \frac{P}{E} \qquad P_{total} = (10\,kW) + (10\,kW)$$
$$I = \frac{10\,kW}{120\,V} \qquad P_{total} = 120\,kW$$
$$I = 83.33\,A \ (\textit{for each load resistor})$$

Instead of a single 240 volt power supply, we use two 120 volt supplies (in phase with each other!) in series to produce 240 volts, then run a third wire to the connection point between the loads to handle the eventuality of one load opening. This is called a *split-phase* power system. Three smaller wires are still cheaper than the two wires needed with the simple parallel design, so we're still ahead on efficiency. The astute observer will note that the neutral wire only has to carry the *difference* of current between the two loads back to the source. In the above case, with perfectly "balanced" loads consuming equal amounts of power, the neutral wire carries zero current.

Notice how the neutral wire is connected to earth ground at the power supply end. This is a common feature in power systems containing "neutral" wires, since grounding the neutral wire ensures the least possible voltage at any given time between any "hot" wire and earth ground.

An essential component to a split-phase power system is the dual AC voltage source. Fortunately, designing and building one is not difficult. Since most AC systems receive their power from a step-down transformer anyway (stepping voltage down from high distribution levels to a user-level voltage like 120 or 240), that transformer can be built with a centre-tapped secondary winding: (Figure below)

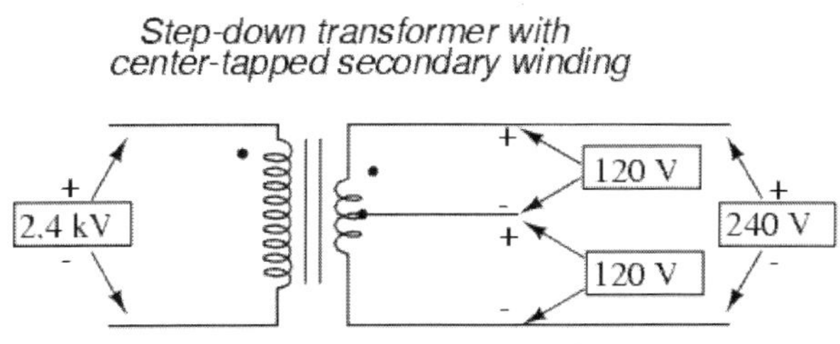

Figure: *American 120/240 Vac power is derived from a centre tapped utility transformer.*

If the AC power comes directly from a generator (alternator), the coils can be similarly centre-tapped for the same effect. The extra expense to include a centre-tap connection in a transformer or alternator winding is minimal.

Here is where the (+) and (–) polarity markings really become important. This notation is often used to reference the phasings of *multiple* AC voltage sources, so it is clear whether they are aiding ("boosting") each other or opposing ("bucking") each other. If not for these polarity markings, phase relations between multiple AC sources might be very confusing. Note that the split-phase sources in the schematic (each one 120 volts – 0°), with polarity marks (+) to (–) just like series-aiding batteries can alternatively be represented as such: (Figure below)

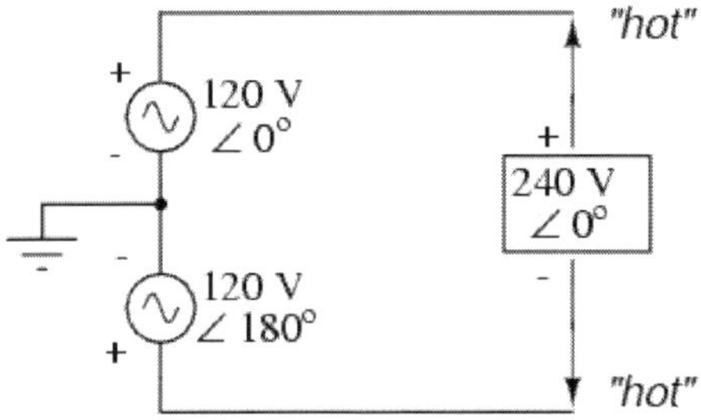

Split phase 120/240 Vac source is equivalent to two series aiding 120 Vac sources.

To mathematically calculate voltage between "hot" wires, we must *subtract* voltages, because their polarity marks show them to be opposed to each other:

Polar	Rectangular
$120\angle 0°$	$120 + \text{jo}\text{V}$
$-120\angle 180°$	$(120 + \text{jo})\,\text{V}$
$240\angle 0°$	$240 + \text{Jo}\text{V}$

If we mark the two sources' common connection point (the neutral wire) with the same polarity mark (-), we must express their relative phase shifts as being 180° apart. Otherwise, we'd be denoting two voltage sources in direct opposition with each other, which would give 0 volts between the two "hot" conductors. Why am I taking the time to elaborate on polarity marks and phase angles? It will make more sense in the next section!

Power systems in American households and light industry are most often of the split-phase variety, providing so-called 120/240 VAC power. The term "split-phase" merely refers to the split-voltage supply in such a system. In a more general sense, this kind of AC power supply is called *single phase* because both voltage waveforms are in phase, or in step, with each other.

The term "single phase" is a counterpoint to another kind of power system called "polyphase" which we are about to investigate in detail. Apologies for the long introduction leading up to the title-topic of this chapter. The advantages of polyphase power systems are more obvious if one first has a good understanding of single phase systems.

Generation of Sinusoidal Voltage

Steady State

"Steady State" means that we are not dealing with turning on or turning off circuits in this section. We are assuming that the circuit was turned on a very long time ago and it is behaving in a pattern. We are computing what the pattern will look like. The "complex frequency" section models turning on and off a circuit with an exponential.

Sinusoidal Forcing Functions

Let us consider a general AC forcing function:

$$v(t) = M \sin(\omega t + \phi)$$

In this equation, the term M is called the "Magnitude", and it acts like a scaling factor that allows the peaks of the sinusoid to be higher or lower than +/- 1. The term ω is what is known as the "Radial Frequency". The term φ is an offset parameter known as the "Phase".

Sinusoidal sources can be current sources, but most often they are voltage sources.

Other Terms

There are a few other terms that are going to be used in many of the following sections, so we will introduce them here:

Period: The period of a sinusoidal function is the amount of time, in seconds, that the sinusoid takes to make a complete wave. The period of a sinusoid is always denoted with a capital T. This is not to be confused with a lower-case t, which is used as the independent variable for time.

Frequency: Frequency is the reciprocal of the period, and is the number of times, per second, that the sinusoid completes an entire cycle. Frequency is measured in Hertz (Hz). The relationship between frequency and the Period is as follows:

$$f = \frac{1}{T}$$

Where f is the variable most commonly used to express the frequency.

Radian Frequency: Radian frequency is the value of the frequency expressed in terms of Radians Per Second, instead of Hertz. Radian Frequency is denoted with the variable ω. The relationship between the Frequency, and the Radian Frequency is as follows:

$$\omega = 2\pi f$$

Phase: The phase is a quantity, expressed in radians, of the time shift of a sinusoid. A sinusoid phase-shifted $\phi = +2\pi$ is moved forward by 1 whole period, and looks exactly the same. An important fact to remember is this:

$$\sin\left(\frac{\pi}{2} - t\right) = \cos(t) \text{ or } \sin(t) = \cos\left(t - \frac{\pi}{2}\right)$$

Phase is often expressed with many different variables, including $\phi, \psi, \theta, \gamma$ etc... This wikibook will try to stick with the symbol ϕ, to prevent confusion.

Lead and Lag

A circuit element may have both a voltage across its terminals and a current flowing through it. If one of the two (current or voltage) is a sinusoid, then the other must also be a sinusoid (remember, voltage is the derivative of the current, and the derivative of a sinusoid is always a sinusoid). However, the sinusoids of the voltage and the current may differ by quantities of magnitude and phase.

If the current has a lower phase angle than the voltage the current is said to lag the voltage. If the current has a higher phase angle then the voltage, it is said to lead the voltage. Many circuits can be classified and examined using lag and lead ideas.

Sinusoidal Response

Reactive components (capacitors and inductors) are going to take energy out of a circuit like a resistor and then pump some of it back into the circuit like a source. The result is initially a mess. But after a while (5 time constants), the circuit starts behaving in a pattern.

The capacitors and inductors get in a rhythm that reflects the driving sources. If the source is sinusoidal, the currents and voltages will be sinusoidal. This is called the "particular" or "steady state" response. In general:

$$A_{in}\cos(\omega_{in}t+\phi_{in})\rightarrow A_{out}\cos(\omega_{out}t+\phi_{out})$$

What happens initially, what happens if the capacitor is initially charged, what happens if sources are switched in and out of a circuit is that there is an energy imbalance. A voltage or current source might be charged by the initial energy in a capacitor. The derivative of the voltage across an Inductor might instantaneously switch polarity. Lots of things are happening. We are going to save this for later. Here we deal with the steady state or "particular" response first.

Sinusoidal Conventions

For the purposes of this book we will generally use cosine functions, as opposed to sine functions. If we absolutely need to use a sine, we can remember the following trigonometric identity:

$$\cos(\omega t)=\sin(\pi/2-\omega t)$$

We can express all sine functions as cosine functions. This way, we don't have to compare apples to oranges per se. This is simply a convention that this wikibook chooses to use to keep things simple. We could easily choose to use all sin () functions, but further down the road it is often more convenient to use cosine functions instead by default.

Sinusoidal Sources

There are two primary sinusoidal sources: wall outlets and oscillators. Oscillators are typically crystals that electrically vibrate and are found in devices that communicate or display video such as TV's, computers, cell phones, radios. An electrical engineer or tech's working area will typically include a "function generator" which can produce oscillations at many frequencies and in shapes that are not just sinusoidal.

RMS or Root mean square is a measure of amplitude that compares with DC magnitude in terms of power, strength of motor, brightness of light, etc. The trouble is that there are several types of AC amplitude:

- peak
- peak to peak
- average
- RMS

Wall outlets are called AC or alternating current. Wall outlets are sinusoidal voltage sources that range from 100 RMS volts, 50 Hz to 240 RMS volts 60 Hz world wide. RMS, rather than peak (which makes more sense mathematically), is used to describe magnitude for several reasons:

- historical reasons related to the competition between Edison (DC power) and Tesla (Sinusoidal or AC power)
- effort to compare/relate AC (wall outlets) to DC (cars, batteries).. 100 RMS volts is approximately 100 DC volts.
- average sinusoidal is zero
- metre movements (physical needles moving on measurement devices) were designed to measure both DC and RMS AC

RMS is a type of average: $p_{\text{rms}} = \sqrt{\frac{1}{T_2 - T_1} \int_{T_1}^{T_2} [p(t)]^2 \, dt}$

Electrical power delivery is a complicated subject that will not be covered in this course. Here we are trying to define terms, design devices that use the power and understand clearly what comes out of wall outlets.

AC Power

Power in an electric circuit is the rate of flow of energy past a given point of the circuit. In alternating current circuits, energy storage elements such as inductance and capacitance may result in periodic reversals of the direction of energy flow. The portion of power that, averaged over a complete cycle of the AC waveform, results in net transfer of energy in one direction is known as real power. The portion of power due to stored energy, which returns to the source in each cycle, is known as reactive power.

Power Factor

The ratio between real power and apparent power in a circuit is called the power factor. It's a practical measure of the efficiency of a power distribution system. For two systems transmitting the same amount of real power, the system with the lower power factor will have higher circulating currents due to energy that returns to the source from energy storage in the load. These higher currents produce higher losses and reduce overall transmission efficiency. A lower power factor circuit will have a higher apparent power and higher losses for the same amount of real power.

The power factor is unity (one) when the voltage and current are in phase. It is zero when the current leads or lags the voltage by 90 degrees. Power factors are usually stated as "leading" or "lagging" to show the sign of the phase angle of current with respect to voltage.

Purely capacitive circuits supply reactive power with the current waveform leading the voltage waveform by 90 degrees, while purely inductive circuits absorb reactive power with the current waveform lagging the voltage waveform by 90 degrees. The result of this is that capacitive and inductive circuit elements tend to cancel each other out.

Where the waveforms are purely sinusoidal, the power factor is the cosine of the phase angle (φ) between the current and voltage sinusoid waveforms. Equipment data sheets and nameplates often will abbreviate power factor as "$\cos\phi$" for this reason.

Example: The real power is 700 W and the phase angle between voltage and current is 45.6°. The power factor is cos(45.6°) = 0.700. The apparent power is then: 700 W / cos(45.6°) = 1000 VA.

Reactive Power Control

Transmission connected generators are generally required to support reactive power flow. For example on the Great Britain transmission system generators are required by the Grid Code Requirements to supply their rated power between the limits of 0.85 power factor lagging and 0.90 power factor leading at the designated terminals. The system operator will perform switching actions to maintain a secure and economical voltage profile while maintaining a reactive power balance equation:

Generator_MVARs + System_gain + Shunt_capacitors = MVAR_Demand + Reactive_losses + Shunt_reactors

The 'System gain' is an important source of reactive power in the above power balance equation, which is generated by the capacitive nature of the transmission network itself. By making decisive switching actions in the early morning before the demand increases, the system gain can be maximized early on, helping to secure the system for the whole day.

To balance the equation some pre-fault reactive generator use will be required. Other sources of reactive power that will also be used include shunt capacitors, shunt reactors, Static VAR Compensators and voltage control circuits.

Unbalanced Polyphase Systems

While real power and reactive power are well defined in any system, the definition of apparent power for unbalanced polyphase systems is considered to be one of the most controversial topics in power engineering. Originally, apparent power arose merely as a figure of merit. Major delineations of the concept are attributed to Stanley's *Phenomena of Retardation in the Induction Coil* (1888) and Steinmetz's *Theoretical Elements of Engineering* (1915). However, with the development of three phase power distribution, it became clear that the definition of apparent power and the power factor could not be applied to unbalanced polyphase systems. In 1920, a "Special Joint Committee of the AIEE and the National Electric Light Association" met to resolve the issue. They considered two definitions:

$$pf = \frac{Pa + Pb + Pc}{|Sa| + |Sb| + |Sc|}$$

that is, the quotient of the sums of the real powers for each phase over the sum of the apparent power for each phase.

$$pf = \frac{Pa + Pb + Pc}{|Pa + Pb + Pc + j(Qa + Qb + Qc)|}$$

that is, the quotient of the sums of the real powers for each phase over the magnitude of the sum of the complex powers for each phase.

The 1920 committee found no consensus and the topic continued to dominate discussions. In 1930 another committee formed and once again failed to resolve the question. The transcripts of their discussions are the lengthiest and most controversial ever published by the AIEE (Emanuel, 1993). Further resolution of this debate did not come until the late 1990s.

Basic Calculations Using Real Numbers

A perfect resistor stores no energy, so current and voltage are in phase. Therefore there is no reactive power and $P = S$. Therefore for a perfect resistor

$$P = S = V_{\text{RMS}} I_{\text{RMS}} = I_{\text{RMS}}^2 R = \frac{V_{\text{RMS}}^2}{R}$$

For a perfect capacitor or inductor there is no net power transfer, so all power is reactive. Therefore for a perfect capacitor or inductor:

$$P = 0$$

$$Q = |S| = V_{\text{RMS}} I_{\text{RMS}} = I_{\text{RMS}}^2 |X| = \frac{V_{\text{RMS}}^2}{|X|}$$

Where X is the reactance of the capacitor or inductor.

If X is defined as being positive for an inductor and negative for a capacitor then we can remove the modulus signs from Q and X and get

$$Q = I_{\text{RMS}}^2 X = \frac{V_{\text{RMS}}^2}{X}$$

Instantaneous power is defined as:

$$P_{inst} = v(t) \times i(t)$$

where v(t) and i(t) are the time varying voltage and current waveforms.

This definition is useful because it applies to all waveforms, whether they are sinusoidal or not. This is particularly useful in power electronics, where nonsinusoidal waveforms are common.

In general, we are interested in the real power averaged over a period of time, whether it is a low frequency line cycle or a high frequency power converter switching period. The simplest way to get that result is to take the integral of the instantaneous calculation over the desired period.

$$P_{avg} = \frac{1}{T_{period}} \int_{t_1}^{t_2} v(t) \times i(t) dt.$$

This method of calculating the average power gives the real power regardless of harmonic content of the waveform. In practical applications, this would be done in the digital domain, where the calculation becomes trivial when compared to the use of rms and phase to determine real power.

$$P_{avg} = \frac{1}{n} * \sum_{k=1}^{n} v[k] \times i[k]$$

Multiple Frequency Systems

Since an RMS value can be calculated for any waveform, apparent power can be calculated from this.

For real power it would at first appear that we would have to calculate loads of product terms and average all of them. However if we look at one of these product terms in more detail we come to a very interesting result.

$$A\cos(\omega_1 t + k_1)\cos(\omega_2 t + k_2)$$

$$= \frac{A}{2}\cos((\omega_1 t + k_1) + (\omega_2 t + k_2)) + \frac{A}{2}\cos((\omega_1 t + k_1) - (\omega_2 t + k_2))$$

$$= \frac{A}{2}\cos((\omega_1 + \omega_2)t + k_1 + k_2) + \frac{A}{2}\cos((\omega_1 - \omega_2)t + k_1 - k_2)$$

however the time average of a function of the form $\cos(\omega t + k)$ is zero provided that ω is nonzero. Therefore the only product terms that have a nonzero average are those where the frequency of voltage and current match. In other words it is possible to calculate real (average) power by simply treating each frequency separately and adding up the answers.

Furthermore, if we assume the voltage of the mains supply is a single frequency (which it usually is), this shows that harmonic currents are a bad thing. They will increase the rms current (since there will be non-zero terms added) and therefore apparent power, but they will have no effect on the real power transferred. Hence, harmonic currents will reduce the power factor.

Harmonic currents can be reduced by a filter placed at the input of the device. Typically this will consist of either just a capacitor (relying on parasitic resistance and inductance in the supply) or a capacitor-inductor network. An active power factor correction circuit at the input would generally reduce the harmonic currents further and maintain the power factor closer to unity.

Three Phase A.C. Circuits

Three-phase electric power is a common method of alternating-current electric power generation, transmission, and distribution. It is a type of polyphase system and is the most common method used by electrical grids worldwide to transfer power. It is also used to power large motors and other heavy loads. A three-phase system is usually more economical than an equivalent single-phase or two-phase system at the same voltage because it uses less conductor material to transmit electrical power. The three-phase system was independently invented by Galileo Ferraris, Mikhail Dolivo-Dobrovolsky and Nikola Tesla in the late 1880s.

Details

In a three-phase system, three circuit conductors carry three alternating currents (of the same frequency) which reach their instantaneous peak values at one third of a cycle from each other. Taking one current as the reference, the other two currents are delayed in time by one third and two thirds of one cycle of the electric current. This delay between phases has the effect of giving constant power transfer over each cycle of the current and also makes it possible to produce a rotating magnetic field in an electric motor.

Three-phase systems may have a neutral wire. A neutral wire allows the three-phase system to use a higher voltage while still supporting lower-voltage single-phase loads. In high-voltage distribution situations, it is common not to have a neutral wire as the loads can simply be connected between phases (phase-phase connection).

Three-phase has properties that make it very desirable in electric power systems:

- The phase currents tend to cancel out one another, summing to zero in the case of a linear balanced load. This makes it possible to reduce the size of the neutral conductor; all the phase conductors carry the same current and so can be the same size, for a balanced load.
- Power transfer into a linear balanced load is constant, which helps to reduce generator and motor vibrations.
- Three-phase systems can produce a magnetic field that rotates in a specified direction, which simplifies the design of electric motors.

Most household loads are single-phase. In North American single-family dwellings, three-phase power generally does not enter the home; multiple-unit apartment blocks may have three-phase power but three-phase power is not used for household appliances. Utilities that supply three-phase power for lower-load-density area homes typically distribute only one phase to individual loads. Some large European appliances may be powered by three-phase power, such as electric stoves and clothes dryers.

Wiring for the three phases is typically identified by colour codes which vary by country. Connection of the phases in the right order is required to ensure correct rotation of three-phase motors. For example, pumps and fans may not work in reverse. Maintaining the identity of phases is required if there is any possibility two sources can be connected at the same time; a direct interconnection between two different phases is a short-circuit.

Generation and Distribution

At the power station, an electrical generator converts mechanical power into a set of three AC electric currents, one from each coil (or winding) of the generator. The windings are arranged such that the currents vary sinusoidally at the same frequency but with the peaks and troughs of their wave forms offset to provide three complementary currents with a phase separation of one-third cycle (120° or $^{2\pi}D\ _{3}$ radians). The generator frequency is typically 50 or 60 Hz, varying by country.

At the power station, transformers change the voltage from generators to a level suitable for transmission minimizing losses. After further voltage conversions in the transmission network, the voltage is finally transformed to the standard utilization before power is supplied to customers.

The majority of automotive alternators produce power as three phase AC power which is rectified to DC through a diode bridge.

Transformer Connections

A "delta" connected transformer winding is connected between phases of a three-phase system. A "wye" ("star") transformer connects each winding from a phase wire to a common neutral point.

In an "open delta" or "V" system, only two sets of transformers are used. A closed delta system can operate as an open delta if one of the transformers have failed or need to be removed. In open delta, each transformer must carry current for its respective phases as well as current for the third phase, therefore capacity is reduced to 87%. With one of three transformers missing and the remaining two at 87% efficiency, the capacity is 58% ((2/3) × 87%).

Where a delta-fed system must be grounded for protection from surge voltages, a grounding transformer (usually a zigzag transformer) may be connected to all three phases; this allows ground fault currents to return from any phase to ground. Another variation is a "corner grounded" delta system, which is a closed delta that is grounded at one of the junctions of transformers.

Three-wire and Four-wire Circuits

There are two basic three-phase configurations: delta or wye (star). Either type can be wired for three or four wires. The fourth wire is provided as a neutral. The '3-wire' and '4-wire' designations do not count the ground wire used on many transmission lines which is solely for fault protection and does not deliver power.

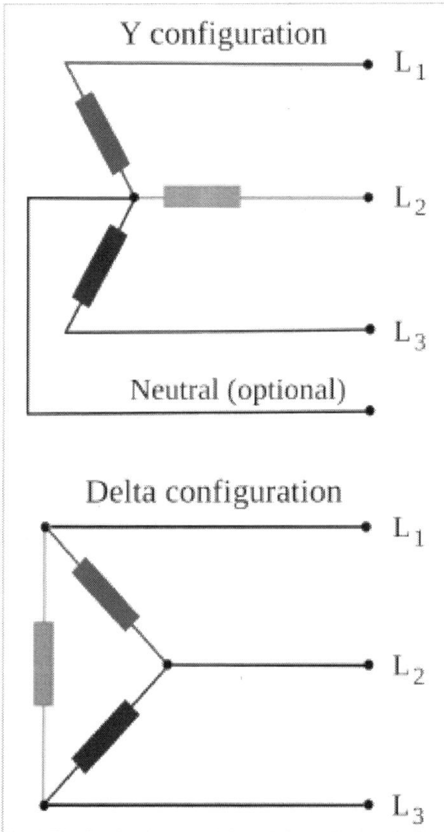

Figure: *Wye (Y) and Delta (Δ) circuits*

A four-wire system with symmetrical voltages between phase and neutral is obtained when the neutral is connected to the "common star point" of an all supply windings. All three phases will have the same magnitude of voltages to the neutral in such a system. Other non-symmetrical systems have been used. In a high-leg delta system, one winding of a delta transformer feeding the system is centre-tapped. This setup produces three voltages. If the voltage between centre tap and the two adjacent phases is 100%, the voltage across any two phases is 200% and neutral to "high leg" is ≈ 173%.

Three-wire distribution systems need one less conductor and help redistribute unbalanced loading during transformation going back to the generation source.

The four-wire wye system is used when ground referenced voltages or the flexibility of more voltage selections are required. Faults on one phase to ground will cause a protection event (fuse or breaker open) locally and not involve other phases or other connected equipment. An example of application is a local distribution in Europe, where each customer is fed a phase and a neutral. When other customers sharing the neutral draw unequal currents, the common neutral wire carries a current as a result of the imbalance. Electrical engineers try to design the system so the loads are balanced as much as possible. By distributing a large number of houses over all three phases, on average a nearly balanced load is seen at the point of supply.

In a *three-phase, four-wire, delta* (high-leg delta) system, the neutral is a centre tap in one of the delta phase supply windings. This can also be supplied by two single-phase transformers in a *V* formation (open delta).

Single-phase Loads

Single-phase loads may be connected to a three-phase system in two ways. Load may be connected across any two phases, or a load can be connected from phase to neutral, if neutral is available.

Single-phase loads should be distributed evenly between the phases of the three-phase system for efficient use of the supply transformer and supply conductors.

In a symmetrical three-phase four-wire, wye system, the three phase conductors have the same voltage to the system neutral. The voltage between line conductors is "3 times the phase conductor to neutral voltage.

$$V_{L-L} = \sqrt{3} V_{L-N}$$

The currents returning from the customers' premises to the supply transformer all share the neutral wire. If the loads are evenly distributed on all three phases, the sum of the returning currents in the neutral wire is approximately zero. Any unbalanced phase loading on the secondary side of the transformer will use the transformer capacity inefficiently.

If the supply neutral is broken, phase-to-neutral voltage is no longer maintained. Phases with higher relative loading will experience reduced voltage and phases with lower relative loading will experience elevated voltage, up to the phase-to-phase voltage.

A high-leg delta provides phase-to-neutral relationship of $V_{L-L} = 2V_{L-N}$, however, L-N load is imposed on one phase. A transformer manufacturer's page suggests that L-N loading to not exceed 5% of transformer capacity.

$\sqrt{3}$is $\approx$ 1.73, so if V_{L-N} was defined as 100%, V_{L-L} would be $\approx$ 100% $\times$ 1.73 = 173% If V_{L-L} was set as 100%, then $V_{L-N} \approx$ 57.7%

Unbalanced Loads

When the currents on the three live wires of a three-phase system are not equal or are not at an exact 120° phase angle, the power-loss is greater than for a perfectly balanced system. The degree of imbalance is expressed by symmetrical components. Three-phase systems are evaluated at generating stations and substations in terms of these three components, of which two are zero in a perfectly balanced system.

Non-linear Loads

With linear loads, the neutral only carries the current due to imbalance between the phases. Devices that utilize rectifier-capacitor front-end such as switch-mode power supplies, computers, office equipment and such produce third order harmonics that are in-phase on all the supply phases. Consequently, such harmonic currents add in the neutral which can cause the neutral current to exceed the phase current.

Three-phase Loads

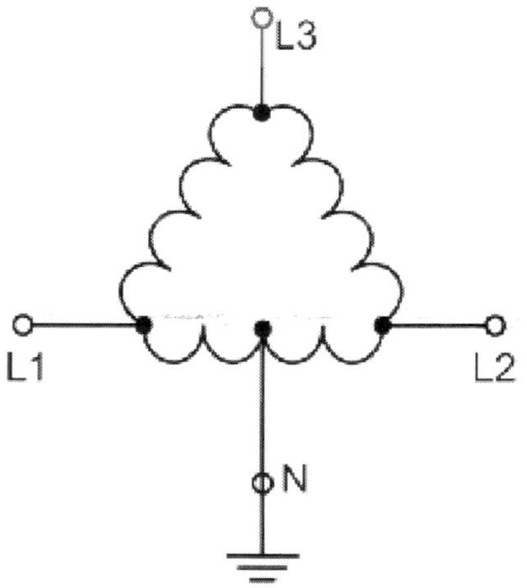

Figure: *A transformer for a high-leg delta system; 200 V 3-phase motors would be connected to L1, L2 and L3. 200 V Single-phase load would be connected L1 and L2. Single phase 100 V load between either L1 or L2 and neutral (N). L3 (wild or high leg) will be 173.2 V to neutral.*

An important class of three-phase load is the electric motor. A three-phase induction motor has a simple design, inherently high starting torque and high efficiency. Such motors are applied in industry for many applications. A three-phase motor is more compact and less costly than a single-phase motor of the same voltage class and rating and single-phase AC motors above 10 HP (7.5 kW) are uncommon. Three-phase motors also vibrate less and hence last longer than single-phase motors of the same power used under the same conditions.

Line frequency flicker in light can be reduced by evenly spreading three phases across line frequency operated light sources so that illuminated area is provided light from all three phases. The effect of line frequency flicker is detrimental to super slow motion cameras used in sports event broadcasting. Three phase lighting has been applied successfully at the 2008 Beijing Olympics to provide consistent light level for each frame for SSM cameras. Resistance heating loads such as electric boilers or space heating may be connected to three-phase systems. Electric lighting may also be similarly connected.

Rectifiers may use a three-phase source to produce a six-pulse DC output. The output of such rectifiers is much smoother than rectified single phase and, unlike single-phase, does not drop to zero between pulses. Such rectifiers may be used for battery charging, electrolysis processes such as aluminium production or for operation of DC motors.

One example of a three-phase load is the electric arc furnace used in steelmaking and in refining of ores.

In Germany, a 1965 publication shows some "full size" stoves are designed for a three-phase feed. However, the individual heating units may be connected between phase and neutral to allow for connection by three individual circuits on the same single-phase supply.

Phase Converters

Phase converters are used when three phase equipment needs to be operated on single phase power source. They are used when three phase power is not available or cost is not justifiable. Such converters may also allow the frequency to be varied (resynthesis) allowing speed control. Some railway locomotives use single phase source to drive three phase motors fed through an electronic drive.

Mechanical

One method to generate three phase power from a single phase source is the rotary phase converter, essentially a three-phase motor with special starting arrangements and power factor correction that produces balanced three-phase voltages. When properly designed, these rotary converters can allow satisfactory operation of three-phase motor on a single phase source. In such a device, the energy storage is performed by the mechanical inertia (flywheel effect) of the rotating components. An external flywheel is sometimes found on one or both ends of the shaft.

A three-phase generator can be driven by a single-phase motor. This motor-generator combination can provide a frequency changer function as well as phase conversion, but requires two machines with all their expense and losses. The motor-generator method can also form an uninterruptable power supply when used in conjunction with a large flywheel and a standby generator set.

Non-mechanical

A second method that was popular in the 1940s and 1950s was the *transformer method*. At that time, capacitors were more expensive than transformers, so an autotransformer was used to apply more power through fewer capacitors. Separated it from another common method, the static converter, as both methods have no moving parts, which separates them from the rotary converters.

Another method often attempted is with a device referred to as a static phase converter. This method of running three-phase equipment is commonly attempted with motor loads though it only supplies 2/3 power and can cause the motor loads to run hot and in some cases overheat. This method does not work when sensitive circuitry is involved such as CNC devices or in induction and rectifier-type loads.

Variable-frequency drives (also known as solid-state inverters) are used to provide precise speed and torque control of three-phase motors. Some models can be powered by a single-phase supply. VFDs work by converting the supply voltage to DC and then converting the DC to a suitable three-phase source for the motor.

Digital phase converters are designed for fixed-frequency operation from a single-phase source. Similar to a variable-frequency drive, they use a microprocessor to control solid-state power switching components to maintain balanced three-phase voltages.

Alternatives to Three-phase

- Split-phase electric power is used when three-phase power is not available and allows double the normal utilization voltage to be supplied for high-power loads.
- Two-phase electric power, like three-phase, gives constant power transfer to a linear load. For loads that connect each phase to neutral, assuming the load is the same power draw,

the two-wire system has a neutral current that is greater than neutral current in a three-phase system. Also motors are not entirely linear, which means that despite the theory, motors running on three-phase tend to run smoother than those on two-phase. The generators in the Adams Power Plant at Niagara Falls that were installed in 1895 were the largest generators in the world at the time and were two-phase machines. True two-phase power distribution is basically obsolete. Special-purpose systems may use a two-phase system for control. Two-phase power may be obtained from a three-phase system (or vice versa) using an arrangement of transformers called a Scott-T transformer, invented by Charles F. Scott.

- *Monocyclic power* was a name for an asymmetrical modified two-phase power system used by General Electric around 1897, championed by Charles Proteus Steinmetz and Elihu Thomson. This system was devised to avoid patent infringement. In this system, a generator was wound with a full-voltage single-phase winding intended for lighting loads and with a small fraction (usually 1/4 of the line voltage) winding that produced a voltage in quadrature with the main windings. The intention was to use this "power wire" additional winding to provide starting torque for induction motors, with the main winding providing power for lighting loads. After the expiration of the Westinghouse patents on symmetrical two-phase and three-phase power distribution systems, the monocyclic system fell out of use; it was difficult to analyze and did not last long enough for satisfactory energy metering to be developed.
- High-phase-order systems for power transmission have been built and tested. Such transmission lines typically would use six phases or twelve phases. High-phase-order transmission lines allow transfer of slightly less than proportionately higher power through a given volume without the expense of a high-voltage direct current (HVDC) converter at each end of the line. However, they require correspondingly more pieces of equipment.

Definition of Phase Sequence

In Electrical Systems, sometimes without identification of phase sequence it is impossible to proceed further. Both students and practicing engineers often find it confusing. There are some important situations where identification of phase sequence is a must. These are when:

- One synchronous generator is to be synchronized to the grid.
- Two systems are to operate in parallel.
- Two transformers are to operate in parallel.
- Connecting two different lines originating from the same source.

In a three phase system the voltage or current sinusoid attain peak values periodically one after another. The sinusoid are displaced 120 degrees from each other. So also phasors representing the three sinusoids for voltage or current waves of three lines are phase displaced by 120 degrees.

Now the question arises what is the sequence ? In which order the voltage or current waves attain the peak values cyclically. In the diagram just look at the ABC Anti Clock Wise phase sequence. Here the phasors are rotating in anti clock wise direction. An imaginary viewer will encounter first phase A, then B, then C again A, then B.....like wise.The sequence is ABCABCABC....... or ABC Anti Clock Wise sequence.

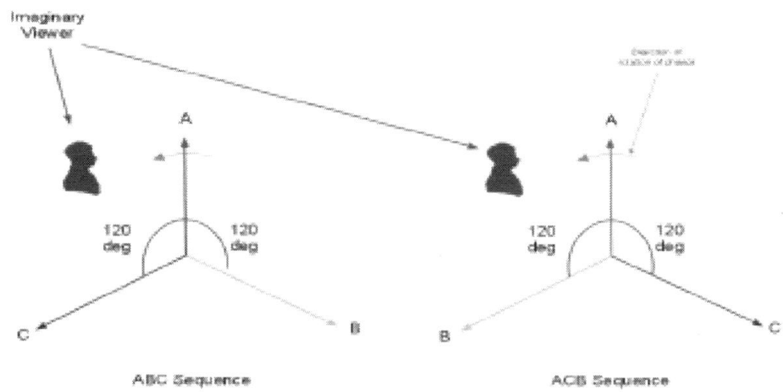

Figure: *ABC and ACD phase sequence, Anti Clock wise Rotation*

You might imagine about the possibility of phase sequence ACB Anti Clock Wise. Yes it can be! In this case the phasors rotating the same anti clock wise direction the imaginary viewer will encounter first phase A, then C, then B. So here the sequence continues like ACBACBACB...... .

You might think that in anti clock wise rotation, do the other sequences possible? You may think why not BCA or BAC or CBA or......?

From the above ABC sequence if you start from B then you can see that BCA is nothing but the same ABC sequence. Similarly BAC and CBA sequence are the same as ACB, only we started from other phase.

Note: If you studied permutation and combination maths then it is easier to appreciate the case.

Hence it is clear that for anti clock wise rotation there are two possible phase sequences ABC or ACB.

Why anti clock wise ? yes it is the convention mostly used. Just recall the school maths when you always measured the trigonometric angle starting from positive x-axis in anticlockwise direction and called it positive angle and in clock wise direction the angle is negative. Accordingly the sine wave is drawn. This is the reason why anti clock wise rotation is so prevalent.

However the Clock Wise ABC and ACB phase sequence can also be used. The phase sequence identification is purely a convention. It helps in identifying the sequence in which three phase voltage or current attain the peak values.

The Anti Clock Wise ABC is equivalent to Clock Wise ACB. Just analyze by placing the imaginary viewer and rotating the phases in respective directions. When any two of the three phase conductors connecting to the three phase induction motor is interchanged the phase sequence of the supply to motor is changed. This results in the rotation of motor in opposite direction. Actually this is the principle used in mechanical phase sequence detectors. The same direction of rotation means same phase sequence. These days solid state sequence detectors are increasingly used.

In some regions of the world other letters may be used for phase sequence, like L1L2L3 or RYB.

It is really confusing when synchronization of two different systems are considered.

In real world, before synchronization or paralleling, the two sides phase sequence is identified by using the same sequence detector. If the same direction of rotation is observed for both sides by the detector, then they are marked accordingly for same sequence. Of course only same sequence is not sufficient. It is also ascertained that terminals of same phase are connected together.

Balanced Supply and Balanced Load

Load balancing, load matching, or daily peak demand reserve refers to the use of various techniques by electrical power stations to store excess electrical power during low demand periods for release as demand rises. The goal would be for the power supply system to see a load factor of 1.

Grid energy storage stores electricity within the transmission grid beyond the customer. Alternatively, the storage can be distributed and involve the customer, for example in storage heaters running demand-response tariffs such as the United Kingdom's Economy 7, or in a vehicle-to-grid system to use storage from electric vehicles during peak times and then replenish it during off peak times. These require incentives for consumers to participate, usually by offering cheaper rates for off peak electricity.

Telephone exchanges often have arrays of batteries in their basements to power equipment and in the past metro systems such as the London Underground had their own power stations, not only giving some redundancy but also using the grid for load balancing. Today these supplies often have been replaced by direct supply from the grid and so are no longer available for the purpose of load balancing.

Future solutions to the load balancing problem focus on "smart grid" technology, in which many consumer and industrial appliances would communicate with the utility using digital means, and could be switched on and off by the utility to run at off-peak hours.

In a very basic demand balancing system, the power company sends a signal down the line or by a dedicated phone chip to turn on a special circuit in the home. Typically, a storage device for space heating or a water heater will be connected to this circuit. The electricity is turned on after the evening peak demand, and turned off in the morning before the morning peak demand starts. The cost for such power is less than the "on-demand" power which makes it worthwhile for the user to subscribe to it.

A far more nuanced system is possible with far greater benefits for the power company and the electricity user. Once home devices contain the appropriate electronics, it will no longer be necessary to have devices connected to a special circuit. The power company can send a signal saying that power is now available at a better rate and this signal will turn on any device (dish washer for instance) that has the dial set for "when available" power (priority 2). There is nothing to stop the device manufacturers from having a number of possible priorities on their machines and the power company sending a number of signals as they need more demand to balance supply. You might dial your washing machine to "wash now" (priority 1) if you were in immediate need of clean dishes. You might dial priority 2 so they will be done sometime during the night or priority 3 if you have sufficient dishes for the next meal but given less expensive electricity you would rather have the dishes washed. For a device such as an electric car you might even have a further setting on the dial of "charge and supply" (priority 4) You are going away for a week and are leaving the electric car at home. On "Charge and supply" your car will get charge when electricity is least expensive and send it back when it is most expensive. Your electric car will generate a small but appreciated income while you are away.

Heating devices can have a special setting. You want your dish washer to finish washing once it has started. On the other hand, a hot water cylinder can be turned on and off frequently as power becomes available or unavailable. This might be "priority 5. Your car could also be charged on priority 5.

The power company benefits by being able to sell more of their power. There is no need to let water flow over the spillway or to feather their wind turbines as long as they can turn devices on that will use the excess power when it is available. Also there is less need to build expensive power stations to "peak shave" when there is a high demand for power. If your water cylinder has been heated or your car charged when cheap power was available, you will not be demanding power when it is in short supply.

8

Electronic Amplifier

An electronic amplifier is used for increasing the power of a signal. It does this by taking energy from a power supply and controlling the output to match the input signal shape but with a larger amplitude. In this sense, an amplifier may be considered as modulating the output of the power supply. The term *amplifier* is applied to anything from a circuit (or stage) using a single active device to a complete system such as a packaged audio hi-fi amplifier.

Types of Amplifier

Amplifiers can be specified according to their input and output properties. They have some kind of gain, or multiplication factor relating the magnitude of the output signal to the input signal. The gain may be specified as the ratio of output voltage to input voltage (voltage gain), output power to input power (power gain), or some combination of current, voltage and power. In many cases, with input and output in the same units, gain will be unitless (although often expressed in decibels); for others this is not necessarily so.

For example, a transconductance amplifier has a gain with units of conductance (output current per input voltage). The power gain of an amplifier depends on the source and load impedances used as well as its voltage gain; while an RF amplifier may have its impedances optimized for power transfer, audio and instrumentation amplifiers are normally employed with amplifier input and output impedances optimized for least loading and highest quality. So an amplifier that is said to have a gain of 20 dB might have a voltage gain of ten times and an available power gain of much more than 20 dB (100 times power ratio), yet be delivering a much lower power gain if, for example, the input is a 600 ohm microphone and the output is a 47 kilohm power amplifier's input socket.

In most cases an amplifier should be linear; that is, the gain should be constant for any combination of input and output signal. If the gain is not constant, e.g., by clipping the output signal at the limits of its capabilities, the output signal will be distorted. There are however cases where variable gain is useful. There are many types of electronic amplifiers, commonly used in radio and television transmitters and receivers, high-fidelity ("hi-fi") stereo equipment, microcomputers and other electronic digital equipment, and guitar and other instrument amplifiers. Critical components include active devices, such as vacuum tubes or transistors. A brief introduction to the many types of electronic amplifier follows.

Power Amplifier

The term *power amplifier* is a relative term with respect to the amount of power delivered to the load and/or sourced by the supply circuit. In general a power amplifier is designated as the last amplifier in a transmission chain (the *output stage*) and is the amplifier stage that typically requires most attention to power efficiency. Efficiency considerations lead to various classes of power amplifier based on the biasing of the output transistors or tubes: see power amplifier classes.

Power amplifiers by application:

- Audio amplifier#PowerAudio power amplifiers
- RF power amplifier, such as for transmitter final stages.
- Servo motor controllers, where linearity is not important.

Power amplifier circuits:

Power amplifier circuits include the following types:

- Vacuum tube/valve, hybrid or transistor power amplifiers
- Push-pull output or single-ended output stages

Vacuum-Tube (Valve) Amplifiers

According to Symons, while semiconductor amplifiers have largely displaced valve amplifiers for low power applications, valve amplifiers are much more cost effective in high power applications such as "radar, countermeasures equipment, or communications equipment" (p. 56). Many microwave amplifiers are specially designed valves, such as the klystron, gyrotron, travelling wave tube, and crossed-field amplifier, and these microwave valves provide much greater single-device power output at microwave frequencies than solid-state devices (p. 59).

Valves/tube amplifiers also have niche uses in other areas, such as:

- electric guitar amplification
- in Russian military aircraft, for their EMP tolerance
- niche audio for their sound qualities (recording, and audiophile equipment)

Transistor Amplifiers

The essential role of this active element is to magnify an input signal to yield a significantly larger output signal. The amount of magnification (the "forward gain") is determined by the external circuit design as well as the active device.

Many common active devices in transistor amplifiers are bipolar junction transistors (BJTs) and metal oxide semiconductor field-effect transistors (MOSFETs). Applications are numerous, some common examples are audio amplifiers in a home stereo or PA system, RF high power generation for semiconductor equipment, to RF and Microwave applications such as radio transmitters.

Transistor-based amplifier can be realised using various configurations: for example with a bipolar junction transistor we can realise common base, common collector or common emitter amplifier; using a MOSFET we can realise common gate, common source or common drain amplifier. Each configuration has different characteristic (gain, impedance...).

Operational Amplifiers (op-amps)

An operational amplifier is an amplifier circuit with very high open loop gain and differential inputs which employs external feedback for control of its transfer function or gain. Although the term is today commonly applied to integrated circuits, the original operational amplifier design was implemented with valves.

Fully Differential Amplifiers

A fully differential amplifier is a solid state integrated circuit amplifier which employs external feedback for control of its transfer function or gain. It is similar to the operational amplifier but it also has differential output pins. These are usually constructed using BJTs or FETs.

Video Amplifiers

These deal with video signals and have varying bandwidths depending on whether the video signal is for SDTV, EDTV, HDTV

720p or 1080i/p etc.. The specification of the bandwidth itself depends on what kind of filter is used and which point (-1 dB or -3 dB for example) the bandwidth is measured. Certain requirements for step response and overshoot are necessary in order for acceptable TV images to be presented.

Oscilloscope vertical amplifiers: These are used to deal with video signals to drive an oscilloscope display tube and can have bandwidths of about 500 MHz. The specifications on step response, rise time, overshoot and aberrations can make the design of these amplifiers extremely difficult. One of the pioneers in high bandwidth vertical amplifiers was the Tektronix company.

Distributed Amplifiers: These use transmission lines to temporally split the signal and amplify each portion separately in order to achieve higher bandwidth than can be obtained from a single amplifying device. The outputs of each stage are combined in the output transmission line. This type of amplifier was commonly used on oscilloscopes as the final vertical amplifier. The transmission lines were often housed inside the display tube glass envelope.

Switched Mode Amplifiers: These nonlinear amplifiers have much higher efficiencies than linear amps, and are used where the power saving justifies the extra complexity.

Negative Resistance Devices: Negative resistances can be used as amplifiers, such as the tunnel diode amplifier.

Microwave Amplifiers

Travelling Wave Tube Amplifiers: Travelling wave tube amplifiers (TWTAs) are used for high power amplification at low microwave frequencies. They typically can amplify across a broad spectrum of frequencies; however, they are usually not as tunable as klystrons.

Klystrons: Klystrons are vacuum-devices that do not have as wide a bandwidth as TWTAs. They generally are also much heavier than TWTAs, and are therefore ill-suited for light-weight mobile applications. Klystrons are tunable, offering selective output within their specified frequency range.

Musical Instrument (Audio) Amplifiers

An audio amplifier is usually used to amplify signals such as music or speech. Several factors are especially important in the selection of musical instrument amplifiers (such as guitar amplifiers) and other audio amplifiers (although the whole of the sound system – components such as microphones to loudspeakers – will impact on these parameters):

- Frequency response – not just the frequency range but the requirement that the signal level varies so little across the audible frequency range that the human ear notices no variation. A typical specification for audio amplifiers may be 20 Hz to 20 kHz +/- 0.5dB.
- Power output – the power level obtainable with little distortion, to obtain a sufficiently loud sound pressure level from the loudspeakers.
- Low distortion – all amplifiers and transducers will distort to some extent; they cannot be perfectly linear, but aim to pass signals without affecting the harmonic content of the sound more than the human ear will tolerate. That tolerance of distortion, and indeed the possibility that some "warmth" or second harmonic distortion (Tube sound) improves the "musicality" of the sound, are subjects of great debate.

Classification of Amplifier Stages and Systems

There are many alternative classifications that address different aspects of amplifier designs, and they all express some particular perspective relating the design parameters to the objectives of the circuit. Amplifier design is always a compromise of numerous factors, such as cost, power consumption, real-world device imperfections, and a multitude of performance specifications. Below are several different approaches to classification:

Common Terminal

One set of classifications for amplifiers is based on which device terminal is common to both the input and the output circuit. In the case of bipolar junction transistors, the three classes are common emitter, common base, and common collector. For field-effect transistors, the corresponding configurations are common source, common gate, and common drain; for triode vacuum devices, *common cathode*, *common grid*, and *common plate*. The output voltage of a common plate amplifier is the same as the input (this arrangement is used as the input presents a high impedance and does not load the signal source, although it does not amplify the voltage), i.e., the output at the cathode follows the input at the grid; consequently it was commonly called a *cathode follower*. By analogy the terms *emitter follower* and *source follower* are sometimes used.

Unilateral or Bilateral

When an amplifier has an output that exhibits no feedback to its input side, it is called 'unilateral'. The input impedance of a unilateral amplifier is independent of the load, and the output impedance is independent of the signal source impedance.

If feedback connects part of the output back to the input of the amplifier it is called a 'bilateral' amplifier. The input impedance of a bilateral amplifier is dependent upon the load, and the output impedance is dependent upon the signal source impedance. All amplifiers are bilateral to some degree; however they may often be modelled as unilateral under operating conditions where feedback is small enough to neglect for most purposes, simplifying analysis.

Negative feedback is often applied deliberately to tailor amplifier behaviour. Some feedback, which may be positive or negative, is unavoidable and often undesirable, introduced, for example, by parasitic elements such as the inherent capacitance between input and output of a device such as a transistor and capacitative coupling due to external wiring.

Excessive frequency-dependent positive feedback may cause what is supposed to be an amplifier to become an oscillator. Linear unilateral and bilateral amplifiers can be represented as two-port networks.

Inverting or Non-Inverting

Another way to classify amps is the phase relationship of the input signal to the output signal. An 'inverting' amplifier produces an output 180 degrees out of phase with the input signal (that is, a polarity inversion or mirror image of the input as seen on an oscilloscope). A 'non-inverting' amplifier maintains the phase of the input signal waveforms. An emitter follower is a type of non-inverting amplifier, indicating that the signal at the emitter of a transistor is following (that is, matching with unity gain but perhaps an offset) the input signal. This description can apply to a single stage of an amplifier, or to a complete amplifier system.

Function

Other amplifiers may be classified by their function or output characteristics. These functional descriptions usually apply to complete amplifier systems or sub-systems and rarely to individual stages.

- A servo amplifier indicates an integrated feedback loop to actively control the output at some desired level. A DC servo indicates use at frequencies down to DC levels, where the rapid fluctuations of an audio or RF signal do not occur. These are often used in mechanical actuators, or devices such as DC motors that must maintain a constant speed or torque. An AC servo amp can do this for some ac motors.

- A linear amplifier responds to different frequency components independently, and does not generate harmonic distortion or Intermodulation distortion. A nonlinear amplifier does generate distortion (e.g. the output is a current to a lamp that must be either fully on or off, but the input is continuously variable; or the amplifier is used in an analog computer where a special transfer function, such as logarithmic, is desired; or a following tuned circuit will remove the harmonics generated by a nonlinear RF amplifier). Even the most linear amplifier will have some nonlinearities, since the amplifying devices – transistors and vacuum tubes – follow nonlinear power laws such as square-laws and rely on circuitry techniques to reduce their effects.
- A wideband amplifier has a precise amplification factor over a wide range of frequencies, and is often used to boost signals for relay in communications systems. A narrowband amp is made to amplify only a specific narrow range of frequencies, to the exclusion of other frequencies.
- An RF amplifier refers to an amplifier designed for use in the radio frequency range of the electromagnetic spectrum, and is often used to increase the sensitivity of a receiver or the output power of a transmitter.
- An audio amplifier is designed for use in reproducing audio frequencies. This category subdivides into small signal amplification, and power amps which are optimised for driving speakers, sometimes with multiple amps grouped together as separate or bridgeable channels to accommodate different audio reproduction requirements. Frequently used terms within audio amplifiers include:
    - preamplifier (preamp), that may include phono preamp with RIAA equalization, or tape head preamps with CCIR equalisation filters; they may include filters or tone control circuitry.
    - power amplifier (normally assumed to drive loudspeakers), headphone amplifiers, and public address amplifiers.
    - stereo amplifiers imply two channels of output (left and right), although the term simply means "solid" sound

(referring to three-dimensional) – so quadraphonic stereo was used for amplifiers with 4 channels; 5.1 and 7.1 systems refer to Home theatre systems with 5 or 7 normal spacial channels, plus a subwoofer channel (that is not very directional).

- Buffer amplifiers, that may include emitter followers, provide a high impedance input for a device (perhaps another amplifier, or perhaps an energy-hungry load such as lights) that would otherwise draw too much current from the source. Line drivers are a type of buffer intended to feed long or interference-prone interconnect cables, possibly with differential outputs if driving twisted pairs of cables.
- A special type of amplifier is widely used in instruments and for signal processing, among many other varied uses. These are known as operational amplifiers or op-amps. This is because this type of amplifier is used in circuits that perform mathematical algorithmic functions, or "operations" on input signals to obtain specific types of output signals. A typical modern op-amp has differential inputs (one "inverting", one "non-inverting") and one output. An idealised op-amp has the following characteristics:
    - o Infinite input impedance (so as to not load circuitry it is sampling as a control input)
    - o Zero output impedance
    - o Infinite gain
    - o Zero propagation delay

The performance of an op-amp with these characteristics would be entirely defined by the (usually passive) components forming a negative feedback loop around it, that is, *the amplifier itself has no effect on the output*. Today, op-amps are usually provided as integrated circuits, rather than constructed from discrete components. All real-world op-amps fall short of the idealised specification above – but some modern components have remarkable performance and come close in some respects.

Interstage Coupling Method

Amplifiers are sometimes classified by the coupling method of the signal at the input, output, or between stages. Different types of these include: Resistive-capacitive (RC) coupled amplifier, using a network of resistors and capacitors. By design these amplifiers cannot amplify

DC signals as the capacitors block the DC component of the input signal. RC-coupled amplifiers were used very often in circuits with vacuum tubes or discrete transistors. In the days of the integrated circuit a few more transistors on a chip are much cheaper and smaller than a capacitor. Inductive-capacitive (LC) coupled amplifier, using a network of inductors and capacitors

This kind of amplifier is most often used in selective radio-frequency circuits. Transformer coupled amplifier, using a transformer to match impedances or to decouple parts of the circuits Quite often LC-coupled and transformer-coupled amplifiers cannot be distinguished as a transformer is some kind of inductor. Direct coupled amplifier, using no impedance and bias matching components This class of amplifier was very uncommon in the vacuum tube days when the anode (output) voltage was at greater than several hundred volts and the grid (input) voltage at a few volts minus. So they were only used if the gain was specified down to DC (e.g., in an oscilloscope). In the context of modern electronics developers are encouraged to use directly coupled amplifiers whenever possible.

Frequency Range

Depending on the frequency range and other properties amplifiers are designed according to different principles.

- Frequency ranges down to DC are only used when this property is needed. DC amplification leads to specific complications that are avoided if possible; DC-blocking capacitors are added to remove DC and sub-sonic frequencies from audio amplifiers.
- Depending on the frequency range specified different design principles must be used. Up to the MHz range only "discrete" properties need be considered; e.g., a terminal has an input impedance.
- As soon as any connection within the circuit gets longer than perhaps 1% of the wavelength of the highest specified frequency (e.g., at 100 MHz the wavelength is 3 m, so the critical connection length is approx. 3 cm) design properties radically change. For example, a specified length and width of a PCB trace can be used as a selective or impedance-matching entity.
- Above a few 100 MHz, it gets difficult to use discrete elements, especially inductors. In most cases PCB traces of very closely defined shapes are used instead.

The frequency range handled by an amplifier might be specified in terms of bandwidth (normally implying a response that is 3 dB down when the frequency reaches the specified bandwidth), or by specifying a frequency response that is within a certain number of decibels between a lower and an upper frequency (e.g. "20 Hz to 20 kHz plus or minus 1 dB").

Implementation

Amplifiers are implemented using active elements of different kinds:

- The first active elements were relays. They were for example used in transcontinental telegraph lines: a weak current was used to switch the voltage of a battery to the outgoing line.
- For transmitting audio, carbon microphones were used as the active element. This was used to modulate a radio-frequency source in one of the first AM audio transmissions, by Reginald Fessenden on Dec. 24, 1906.
- In the 1960s, the transistor started to take over. These days, discrete transistors are still used in high-power amplifiers and in specialist audio devices.
- Up to the early 1970s, most amplifiers used vacuum tubes. Today, tubes are used for specialist audio applications such as guitar amplifiers and audiophile amplifiers. Many broadcast transmitters still use vacuum tubes.
- Beginning in the 1970s, more and more transistors were connected on a single chip therefore creating the integrated circuit. A large number of amplifiers commercially available today are based on integrated circuits.

For exotic purposes, other active elements have been used. For example, in the early days of the communication satellite parametric amplifiers were used. The core circuit was a diode whose capacity was changed by an RF signal created locally. Under certain conditions, this RF signal provided energy that was modulated by the extremely weak satellite signal received at the earth station. The operating principle of a parametric amplifier is somewhat similar to the principle by which children keep their swings in motion: as long as the swing moves you only need to change a parameter of the swinging entity; e.g., you must move your centre of gravity up and down. In our case, the capacity of the diode is changed periodically.

Power Aplifier Classes

Angle of Flow or Conduction Angle

Power amplifier circuits (output stages) are classified as A, B, AB and C for analog designs, and class D and E for switching designs based upon the conduction angle or *angle of flow*, È, of the input signal through the (or each) output amplifying device, that is, the portion of the input signal cycle during which the amplifying device conducts. The image of the conduction angle is derived from amplifying a sinusoidal signal. (If the device is always on, È = 360°.) The angle of flow is closely related to the amplifier power efficiency. The various classes are introduced below, followed by more detailed discussion under individual headings later on.

Class A

100% of the input signal is used (conduction angle È = 360° or 2π); i.e., the active element remains conducting (works in its "linear" range) all of the time. Where efficiency is not a consideration, most small signal linear amplifiers are designed as class A. Class-A amplifiers are typically more linear and less complex than other types, but are very inefficient. This type of amplifier is most commonly used in small-signal stages or for low-power applications (such as driving headphones). Subclass A2 is sometimes used to refer to vacuum-tube class-A stages where the grid is allowed to be driven slightly positive on signal peaks, resulting in slightly more power than normal class A (A1; where the grid is always negative), but incurring more distortion.

Class B

50% of the input signal is used (È = 180° or π; i.e., the active element works in its linear range half of the time and is more or less turned off for the other half). In most class B, there are two output devices (or sets of output devices), each of which conducts alternately (push–pull) for exactly 180° (or half cycle) of the input signal; selective RF amplifiers can also be implemented using a single active element. These amplifiers are subject to *crossover distortion* if the transition from one active element to the other is not perfect, as when two complementary transistors (i.e., one PNP, one NPN) are connected as two emitter followers with their base and emitter terminals in common, requiring the base voltage to slew across the region where both devices are turned off.

Class AB

Class AB is intermediate between class A and B, with better power efficiency than class A and less distortion than class B. The two active elements conduct more than half of the time, producing less cross-over distortion than class-B amplifiers. In the example of the complementary emitter followers, a bias network allows the quiescent current to be adjusted, providing an operating point somewhere between class A and class B. Sometimes a figure is added (e.g., AB_1 or AB_2) for vacuum-tube stages where the grid voltage is always negative with respect to the cathode (class AB_1) or may be slightly positive (hence drawing grid current, adding more distortion, but giving slightly higher output power) on signal peaks (class AB_2). Class-AB circuits with large negative feedback provide excellent distortion characteristics with good power efficiency, and are widely used for solid-state amplifiers.

Class C

Less than 50% of the input signal is used (conduction angle È < 180°). Efficiency is high, but so is distortion.

Class D

These use switching to achieve a very high power efficiency (more than 90% in modern designs). By allowing each output device to be either fully on or off, losses are minimised. The analog output is created by pulse-width modulation; i.e., the active element is switched on for shorter or longer intervals instead of modifying its resistance. There are more complicated switching schemes such as sigma-delta modulation, to improve performance aspects such as distortions or efficiency.

Additional Classes

There are several other amplifier classes, although they are mainly variations of the previous classes. For example, class-G and class-H amplifiers are marked by variation of the supply rails (in discrete steps or in a continuous fashion, respectively) following the input signal. Wasted heat on the output devices can be reduced as excess voltage is kept to a minimum.

The amplifier that is fed with these rails itself can be of any class. These kinds of amplifiers are more complex, and are mainly used for specialised applications, such as very high-power units. Also, class-E and class-F amplifiers are commonly described in literature for radio-frequency applications where efficiency of the traditional classes is important, yet several aspects deviate substantially from their ideal values. These classes use harmonic tuning of their output networks to achieve higher efficiency and can be considered a subset of class C due to their conduction-angle characteristics.

The classes can be most easily understood using the diagrams in each section below. For the sake of illustration, a bipolar junction transistor is shown as the amplifying device, but in practice this could be a MOSFET or vacuum-tube device. In an analog amplifier (the most common kind), the signal is applied to the input terminal of the device (base, gate or grid), and this causes a proportional output drive current to flow out of the output terminal. The output drive current comes from the power supply.

Class A

Amplifying devices operating in class A conduct over the whole of the input cycle. A *class-A amplifier* is distinguished by the *output stage* being biased into class A.

Advantages of class-A amplifiers

- Class-A designs are simpler than other classes; for example class-AB and -B designs require two devices (push–pull output) to handle both halves of the waveform; class A can use a single device single-ended.
- The amplifying element is biased so the device is always conducting to some extent, normally implying the quiescent (small-signal) collector current (for transistors; drain current for FETs or anode/plate current for vacuum tubes) is close to the most linear portion of its transconductance curve.
- Because the device is never shut off completely there is no "turn on" time, little problem with charge storage, and generally better high frequency performance and feedback loop stability (and usually fewer high-order harmonics).
- The point at which the device comes closest to being cut off is not close to zero signal, so the problem of crossover distortion associated with class-AB and -B designs is avoided.

Disadvantage of class-A amplifiers

- They are very inefficient; a theoretical maximum of 50% is obtainable with inductive output coupling and only 25% with capacitive coupling, unless deliberate use of nonlinearities is made (such as in square-law output stages). In a power amplifier this not only wastes power and limits battery operation, it may place restrictions on the output devices that can be used (for example: ruling out some audio triodes if modern low-efficiency loudspeakers are to be used), and will increase costs. Inefficiency comes not just from the fact that the device is always conducting to some extent (that happens even with class AB, yet its efficiency can be close to that of class B); it is that the standing current is roughly half the maximum output current (although this can be less with square law output stage), together with the problem that a large part of the power supply voltage is developed across the output device at low signal levels (as with classes AB and B, but unlike output stages such as class D). If high output powers are needed from a class-A circuit, the power waste (and the accompanying heat) will become significant. For every watt delivered to the load, the amplifier itself will, *at best*, dissipate another watt. For large powers this means very large and expensive power supplies and heat sinking.

Class-A designs have largely been superseded by the more efficient designs for power amplifiers, though they remain popular with some hobbyists, mostly for their simplicity. Also, many audiophiles believe that class A gives the best sound quality (for their absence of crossover distortion and reduced odd-harmonic and high-order harmonic distortion) which provides a good market for expensive high fidelity class-A amps.

Single-ended and Triode Class-A Amplifiers

Some aficionados who prefer class-A amplifiers also prefer the use of thermionic valve (or "tube") designs instead of transistors, especially in Single-ended triode output configurations for several claimed reasons:

- Single-ended output stages (be they tube or transistor) have an asymmetrical transfer function, meaning that even order harmonics in the created distortion tend not to be canceled (as they are in push–pull output stages); by using tubes OR FETs most of the distortion is from the square law transfer characteristic and so second-order, which some consider to be "warmer" and more pleasant.
- For those who prefer low distortion figures, the use of tubes with class A (generating little odd-harmonic distortion, as mentioned above) together with symmetrical circuits (such as push–pull output stages, or balanced low-level stages) results in the cancellation of most of the even distortion harmonics, hence the removal of most of the distortion.
- Distortion is characteristic of the sound of electric guitar amplifiers.
- Historically, valve amplifiers often used a class-A power amplifier simply because valves are large and expensive; many class-A designs use only a single device.

Transistors are much cheaper, and so more elaborate designs that give greater efficiency but use more parts are still cost-effective. A classic application for a pair of class-A devices is the long-tailed pair, which is exceptionally linear, and forms the basis of many more complex circuits, including many audio amplifiers and almost all op-amps.

Class-A amplifiers are often used in output stages of high quality op-amps (although the accuracy of the bias in low cost op-amps such as the 741 may result in class A or class AB or class B, varying from device to device or with temperature). They are sometimes used as medium-power, low-efficiency, and high-cost audio amplifiers. The power consumption is unrelated to the output power. At idle (no input), the power consumption is essentially the same as at high output volume. The result is low efficiency and high heat dissipation.

Class B and AB

Class-B or -AB push–pull circuits are the most common design type found in audio power amplifiers. Class AB is widely considered a good compromise for audio amplifiers, since much of the time the music is quiet enough that the signal stays in the "class A" region, where it is amplified with good fidelity, and by definition if passing out of this region, is large enough that the distortion products typical of class B are relatively small. The crossover distortion can be reduced further by using negative feedback. Class-B and -AB amplifiers are sometimes used for RF linear amplifiers as well. Class-B amplifiers are also favoured in battery-operated devices, such as transistor radios.

Class B

Class-B amplifiers only amplify half of the input wave cycle, thus creating a large amount of distortion, but their efficiency is greatly improved and is much better than class A. Class B has a maximum theoretical efficiency of $\pi/4$. (i.e. 78.5%) This is because the amplifying element is switched off altogether half of the time, and so cannot dissipate power. A single class-B element is rarely found in practice, though it has been used for driving the loudspeaker in the early IBM Personal Computers with beeps, and it can be used in RF power amplifier where the distortion levels are less important. However, class C is more commonly used for this.

A practical circuit using class-B elements is the push–pull stage, such as the very simplified complementary pair arrangement shown below. Here, complementary or quasi-complementary devices are each used for amplifying the opposite halves of the input signal, which is then recombined at the output. This arrangement gives excellent efficiency, but can suffer from the drawback that there is a small mismatch in the cross-over region – at the "joins" between the two halves of the signal, as one output device has to take over supplying power exactly as the other finishes. This is called crossover distortion. An improvement is to bias the devices so they are not completely off when they're not in use. This approach is called *class AB* operation.

Class AB

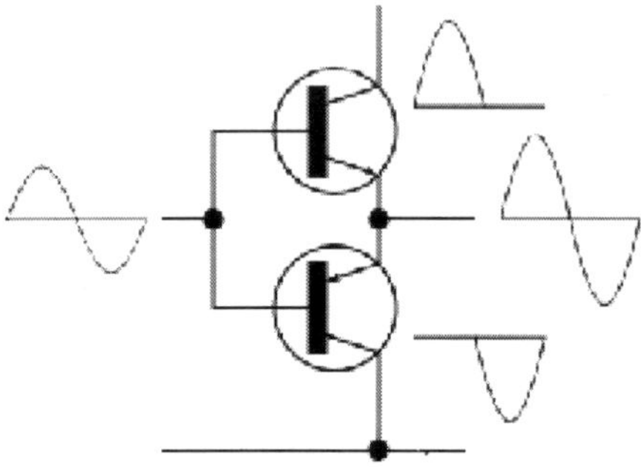

Figure: *Class-B push–pull amplifier*

In class-AB operation, each device operates the same way as in class B over half the waveform, but also conducts a small amount on the other half. As a result, the region where both devices simultaneously are nearly off (the "dead zone") is reduced. The result is that when the waveforms from the two devices are combined, the crossover is greatly minimised or eliminated altogether. The exact choice of quiescent current, the standing current through both devices when there is no signal, makes a large difference to the level of distortion (and to the risk of thermal runaway, that may damage the devices); often the bias voltage applied to set this quiescent current has to be adjusted with the temperature of the output transistors (for example in the circuit at the beginning of the article the diodes would be mounted physically close to the output transistors, and chosen to have a matched temperature coefficient). Another approach (often used as well as thermally tracking bias voltages) is to include small value resistors in series with the emitters.

Class AB sacrifices some efficiency over class B in favour of linearity, thus is less efficient (below 78.5% for full-amplitude sinewaves in transistor amplifiers, typically; much less is common in class-AB vacuum-tube amplifiers). It is typically much more efficient than class A.

Class C

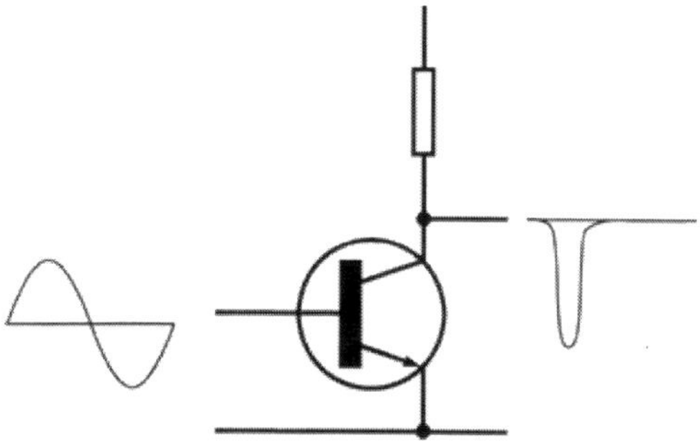

Figure: *Class-C amplifier*

Class-C amplifiers conduct less than 50% of the input signal and the distortion at the output is high, but high efficiencies (up to 90%) are possible. The usual application for class-C amplifiers is in RF transmitters operating at a single fixed carrier frequency, where the distortion is controlled by a tuned load on the amplifier. The input signal is used to switch the active device causing pulses of current to flow through a tuned circuit forming part of the load.

The class-C amplifier has two modes of operation: tuned and untuned. The diagram shows a waveform from a simple class-C circuit without the tuned load. This is called untuned operation, and the analysis of the waveforms shows the massive distortion that appears in the signal. When the proper load (e.g., an inductive-capacitive filter plus a load resistor) is used, two things happen. The first is that the output's bias level is clamped with the average output voltage equal to the supply voltage.

This is why tuned operation is sometimes called a *clamper*. This allows the waveform to be restored to its proper shape despite the amplifier having only a one-polarity supply. This is directly related to the second phenomenon: the waveform on the centre frequency becomes less distorted. The residual distortion is dependent upon the bandwidth of the tuned load, with the centre frequency seeing very little distortion, but greater attenuation the farther from the tuned frequency that the signal gets.

The tuned circuit resonates at one frequency, the fixed carrier frequency, and so the unwanted frequencies are suppressed, and the wanted full signal (sine wave) will be extracted by the tuned load. The signal bandwidth of the amplifier is limited by the Q-factor of the tuned circuit but this is not a serious limitation. Any residual harmonics can be removed using a further filter.

In practical class-C amplifiers a tuned load is invariably used. In one common arrangement the resistor shown in the circuit above is replaced with a parallel-tuned circuit consisting of an inductor and capacitor in parallel, whose components are chosen to resonate the frequency of the input signal.

Power can be coupled to a load by transformer action with a secondary coil wound on the inductor. The average voltage at the drain is then equal to the supply voltage, and the signal voltage appearing across the tuned circuit varies from near zero to near twice the supply voltage during the rf cycle. The input circuit is biassed so that the active element (e.g. transistor) conducts for only a fraction of the rf cycle, usually one third (120 degrees) or less.

The active element conducts only while the drain voltage is passing through its minimum. By this means, power dissipation in the active device is minimised, and efficiency increased. Ideally, the active element would pass only an instantaneous current pulse while the voltage across it is zero: it then disspates no power and 100% efficiency is achieved. However practical devices have a limit to the peak current they can pass, and the pulse must therefore be widened, to around 120 degrees, to obtain a reasonable amount of power, and the efficiency is then 60-70%.

Class D

In the class-D amplifier the input signal is converted to a sequence of higher voltage output pulses. The averaged-over-time power values of these pulses are directly proportional to the instantaneous amplitude of the input signal. The frequency of the output pulses is typically ten or more times the highest frequency in the input signal to be amplified. The output pulses contain inaccurate spectral components (that is, the pulse frequency and its harmonics) which must be removed by a low-pass passive filter. The resulting filtered signal is then an amplified replica of the input.

These amplifiers use pulse width modulation, pulse density modulation (sometimes referred to as pulse frequency modulation) or a more advanced form of modulation such as Delta-sigma modulation (for example, in the Analog Devices AD1990 class-D audio power amplifier). Output stages such as those used in pulse generators are examples of class-D amplifiers. The term *class D* is usually applied to devices intended to reproduce signals with a bandwidth well below the switching frequency. Class-D amplifiers can be controlled by either analog or digital circuits. The digital control introduces additional distortion called *quantization error* caused by its conversion of the input signal to a digital value.

The main advantage of a class-D amplifier is power efficiency. Because the output pulses have a fixed amplitude, the switching elements (usually MOSFETs, but valves (vacuum tubes) and bipolar transistors were once used) are switched either completely on or completely off, rather than operated in linear mode. A MOSFET operates with the lowest resistance when fully on and thus has the lowest power dissipation when in that condition, except when fully off. When operated in a linear mode the MOSFET has variable amounts of resistance that vary linearly with the input voltage and the resistance is something other than the minimum possible, therefore more electrical energy is dissipated as heat. Compared to class-AB operation, class D's lower losses permit the use of a smaller heat sink for the MOSFETS while also reducing the amount of AC power supply power required. Thus, class-D amplifiers do not need as large or as heavy power supply transformers or heatsinks, so they are smaller and more compact in size than an equivalent class-AB amplifier.

Class-D amplifiers have been widely used to control motors, and almost exclusively for small DC motors, but they are now also used as audio amplifiers, with some extra circuitry to allow analogue to be converted to a much higher frequency pulse width modulated signal.

High quality class-D audio amplifiers have now appeared in the market and these revised designs have been said to rival good traditional AB amplifiers in terms of quality. Before these higher quality designs existed an earlier use of class-D amplifiers and prolific area of application was high-powered, subwoofer amplifiers in cars. Because subwoofers are generally limited to a bandwidth of no higher than 150 Hz, the switching speed for the amplifier does not have to be as high as for a full range amplifier. Class-D amplifiers for driving subwoofers are relatively inexpensive, in comparison to class-AB amplifiers.

The letter *D* used to designate this amplifier class is simply the next letter after *C*, and does not stand for *digital*. Class-D and class-E amplifiers are sometimes mistakenly described as "digital" because the output waveform superficially resembles a pulse-train of digital symbols, but a class-D amplifier merely converts an input waveform into a continuously pulse-width modulated (square wave) analog signal. (A digital waveform would be pulse-code modulated.)

Additional Classes

Class E

The class-E/F amplifier is a highly efficient switching power amplifier, typically used at such high frequencies that the switching time becomes comparable to the duty time. As said in the class-D amplifier, the transistor is connected via a serial LC circuit to the load, and connected via a large L (inductor) to the supply voltage. The supply voltage is connected to ground via a large capacitor to prevent any RF signals leaking into the supply. The class-E amplifier adds a C (capacitor) between the transistor and ground and uses a defined L_1 to connect to the supply voltage.

The following description ignores DC, which can be added easily afterwards. The above mentioned C and L are in effect a parallel LC circuit to ground. When the transistor is on, it pushes through the serial LC circuit into the load and some current begins to flow to the parallel LC circuit to ground. Then the serial LC circuit swings back and compensates the current into the parallel LC circuit. At this point the current through the transistor is zero and it is switched off. Both LC circuits are now filled with energy in C and L_0. The whole circuit performs a damped oscillation. The damping by the load has been adjusted so that some time later the energy from the Ls is gone into the load, but the energy in both C_0 peaks at the original value to in turn restore the original voltage so that the voltage across the transistor is zero again and it can be switched on.

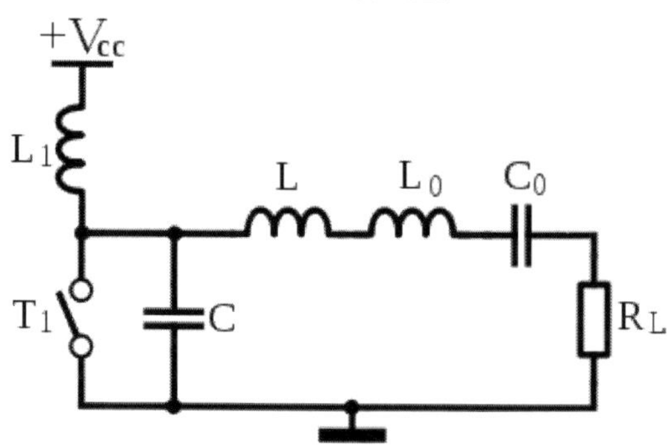

Figure: *Class-E amplifier*

With load, frequency, and duty cycle (0.5) as given parameters and the constraint that the voltage is not only restored, but peaks at the original voltage, the four parameters (L, L_0, C and C_0) are determined. The class-E amplifier takes the finite on resistance into account and tries to make the current touch the bottom at zero. This means that the voltage and the current at the transistor are symmetric with respect to time. The Fourier transform allows an elegant formulation to generate the complicated LC networks and says that the first harmonic is passed into the load, all even harmonics are shorted and all higher odd harmonics are open.

Class E uses a significant amount of second-harmonic voltage. The second harmonic can be used to reduce the overlap with edges with finite sharpness. For this to work, energy on the second harmonic has to flow from the load into the transistor, and no source for this is visible in the circuit diagram. In reality, the impedance is mostly reactive and the only reason for it is that class E is a class F amplifier with a much simplified load network and thus has to deal with imperfections. In many amateur simulations of class-E amplifiers, sharp current edges are assumed nullifying the very motivation for class E and measurements near the transit frequency of the transistors show very symmetric curves, which look much similar to class-F simulations. The class-E amplifier was invented in 1972 by Nathan O. Sokal and Alan D. Sokal, and details were first published in 1975. Some earlier reports on this operating class have been published in Russian.

Class F

In push–pull amplifiers and in CMOS, the even harmonics of both transistors just cancel. Experiment shows that a square wave can be generated by those amplifiers. Theoretically square waves consist of odd harmonics only. In a class-D amplifier, the output filter blocks all harmonics; i.e., the harmonics see an open load. So even small currents in the harmonics suffice to generate a voltage square wave. The current is in phase with the voltage applied to the filter, but the voltage across the transistors is out of phase. Therefore, there is a minimal overlap between current through the transistors and voltage across the transistors. The sharper the edges, the lower the overlap.

While in class D, transistors and the load exist as two separate modules, class F admits imperfections like the parasitics of the transistor and tries to optimise the global system to have a high impedance at the harmonics.

Of course there has to be a finite voltage across the transistor to push the current across the on-state resistance. Because the combined current through both transistors is mostly in the first harmonic, it looks like a sine. That means that in the middle of the square the maximum of current has to flow, so it may make sense to have a dip in the square or in other words to allow some overswing of the voltage square wave. A class-F load network by definition has to transmit below a cutoff frequency and reflect above.

Any frequency lying below the cutoff and having its second harmonic above the cutoff can be amplified, that is an octave bandwidth. On the other hand, an inductive-capacitive series circuit with a large inductance and a tunable capacitance may be simpler to implement. By reducing the duty cycle below 0.5, the output amplitude can be modulated. The voltage square waveform will degrade, but any overheating is compensated by the lower overall power flowing. Any load mismatch behind the filter can only act on the first harmonic current waveform, clearly only a purely resistive load makes sense, then the lower the resistance, the higher the current. Class F can be driven by sine or by a square wave, for a sine the input can be tuned by an inductor to increase gain. If class F is implemented with a single transistor, the filter is complicated to short the even harmonics. All previous designs use sharp edges to minimise the overlap.

Classes G and H

There are a variety of amplifier designs that enhance class-AB output stages with more efficient techniques to achieve greater efficiencies with low distortion. These designs are common in large audio amplifiers since the heatsinks and power transformers would be prohibitively large (and costly) without the efficiency increases. The terms "class G" and "class ≈ are used interchangeably to refer to different designs, varying in definition from one manufacturer or paper to another.

Class-G amplifiers (which use "rail switching" to decrease power consumption and increase efficiency) are more efficient than class-AB amplifiers. These amplifiers provide several power rails at different voltages and switch between them as the signal output approaches each level. Thus, the amplifier increases efficiency by reducing the wasted power at the output transistors. Class-G amplifiers are more efficient than class AB but less efficient when compared to class D, without the negative EMI effects of class D.

Class-H amplifiers take the idea of class G one step further creating an infinitely variable supply rail. This is done by modulating the supply rails so that the rails are only a few volts larger than the output signal at any given time. The output stage operates at its maximum efficiency all the time. Switched-mode power supplies can be used to create the tracking rails. Significant efficiency gains can be achieved but with the drawback of more complicated supply design and reduced THD performance. In common designs, a voltage drop of about 10V is maintained over the output transistors in Class H circuits. The picture above shows positive supply voltage of the output stage and the voltage at the speaker output. The boost of the supply voltage is shown for a real music signal.

The voltage signal shown is thus a larger version of the input, but has been changed in sign (inverted) by the amplification. Other arrangements of amplifying device are possible, but that given (that is, common emitter, common source or common cathode) is the easiest to understand and employ in practice. If the amplifying element is linear, then the output will be faithful copy of the input, only larger and inverted. In practice, transistors are not linear, and the output will only approximate the input. nonlinearity from any of several sources is the origin of distortion within an amplifier. Which class of amplifier (A, B, AB or C) depends on how the amplifying device is biased – in the diagrams the bias circuits are omitted for clarity.

Any real amplifier is an imperfect realisation of an ideal amplifier. One important limitation of a real amplifier is that the output it can generate is ultimately limited by the power available from the power supply. An amplifier will saturate and clip the output if the input signal becomes too large for the amplifier to reproduce or if operational limits for a device are exceeded.

Doherty Amplifiers

A hybrid configuration receiving new attention is the Doherty amplifier, invented in 1934 by William H. Doherty for Bell Laboratories (whose sister company, Western Electric, was then an important manufacturer of radio transmitters). The Doherty amplifier consists of a class-B *primary* or *carrier* stages in parallel with a class-C *auxiliary* or *peak* stage. The input signal is split to drive the two amplifiers and a combining network sums the two output signals. Phase shifting networks are employed in the inputs and the outputs. During periods of low signal level, the class-B amplifier efficiently operates on the signal and the class-C amplifier is cutoff and consumes little power. During periods of high signal level, the class-B amplifier delivers its maximum power and the class-C amplifier delivers up to its maximum power. The efficiency of previous AM transmitter designs was proportional to modulation but, with average modulation typically around 20%, transmitters were limited to less than 50% efficiency. In Doherty's design, even with zero modulation, a transmitter could achieve at least 60% efficiency.

As a successor to Western Electric for broadcast transmitters, the Doherty concept was considerably refined by Continental Electronics Manufacturing Company of Dallas, TX. Perhaps, the ultimate refinement was the screen-grid modulation scheme invented by Joseph B. Sainton. The Sainton amplifier consists of a class-C primary or carrier stage in parallel with a class-C auxiliary or peak stage. The stages are split and combined through 90-degree phase shifting networks as in the Doherty amplifier. The unmodulated radio frequency carrier is applied to the control grids of both tubes. Carrier modulation is applied to the screen grids of both tubes. The bias point of the carrier and peak tubes is different, and is established such that the peak tube is cutoff when modulation is absent (and the amplifier is producing rated unmodulated carrier power) whereas both tubes contribute twice the rated carrier power during 100% modulation (as four times the carrier power is required to achieve 100% modulation). As both tubes operate in class C, a significant improvement in efficiency is thereby achieved in the final stage. In addition, as the tetrode carrier and peak tubes require very little drive power, a significant improvement in efficiency within the driver stage is achieved as well (317C, et al.). The released version of the Sainton amplifier employs a cathode-follower modulator, not a push–pull modulator. Previous Continental Electronics designs, by James O. Weldon and others, retained most of the characteristics of the Doherty amplifier but added screen-grid modulation of the driver (317B, et al.).

The Doherty amplifier remains in use in very-high-power AM transmitters, but for lower-power AM transmitters, vacuum-tube amplifiers in general were eclipsed in the 1980s by arrays of solid-state amplifiers, which could be switched on and off with much finer granularity in response to the requirements of the input audio. However, interest in the Doherty configuration has been revived by cellular-telephone and wireless-Internet applications where the sum of several constant envelope users creates an aggregate AM result. The main challenge of the Doherty amplifier for digital transmission modes is in aligning the two stages and getting the class-C amplifier to turn on and off very quickly.

Recently, Doherty amplifiers have found widespread use in cellular base station transmitters for GHz frequencies. Implementations for transmitters in mobile devices have also been demonstrated.

Special Classes

Various newer classes of amplifier, as defined by the technical details of their topology, have been developed on the basis of previously existing operating classes. For example, Crown's K and I-Tech Series as well as several other models utilise Crown's patented class I (or BCA) technology. Lab.gruppen use a form of class-D amplifier called class TD or tracked class D which tracks the waveform to more accurately amplify it without the drawbacks of traditional class-D amplifiers.

"Class S" was the name of a design published by A M Sandman in *Wireless World* (sept. 1982), which had some elements in common with a current dumping design. It comprises a class A input stage coupled to a class B output stage, with a specific feedback design. A modified design was used in Technics' class AA (marketed) output stage.

"Class T" was a trademark of TriPath company which manufactures audio amplifier ICs. This new class T is a revision of the common class-D amplifier, but with changes to ensure fidelity over the full audio spectrum, unlike traditional class-D designs. It operates at different frequencies depending on the power output, with values ranging from as low as 200 kHz to 1.2 MHz, using a proprietary modulator. Tripath ceased operations in 2007, its patents acquired by Cirrus Logic for their Mixed-Signal Audio division. Some Kenwood Recorder use class-W amplifiers. "Class Z" is a trademark of Zetex Semiconductors (now part of Diodes Inc. of Dallas, TX) and is a direct-digital-feedback technology. Zetex-patented circuits are being utilised in the latest power amplifiers by NAD Electronics of Canada.

Amplifier Circuit

The practical amplifier circuit to the right could be the basis for a moderate-power audio amplifier. It features a typical (though substantially simplified) design as found in modern amplifiers, with a class-AB push–pull output stage, and uses some overall negative feedback. Bipolar transistors are shown, but this design would also be realisable with FETs or valves.

The input signal is coupled through capacitor C1 to the base of transistor Q1. The capacitor allows the AC signal to pass, but blocks the DC bias voltage established by resistors R1 and R2 so that any preceding circuit is not affected by it. Q1 and Q2 form a differential amplifier (an amplifier that multiplies the difference between two inputs by some constant), in an arrangement known as a long-tailed pair. This arrangement is used to conveniently allow the use of negative feedback, which is fed from the output to Q2 via R7 and R8.

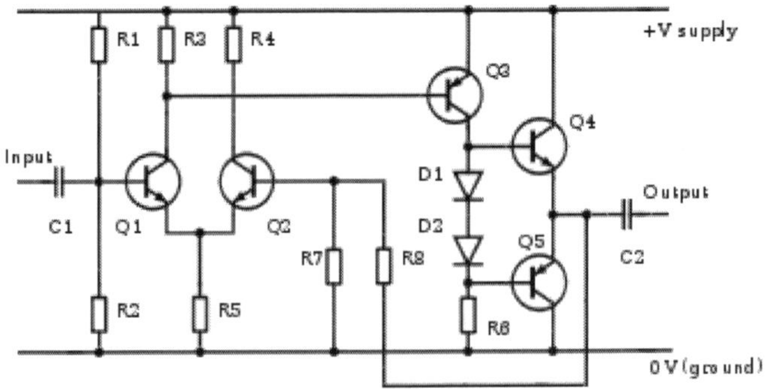

The negative feedback into the difference amplifier allows the amplifier to compare the input to the actual output. The amplified signal from Q1 is directly fed to the second stage, Q3, which is a common emitter stage that provides further amplification of the signal and the DC bias for the output stages, Q4 and Q5. R6 provides the load for Q3 (A better design would probably use some form of active load here, such as a constant-current sink). So far, all of the amplifier is operating in class A. The output pair are arranged in class-AB push–pull, also called a complementary pair. They provide the majority of the current amplification (while consuming low quiescent current) and directly drive the load, connected via DC-blocking capacitor C2.

The diodes D1 and D2 provide a small amount of constant voltage bias for the output pair, just biasing them into the conducting state so that crossover distortion is minimised. That is, the diodes push the output stage firmly into class-AB mode (assuming that the base-emitter drop of the output transistors is reduced by heat dissipation). This design is simple, but a good basis for a practical design because it automatically stabilises its operating point, since feedback internally operates from DC up through the audio range and beyond.

Further circuit elements would probably be found in a real design that would roll off the frequency response above the needed range to prevent the possibility of unwanted oscillation. Also, the use of fixed diode bias as shown here can cause problems if the diodes are not both electrically and thermally matched to the output transistors – if the output transistors turn on too much, they can easily overheat and destroy themselves, as the full current from the power supply is not limited at this stage.

A common solution to help stabilise the output devices is to include some emitter resistors, typically an ohm or so. Calculating the values of the circuit's resistors and capacitors is done based on the components employed and the intended use of the amp. For the basics of radio frequency amplifiers using valves, see Valved RF amplifiers.

Notes on Implementation

Real world amplifiers are imperfect.

- One consequence is that the power supply itself may influence the output, and must itself be considered when designing the amplifier
- The amplifier circuit has an "open loop" performance, that can be described as various parameters (gain, slew rate, output impedance, distortion, bandwidth, signal to noise ratio, etc.)
- Many modern amplifiers use negative feedback techniques to hold the gain at the desired value.

Different methods of supplying power result in many different methods of bias. Bias is a technique by which the active devices are set up to operate in a particular regime, or by which the DC component of the output signal is set to the midpoint between the maximum voltages available from the power supply. Most amplifiers use several devices at each stage; they are typically matched in specifications except for polarity. Matched inverted polarity devices are called complementary pairs. Class-A amplifiers generally use only one device, unless the power supply is set to provide both positive and negative voltages, in which case a dual device symmetrical design may be used. Class-C amplifiers, by definition, use a single polarity supply. Amplifiers often have multiple stages in cascade to increase gain. Each stage of these designs may be a different type of amp to suit the needs of that stage. For instance, the first stage might be a class-A stage, feeding a class-AB push–pull second stage, which then drives a class-G final output stage, taking advantage of the strengths of each type, while minimising their weaknesses.

Dynamic Range Compression

This article is about a process that intentionally reduces the dynamic range of audio signals. For similar reductions caused by circuit imperfections, see Gain compression. For processes that reduce the size of digital audio files, see Audio compression (data). For processes that reduce the size of data files in general, see Data compression.

Peak vs RMS Sensing

A peak sensing compressor responds to the instantaneous level of the input signal. While providing tighter peak control, peak sensing might yield very quick changes in gain reduction, more evident compression or sometimes even distortion. Some compressors will apply an averaging function (commonly RMS) on the input signal before its level is compared to the threshold. This allows a more relaxed compression that also more closely relates to our perception of loudness.

Stereo Linking

A compressor in stereo linking mode applies the same amount of gain reduction to both the left and right channels. This is done to prevent image shifting that can occur if both channels are compressed individually. It becomes noticeable when a loud element that is panned to either edge of the stereo field raises the level of the program to the compressor's threshold, causing its image to shift toward the centre of the stereo field. Stereo linking can be achieved in two ways: Either the compressor sums to mono the left and right channel at the input, then only the left channel controls are functional; or, the compressor still calculates the required amount of gain reduction independently for each channel and then apply the highest amount of gain reduction to both (in such case it could still make sense to dial different setting on left and right channels as one might wish to have less compression for left-side events).

Use

An audio engineer might use a compressor to reduce the dynamic range of source material in order to allow it to be recorded optimally on a medium with a more limited dynamic range than the source signal or else in order to change the character of an instrument being processed. Engineers wishing to achieve dynamic range reduction with few obvious effects might choose a relatively low threshold and low compression ratio so that the source material is being compressed very slightly most of the time. To deliberately soften the attack of a snare drum, they might choose a fast attack time and a moderately fast release time combined with a higher threshold. To accentuate the attack of the snare, they might choose a slower attack time to avoid affecting the initial transient. It is easier to apply these controls with a basic knowledge of acoustics.

Limiting

Compression and limiting are not different in process but in degree and perceived effect. A limiter is a compressor with a high ratio and, generally, a fast attack time. Most engineers consider compression with ratio of 10:1 or more as limiting. Engineers sometimes refer to soft and hard limiting which are differences of degree. The "harder" a limiter, the higher its ratio and the faster its attack and release times. *Brick wall limiting* has a very high ratio and a very fast attack time. Ideally, this ensures that an audio signal never exceeds the amplitude of the threshold. Ratios of 20:1 all the way up to ":1 are considered to be 'brick wall'. The sonic results of more than momentary and infrequent hard/brick-wall limiting are harsh and unpleasant, thus it is more common as a safety device in live sound and broadcast applications. Some modern consumer electronics devices incorporate limiters. Sony uses the Automatic Volume Limiter System (AVLS), on some audio products and the PlayStation Portable.

Parallel Compression

One technique is to insert the compressor in a parallel signal path. This is known as parallel compression and can give a measure of dynamic control without significant audible side effects, if the ratio is relatively low and the compressor's sound is relatively neutral. On the other hand, a high compression ratio with significant audible artifacts can be chosen in one of the two parallel signal paths—this is used by some concert mixers and recording engineers as an artistic effect called *New York compression* or *Motown compression*. Combining a linear signal with a compressor and then reducing the output gain of the compression chain results in low-level detail enhancement without any peak reduction (since the compressor will significantly add to the combined gain at low levels only). This will often be beneficial when compressing transient content, since high-level dynamic liveliness is still maintained, despite the overall dynamic range reduction.

Multiband Compression

Multiband (also spelled multi-band) compressors can act differently on different frequency bands. The advantage of multiband compression over full-bandwidth (full-band, or single-band) compression is that unneeded audible gain changes or "pumping" in other frequency bands is not caused by changing signal levels in a single frequency band. Multiband compressors work by first splitting the signal through some number of bandpass filters or crossover filters. The frequency ranges or crossover frequencies may be adjustable. Each split signal then passes through its own compressor and is independently adjustable for threshold, ratio, attack, and release. The signals are then recombined and an additional limiting circuit may be employed to ensure that the combined effects do not create unwanted peak levels. Software plug-ins or DSP emulations of multiband compressors can be complex, with many bands, and require corresponding computing power.

Multiband compressors are primarily an audio mastering tool, but their inclusion in digital audio workstation plug-in sets is increasing their use among mix engineers. Hardware multiband compressors are also commonly used in the on-air signal chain of a radio station, either AM or FM, in order to increase the station's apparent loudness without fear of overmodulation. Having a louder sound is often considered an advantage in commercial competition. However, adjusting a multiband output compressor of a radio station also requires some artistic sense of style, plenty of time and a good pair of ears. This is because the constantly changing spectral balance between audio bands may have an equalizing effect on the output, by dynamically modifying the on-air frequency response. A further development of this approach is programmable radio output processing, where the parameters of the multiband compressor automatically change between different settings according to the current programme block style or the time of day.

Serial Compression

Serial compression is a technique used in sound recording and mixing. Serial compression is achieved by using two fairly different compressors in a signal chain. One compressor will generally stabilise the dynamic range while the other will more aggressively compress stronger peaks. This is the normal internal signal routing in common combination devices marketed as "compressor-limiters", where an RMS compressor (for general gain control) would be directly followed by a fast peak sensing limiter (for overload protection). Done properly, even heavy serial compression can sound very natural in a way not possible with a single compressor. It is most often used to even out erratic vocals and guitars.

Common Uses

Public Spaces

Compression is often used to make music sound louder without increasing its peak amplitude. By compressing the peak (or loudest) signals, it becomes possible to increase the overall gain (or volume) of a signal without exceeding the dynamic limits of a reproduction device or medium. The net effect, when compression is applied along with a gain boost, is that relatively quiet sounds become louder, while louder sounds remain unchanged. Compression is often applied in this manner in audio systems for restaurants, retail, and similar public environments, where background music is played at a relatively low volume and needs to be compressed not just to keep the volume fairly constant, but also in order for relatively quiet parts of the music to be audible over ambient noise, or audible at all. Compression can be used to increase the average output gain of a power amplifier by 50 to 100% with a reduced dynamic range. For paging and evacuation systems, this adds clarity under noisy circumstances and saves on the number of amplifiers required.

Music Production

Compression is often used in music production to make performances more consistent in dynamic range so that they "sit" in the mix of other instruments better and maintain consistent attention from the listener. Vocal performances in rock music or pop music are usually compressed in order to make them stand out from the surrounding instruments and to add to the clarity of the vocal performance. Compression can also be used on instrument sounds to create effects not primarily focused on boosting loudness. For instance, drum and cymbal sounds tend to decay quickly, but a compressor can make the sound appear to have a more sustained tail. Guitar sounds are often compressed in order to obtain a fuller, more sustained sound. In dance music, side-chaining is often used on basslines, controlled by the kick drum or a similar percussive trigger, to prevent the two conflicting, and provide a pulsating, rhythmic dynamic to the sound. Most devices capable of compressing audio dynamics can also be used to reduce the volume of one audio source when another audio source reaches a certain level; see Side-Chaining above.

Broadcasting

Compression is used extensively in broadcasting to boost the perceived volume of sound while reducing the dynamic range of source audio (typically CDs) to a range that can be accommodated by the narrower-range broadcast signal. Broadcasters in most countries have legal limits on instantaneous peak volume they may broadcast. Normally these limits are met by permanently inserted hardware in the on-air chain. As was alluded to above, the use of compressors to boost perceived volume is a favourite trick of broadcasters who want their station to sound "louder" at the same volume than comparable stations on the dial. The effect is to make the more heavily compressed station "jump out" at the listener at a given volume setting.

But loudness jumps are not limited to inter-channel differences; they also exist between programme material within the same channel. Loudness differences are a frequent source of audience complaints, especially TV commercials and promos which are known to be 'too loud'. One complicating factor is that many broadcasters use (quasi-)peak metres and peak-levelling. Unfortunately the peak level reading does not correlate very well with the perceived loudness. It basically should only be used to prevent overmodulation.

The European Broadcasting Union has been addressing this issue in the EBU PLOUD Group, which consist of over 240 audio professionals, many from broadcasters and equipment manufacturers. In 2010, the EBU published EBU Recommendation R 128, which introduces a new way of metring and normalising audio. The Recommendation is based on ITU-R BS.1770 and could be called a real 'audio revolution'. Several European TV stations have already announced to support the new norm and over 20 manufacturers have announced products supporting the new 'EBU Mode' Loudness metres (EBU Tech 3341).

To help audio engineers understand what Loudness Range their material consists of (e.g. to check if some compression may be needed to fit it into the channel of a specific delivery platform), the EBU also introduced the Loudness Range Descriptor (EBU Tech 3342).

Other Uses

A compressor is sometimes used to reduce the dynamic range of a signal for transmission, to be expanded afterward. This reduces the effects of a channel with limited dynamic range. See Companding. Gain pumping, where a regular amplitude peak (such as a kick drum) causes the rest of the mix to change in volume due to the compressor, is generally avoided in music production. However, many dance and hip-hop musicians purposefully use this phenomenon, causing the mix to alter in volume rhythmically in time with the beat.

A compressor is used in hearing aids to bring the audio volume into the listener's hearing range. To enable the patient to perceive the direction from which the sound is coming, binaural compression may be required. Compressors are also used in some active sound protection earmuffs, to allow sounds at ordinary volumes to be heard normally while attenuating louder sounds. This allows, for example, shooters wearing hearing protection at a shooting range to converse normally, while sharply attenuating the much louder sounds of the gunshots.

Audio Crossover

Audio crossovers are a class of electronic filter used in audio applications. Most individual loudspeaker drivers are incapable of covering the entire audio spectrum from low frequencies to high frequencies with acceptable relative volume and lack of distortion so most hi-fi speaker systems use a combination of multiple loudspeakers drivers, each catering to a different frequency band. Crossovers split the audio signal into separate frequency bands that can be separately routed to loudspeakers optimized for those bands. Active crossovers allow drivers covering different frequency ranges to be powered by separate amplifiers, a configuration known as bi-amping. Signal crossovers allow the audio signal is split into bands that are adjusted (equalized, compressed, echoed, etc.) separately before they are mixed together again. Some examples are: multiband dynamics (compression, limiting, de-essing), multiband distortion, bass enhancement, high frequency exciters, and noise reduction (for example: Dolby A noise reduction).

Classification

Classification Based on the Number of Filter Sections

In loudspeaker specifications, one often sees a speaker classified as an "N-way" speaker. N is a positive whole number greater than 1, and it indicates the number of filter sections. A 2-way crossover consists of a low-pass and a high-pass filter. A 3-way crossover is constructed as a combination of low-pass, band-pass and high-pass filters (LPF, BPF and HPF respectively). The BPF section is in turn a combination of HPF and LPF sections. 4 (or more) way crossovers are not very common in speaker design, primarily due to the complexity involved, which is not generally justified by better acoustic performance.

An extra HPF section may be present in an "N-way" loudspeaker crossover to protect the lowest-frequency driver from frequencies lower than it can safely handle. Such a crossover would then have a bandpass filter for the lowest-frequency driver. Similarly, the highest-frequency driver may have a protective LPF section to prevent high frequency damage, though this is far less common. Recently, a number of manufacturers have begun using what is often called "N.5-way" crossover techniques for stereo loudspeaker crossovers. This usually indicates the addition of a second woofer that plays the same bass range as the main woofer but rolls off far before the main woofer does.

Remark: Filter sections mentioned here is not to be confused with the individual 2-pole filter sections that a higher order filter consists of.

Classification Based on Components

Crossovers can also be classified based on the design approach; by the type of components used.

Passive: A passive crossover is made entirely of passive components, arranged most commonly in a Cauer topology to achieve a Butterworth filter. Passive filters use non-reactive resistors combined with reactive components such as capacitors and inductors. Very high performance passive crossovers are likely to be more expensive than active crossovers since individual components capable of good performance at the high currents and voltages at which speaker systems are driven are hard to make, and expensive. Polypropylene, metalized polyester foil, and paper-electrolytic capacitors are common.

Inductors may have air cores, powdered metal cores, ferrite cores, or laminated silicon steel cores, and most are wound with enamelled copper wire. Some passive networks include devices such as fuses, PTC devices, bulbs or circuit breakers to protect the loudspeaker drivers from accidental overpowering. Modern passive crossovers increasingly incorporate equalization networks (e.g., Zobel networks) that compensate for the changes in impedance with frequency inherent in virtually all loudspeakers. The issue is complex, as part of the change in impedance is due to acoustic loading changes across a driver's passband.

On the negative side, passive networks may be bulky and cause power loss. They are not only frequency specific, but also impedance specific. This prevents interchangeability with speaker systems of different impedances. Ideal crossover filters, including impedance compensation and equalization networks, can be very difficult to design, as the components interact in complex ways. Crossover design expert Siegfried Linkwitz said of them that "the only excuse for passive crossovers is their low cost. Their behaviour changes with the signal level dependent dynamics of the drivers. They block the power amplifier from taking maximum control over the voice coil motion. They are a waste of time, if accuracy of reproduction is the goal." Alternatively, passive components can be utilised to construct filter circuits before the amplifier. This is called passive line-level crossover.

Active: An active crossover contains active components (i.e., those with gain) in its filters. In recent years, the most commonly used active device is an op-amp; active crossovers are operated at levels suited to power amplifier inputs in contrast to passive crossovers which operate after the power amplifier's output, at high current and in some cases high voltage. On the other hand, all circuits with gain introduce noise, and such noise has a more deleterious effect when introduced prior to the signal being amplified by the power amplifiers.

Active crossovers always require the use of power amplifiers for each output band. Thus a 2-way active crossover needs two amplifiers—one each for the woofer and tweeter. This means that an active crossover based system will often cost more than a passive crossover based system, although none of the amplifiers needs to provide output as high as for an equivalent sound level full-frequency, power amplifier, which reduces cost. The cost and complication disadvantages of active crossovers are offset by the following gains:

- a frequency response independent of the dynamic changes in a driver's electrical characteristics.
- typically, the possibility of an easy way to vary or fine tune each frequency band to the specific drivers used. Examples would be crossover slope, filter type (e.g., Bessel, Butterworth, etc.), relative levels,...
- isolation of each driver from signals handled by drivers, thus reducing intermodulation distortion and overdriving
- The power amplifiers are directly connected to the speaker drivers, thereby maximising amplifier damping control of the speaker voice coil, reducing consequences of dynamic changes in driver electrical characteristics, all of which are likely to improve the transient response of the system
- reduction in power amplifier output requirement. With no energy being lost in passive components, amplifier requirements are reduced considerably (up to 1/2 in some cases), reducing costs, and potentially increasing quality.

Digital: Active crossovers can be implemented digitally using a DSP chip or other microprocessor. They either use digital approximations to traditional analog circuits, known as IIR filters (Bessel, Butterworth, Linkwitz-Riley etc.), or they use Finite impulse response (FIR) filters. IIR filters have many similarities with analog filters and are relatively undemanding of CPU resources; FIR filters on the other hand usually have a higher order and therefore require more resources for similar characteristics.

They can be designed and built so that they have a linear phase response, which is thought desirable by many involved in sound reproduction. There are drawbacks though—in order to achieve linear phase response, a longer delay time is incurred than would be necessary with an IIR or minimum phase FIR filters. IIR filters, which are by nature recursive have the drawback that if not carefully designed they may enter limit cycles resulting in non-linear distortion.

Mechanical: This crossover type is mechanical and uses the properties of the materials in a driver diaphragm to achieve the necessary filtering. Such crossovers are commonly found in full-range speakers which are designed to cover as much of the audio band as possible. One such is constructed by coupling the cone of the speaker to the voice coil bobbin through a compliant section and directly attaching a small lightweight *whizzer* cone to the bobbin. This compliant section serves as a compliant filter, so the main cone is not vibrated at higher frequencies.

The whizzer cone responds to all frequencies, but due to its smaller size only gives a useful output at higher frequencies, thereby implementing a mechanical crossover function. Careful selection of materials used for the cone, whizzer and suspension elements determines the crossover frequency and the effectiveness of the crossover. Such mechanical crossovers are complex to design, especially if high fidelity is desired. Computer aided design has largely replaced the labourious trial and error approach that was historically used. Over several years, the compliance of the materials may change, negatively affecting the frequency response of the speaker.

A more common approach is to employ the dust cap as a high frequency radiator. The dust cap radiates low frequencies, moving as part of the main assembly, but due to low-mass and reduced damping, radiates increased energy at higher frequencies. As with whizzer cones, careful selection of material, shape and position are required to provide smooth, extended output. High frequency dispersion is somewhat different for this approach than for whizzer cones. A related approach is to shape the main cone with such profile, and of such materials, that the neck area remains more rigid, radiating all frequencies, while the outer areas of the cone are selectively decoupled, radiating only at lower frequencies. Cone profiles and materials can be modelled in FEA software and the results predicted to excellent tolerances.

Speakers which use these mechanical crossovers have some advantages in sound quality despite the difficulties of designing and manufacturing them, and despite the inevitable output limitations. Full-range drivers have a single acoustic centre, and can have relatively modest phase change across the audio spectrum. For best performance at low frequencies, these drivers require careful enclosure design. Their small size (typically 165 to 200 mm) requires considerable cone excursion to reproduce bass effectively, but the short voice coils required for reasonable high frequency performance can only move over a limited range. Nevertheless, within these constraints, cost and complications are reduced, as no crossovers are required.

Classification Based on Filter Order or Slope

Just as filters have different orders, so do crossovers, depending on the filter slope they implement. The final acoustic slope may be completely determined by the electrical filter or may be achieved by combining the electrical filter's slope with the natural characteristics of the driver. In the former case, the only requirement is that each driver has a flat response at least to the point where its signal is approximately "10dB down from the passband.

In the latter case, the final acoustic slope is usually steeper than that of the electrical filters used. A third- or fourth-order acoustic crossover often has just a second order electrical filter. This requires that speaker drivers be well behaved a considerable way from the nominal crossover frequency, and further that the high frequency driver be able to survive a considerable input in a frequency range below its crossover point. This is difficult in actual practice. In the discussion below, the characteristics of the electrical filter order is discussed, followed by a discussion of crossovers having that acoustic slope and their advantages or disadvantages.

Most audio crossovers use first to fourth order electrical filters. Higher orders are not generally implemented in passive crossovers for loudspeakers, but are sometimes found in electronic equipment under circumstances for which their considerable cost and complexity can be justified.

First Order

First-order filters have a 20 dB/decade (or 6 dB/octave) slope. All first-order filters have a Butterworth filter characteristic. First-order filters are considered by many audiophiles to be ideal for crossovers. This is because this filter type is 'transient perfect', meaning it passes both amplitude and phase unchanged across the range of interest. It also uses the fewest parts and has the lowest insertion loss (if passive).

A first-order crossover allows more signals of unwanted frequencies to get through in the LPF and HPF sections than do higher order configurations.

While woofers can easily take this (aside from generating distortion at frequencies above those they can properly handle), smaller high frequency drivers (especially tweeters) are more likely to be damaged since they are not capable of handling large power inputs at frequencies below their crossovers. In practice, speaker systems with true first order acoustic slopes are difficult to design because they require large overlapping driver bandwidth, and the shallow slopes mean that non-coincident drivers interfere over a wide frequency range and cause large response shifts off-axis.

Second Order

Second-order filters have a 40 dB/decade (or 12 dB/octave) slope. Second-order filters can have a Bessel, Linkwitz-Riley or Butterworth characteristic depending on design choices and the components used. This order is commonly used in passive crossovers as it offers a reasonable balance between complexity, response, and higher frequency driver protection. When designed with time aligned physical placement, these crossovers have a symmetrical polar response, as do all even order crossovers.

It is commonly thought that there will always be a phase difference of 180° between the outputs of a (second order) low-pass filter and a high-pass filter having the same crossover frequency. And so, in a 2-way system, the high-pass section's output is usually connected to the high frequency driver 'inverted', to correct for this phase problem. For passive systems, the tweeter is wired with opposite polarity to the woofer; for active crossovers the high-pass filter's output is inverted. In 3-way systems the mid-range driver or filter is inverted. However, this is generally only true when the speakers have a wide response overlap and the acoustic centres are physically aligned.

Third Order

Third-order filters have a 60 dB/decade (or 18 dB/octave) slope. These crossovers usually have Butterworth filter characteristics; phase response is very good, the level sum being flat and in phase quadrature, similar to a first order crossover. The polar response is asymmetric. In the original D'Appolito MTM arrangement, a symmetrical arrangement of drivers is used to create a symmetrical off-axis response when using third-order crossovers. Third-order acoustic crossovers are often built from first- or second-order filter circuits.

Fourth Order

Fourth-order filters have an 80 dB/decade (or 24 dB/octave) slope. These filters are complex to design in passive form, as the components interact with each other. Steep-slope passive networks are less tolerant of parts value deviations or tolerances, and more sensitive to mis-termination with reactive driver loads. A 4th order crossover with "6 dB crossover point and flat summing is also known as a Linkwitz-Riley crossover (named after its inventors), and can be constructed in active form by cascading two 2nd order Butterworth filter sections. The output signals of this crossover order are in phase, thus avoiding partial phase inversion if the crossover bandpasses are electrically summed, as they would be within the output stage of a multiband compressor. Crossovers used in loudspeaker design do not require the filter sections to be in phase: smooth output characteristics are often achieved using non-ideal, asymmetric crossover filter characteristics. Bessel, Butterworth and Chebyshev are among the possible crossover topologies.

Such steep-slope filters have greater problems with overshoot and ringing but there are several key advantages, even in their passive form, such as the potential for a lower crossover point and increased power handling for tweeters, together with less overlap between drivers, dramatically reducing lobing, or other unwelcome off-axis effects. With less overlap between adjacent drivers, their location relative to each other becomes less critical and allows more latitude in speaker system cosmetics or (in car audio) practical installation constraints.

Higher Order

Passive crossovers giving acoustic slopes higher than fourth-order are not common because of cost and complexity. Filters of up to 96 dB per octave are available in active crossovers and loudspeaker management systems.

9

Transformers

A transformer is a static electrical device that transfers energy by inductive coupling between its winding circuits. A varying current in the *primary* winding creates a varying magnetic flux in the transformer's core and thus a varying magnetic flux through the *secondary* winding. This varying magnetic flux induces a varying electromotive force (emf) or voltage in the secondary winding.

Figure: *Pole-mounted distribution transformer with center-tapped secondary winding used to provide 'split-phase' power for residential and light commercial service, which in North America is typically rated 120/ 240 volt.*

Transformers range in size from thumbnail-sized used in microphones to units weighing hundreds of tons interconnecting the power grid. A wide range of transformer designs are used in electronic and electric power applications. Transformers are essential for the transmission, distribution, and utilization of electrical energy.

Basic Principles

The Ideal Transformer

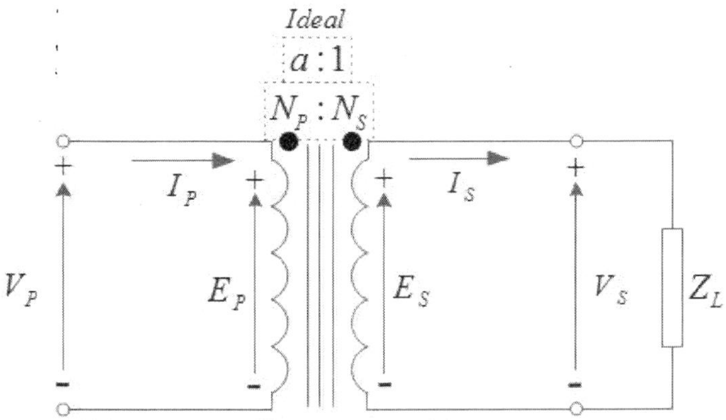

$$\frac{V_P}{V_S} = \frac{I_S}{I_P} = \frac{N_P}{N_S} = a$$

Figure: *Ideal transformer circuit diagram*

Consider the ideal, lossless, perfectly-coupled transformer shown in the circuit diagram at right having primary and secondary windings with N_P and N_S turns, respectively.

The ideal transformer induces secondary voltage $E_S = V_S$ as a proportion of the primary voltage $V_P = E_P$ and respective winding turns as given by the equation

$$\frac{V_P}{V_S} = \frac{E_P}{E_S} = \frac{N_P}{N_S} = a,$$

where,

- $V_P/V_S = E_P/E_S$ = a is the *voltage ratio* and N_P/N_S = a is the winding *turns ratio*, the value of these ratios being respectively higher and lower than unity for step-down and step-up transformers,

- V_P designates source impressed voltage,

- V_S designates output voltage, and,

- E_P & E_S designate respective emf induced voltages.

Any load impedance Z_L connected to the ideal transformer's secondary winding causes current to flow without losses from primary to secondary circuits, the resulting input and output apparent power therefore being equal as given by the equation

$$I_P \times V_P = I_S \times V_S .$$

Combining the two equations yields the following ideal transformer identity

$$\frac{V_P}{V_S} = \frac{I_S}{I_P} = \frac{N_P}{N_S} = a .$$

This formula is a reasonable approximation for the typical commercial transformer, with voltage ratio and winding turns ratio both being inversely proportional to the corresponding current ratio.

The load impedance Z_L is defined in terms of secondary circuit voltage and current as follows

$$Z_L = \frac{V_L}{I_L} = \frac{V_S}{I_S} .$$

The apparent impedance $Z_L^{'}$ of this secondary circuit load *referred* to the primary winding circuit is governed by a squared turns ratio multiplication factor relationship derived as follows

$$Z_L^{'} = \frac{V_P}{I_P} = \frac{aV_S}{I_S / a} = a^2 \times \frac{V_S}{I_S} = a^2 \times Z_L .$$

Induction Law

The transformer is based on two principles: first, that an electric current can produce a magnetic field and second that a changing magnetic field within a coil of wire induces a voltage across the ends of the coil (electromagnetic induction). Changing the current in the primary coil changes the magnetic flux that is developed. The changing magnetic flux induces a voltage in the secondary coil.

Referring to the two figures here, current passing through the primary coil creates a magnetic field. The primary and secondary coils are wrapped around a core of very high magnetic permeability, usually iron, so that most of the magnetic flux passes through both the primary and secondary coils. Any secondary winding connected load causes current and voltage induction from primary to secondary circuits in indicated directions.

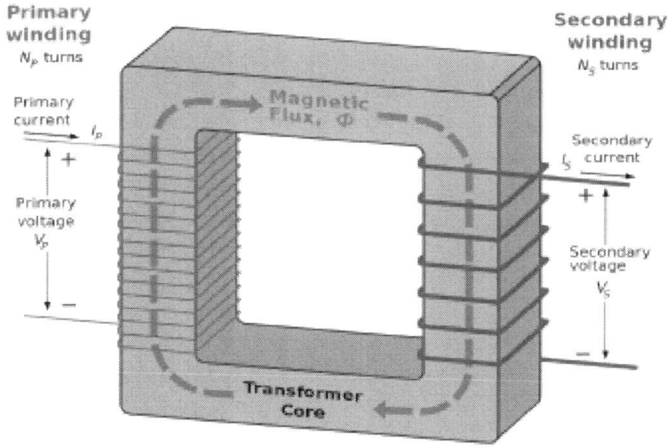

Figure: *Ideal transformer and induction law*

The voltage induced across the secondary coil may be calculated from Faraday's law of induction, which states that:

$$V_S = E_S = N_S \frac{d\Phi}{dt}.$$

where $V_s = E_s$ is the instantaneous voltage, N_s is the number of turns in the secondary coil, and $d\Phi/dt$ is the derivative of the magnetic flux Φ through one turn of the coil. If the turns of the coil are oriented perpendicularly to the magnetic field lines, the flux is the product of the magnetic flux density *B* and the area *A* through which it cuts. The area is constant, being equal to the cross-sectional area of the transformer core, whereas the magnetic field varies with time according to the excitation of the primary. Since the same magnetic flux passes through both the primary and secondary coils in an ideal transformer, the instantaneous voltage across the primary winding equals

$$V_P = E_P = N_P \frac{d\Phi}{dt}.$$

Taking the ratio of the above two equations gives the same voltage ratio and turns ratio relationship shown above, that is,

$$\frac{V_P}{V_S} = \frac{E_P}{E_S} = \frac{N_P}{N_S} = a.$$

The changing magnetic field induces an emf across each winding. The primary emf, acting as it does in opposition to the primary voltage, is sometimes termed the counter emf. This is in accordance with Lenz's law, which states that induction of emf always opposes development of any such change in magnetic field.

As still lossless and perfectly-coupled, the transformer still behaves as described above in the ideal transformer.

Polarity

Figure: *Instrument transformer, with polarity dot and X1 markings on LV side terminal*

A dot convention is often used in transformer circuit diagrams, nameplates or terminal markings to define the relative polarity of transformer windings. Positively-increasing instantaneous current entering the primary winding's dot end induces positive polarity voltage at the secondary winding's dot end.

The Real Transformer

Real Transformer Deviations from Ideal

The ideal model neglects the following basic linear aspects in real transformers:

Core losses collectively called magnetizing current losses consisting of:

- Hysteresis losses due to nonlinear application of the voltage applied in the transformer core

- Eddy current losses due to joule heating in core proportional to the square of the transformer's applied voltage.

Whereas the ideal windings have no impedance, the windings in a real transformer have finite non-zero impedances in the form of:

- Joule losses due to resistance in the primary and secondary windings
- Leakage flux that escapes from the core and passes through one winding only resulting in primary and secondary reactive impedance.

Leakage Inductance

Leakage inductance derives from the electrical property of an imperfectly-coupled transformer whereby each winding behaves as a self-inductance constant in series with the winding's respective ohmic resistance constant, these four winding constants also interacting with the transformer's mutual inductance constant. The winding self-inductance constant and associated leakage inductance is due to leakage flux not linking with all turns of each imperfectly-coupled winding.

The leakage flux alternately stores and discharges magnetic energy with each electrical cycle acting as an inductor in series with each of the primary and secondary circuits. Leakage inductance depends on the geometry of the core and the windings. Voltage drop across the leakage reactance results in often undesirable supply regulation with varying transformer load. Although discussed exclusively in relation to transformers in this article, leakage inductance applies to any imperfectly-coupled magnetic circuit device including especially motors.

Leakage Inductance and Coupling Coefficient

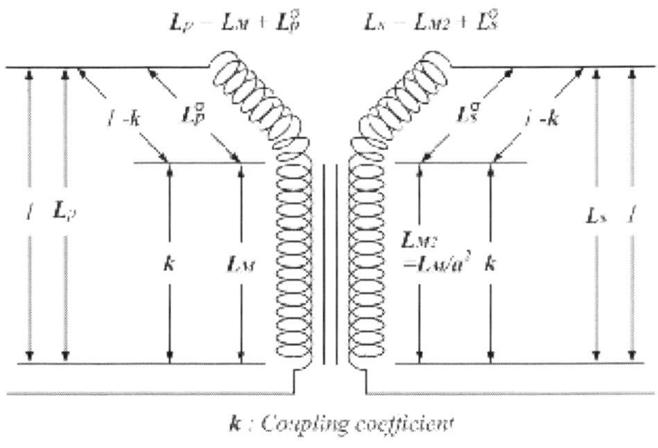

Figure: *$L_P^s$and L_S^σ are primary and secondary leakage inductances*

The magnetic circuit's flux that does not interlink both windings is the leakage flux corresponding to primary leakage inductance L_P^σ and secondary leakage inductance L_S^σ. These leakage inductances are defined in terms of transformer winding open-circuit inductances as well as the transformer's coupling coefficient k, the primary open-circuit self-inductance being given by

$$L_{oc}^{pri} = L_P = L_P \cdot (1-k) + L_P \cdot k$$

where

L_{oc}^{pri} = Primary leakage inductance L_P^σ + Magnetizing inductance L_M

L_P = Primary self-inductance

L_P^σ = Primary leakage inductance = $L_P.(1-k)$

L_M = Magnetizing inductance referred to the primary = $L_P.k$.

It therefore follows that the transformer secondary open-circuit self, magnetizing and leakage inductances are given by

$$L_{oc}^{sec} = L_S = L_S \cdot (1-k) + L_S \cdot k$$

where

L_{oc}^{sec} = Secondary leakage inductance L_S^σ + Magnetizing inductance L_M/a^2

L_S = Secondary self-inductance

L_S^σ = Secondary leakage inductance = $L_S.(1-k)$

$\frac{L_M}{a^2}$ = Magnetizing inductance referred to the secondary = L_S. k

a = Winding turns ratio.

The electric validity of the above transformer diagram depends strictly on open circuit conditions for the respective winding inductances considered, more generalized circuit conditions being as developed in the next two sections.

Leakage Factor and Inductance

A real linear two-winding transformer can be represented by two mutual inductance coupled circuit loops linking the transformer's five impedance constants, where,

- M is mutual inductance
- L_P & L_S are primary and secondary winding self-inductances

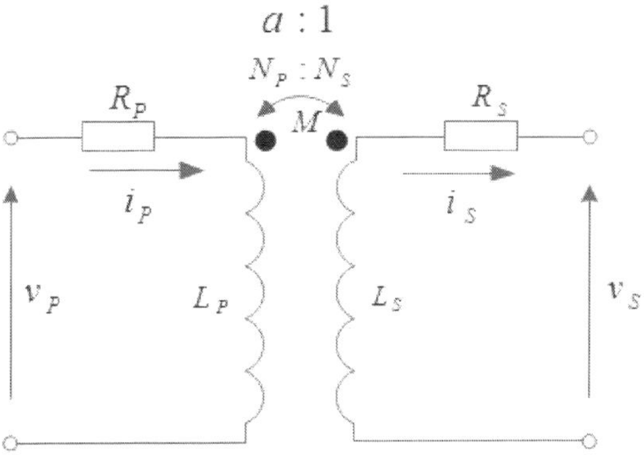

Figure: *Real transformer circuit diagram*

- R_P & R_S are primary and secondary winding resistances
- Constants M, L_P, L_S, R_P & R_S are measurable at the transformer's terminals
- Coupling coefficient k is given as

  $k = M / \sqrt{L_P L_S}$, with $0 < k < 1$

- Winding turns ratio a is in practice given as

  $a = N_P / N_S = v_P / v_S = i_S / i_P = \sqrt{L_P / L_S}$.

The two circuit loops can be expressed by the following voltage and flux linkage equations,

$$v_P = R_P i_P + \frac{d\Psi_P}{dt}$$

$$v_S = -R_S i_S - \frac{d\Psi_S}{dt}$$

$$\Psi_P = L_P i_P - M i_S$$

$$\Psi_S = L_S i_S - M i_P,$$

where

- ψ is flux linkage
- $d\psi/dt$ is derivative of flux linkage with respect to time.

These equations can be developed to show that, neglecting associated winding resistances, the ratio of a winding circuit's inductances and currents with the other winding short circuited and at no-load is as follows,

$$\sigma = 1 - \frac{M^2}{L_P L_S} = 1 - k^2 = \frac{L_{sc}}{L_{oc}} = \frac{L_{sc}^{sec}}{L_P} = \frac{L_{sc}^{pri}}{L_S} = \frac{i_{oc}}{i_{sc}},$$

where,

- σ is the leakage factor or Heyland factor
- i_{oc} & i_{sc} are no-load and short circuit currents
- L_{oc} & L_{sc} are no-load and short circuit inductances.

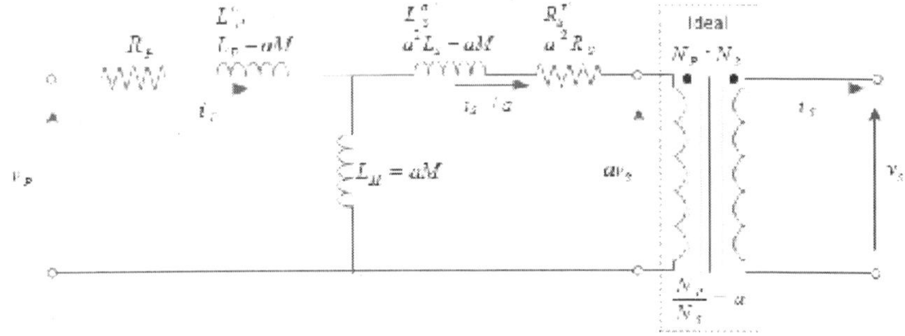

Figure: *Real transformer equivalent circuit*

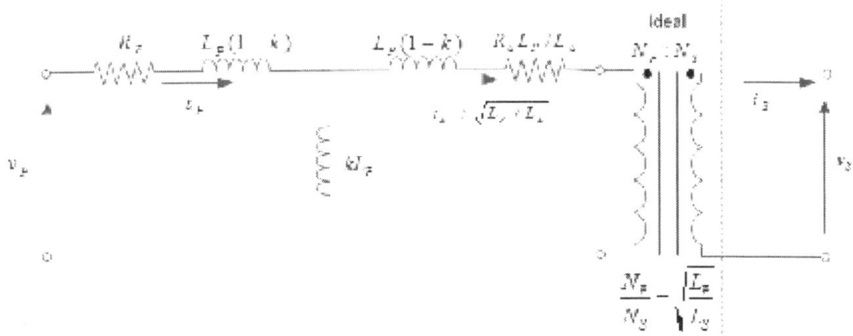

Figure: *Real transformer equivalent circuit in terms of coupling coefficient k*

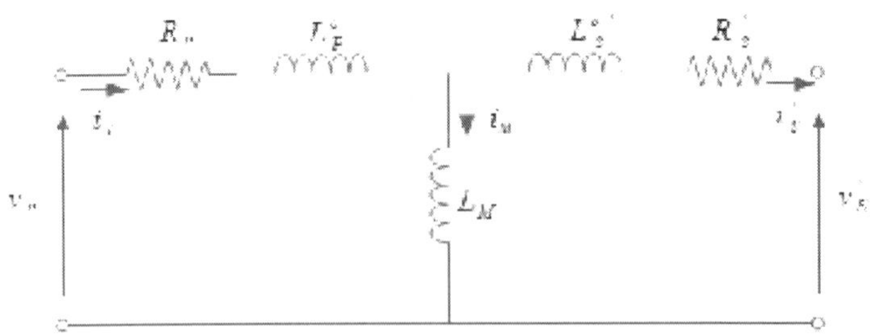

Figure: *Simplified real transformer equivalent circuit*

The transformer can thus be further defined in terms of the three inductance constants as follows,

$$L_M = aM$$

$$L_P^\sigma = L_P - aM$$

$$L_S^\sigma = L_S - aM \ ,$$

where,

- L_M is magnetizing inductance, corresponding to magnetizing reactance X_M
- $L_P{}^\sigma$ & $L_S{}^\sigma$ are primary & secondary leakage inductances, corresponding to primary & secondary leakage reactances $X_P{}^\sigma$ & $X_S{}^\sigma$.

The transformer can be expressed more conveniently as the first shown equivalent circuit with secondary constants referred (i.e., with prime superscript notation) to the primary,

$$L_S^{\sigma'} = a^2 L_2 - aM$$

$$R_S^{'} = a^2 R_S$$

$$V_S^{'} = aV_S$$

$$I_S^{'} = I_S / a \, .$$

Since

$$k = M / \sqrt{L_P L_S}$$

and

$$a = \sqrt{L_P / L_S} \, ,$$

we have

$$aM = \sqrt{L_P / L_S} * k * \sqrt{L_P L_S} = kL_P \, ,$$

which allows expression as second shown equivalent circuit with winding leakage and magnetizing inductance constants as follows,

$$L_P^\sigma = L_S^{\sigma'} = L_P * (1 - k) \quad L_M = kL_P \, .$$

Expanded Leakage Factor

The real transformer can be simplified, with secondary constants referred to the primary and without ideal transformer isolation, where,

$$i_M = i_P - i_S^{'}$$

i_M is magnetizing current excited by flux Φ_M that links both primary and secondary windings.

Referring to the flux diagram at right, the winding-specific leakage factor equations can be defined as follows,

$$\sigma_P = \Phi_P^{\sigma}/\Phi_M = L_P^{\sigma}/L_M$$
$$\sigma_S = \Phi_S^{\sigma'}/\Phi_M = L_S^{\sigma'}/L_M$$
$$\Phi_P = \Phi_M + \Phi_P^{\sigma} = (1 + \sigma_P)\Phi_M$$
$$\Phi_S^{'} = \Phi_M + \Phi_S^{\sigma'} = (1 + \sigma_S)\Phi_M$$
$$L_P = L_M + L_P^{\sigma} = (1 + \sigma_P)L_M$$
$$L_S^{'} = L_M + L_S^{\sigma'} = (1 + \sigma_S)L_M,$$

where

- σ_P is primary leakage factor
- σ_S is secondary leakage factor
- Φ is magnetic flux.

The leakage factor σ can thus be expanded in terms of the interrelationship of above winding-specific inductance and leakage factor equations as follows:

$$\sigma = 1 - \frac{M^2}{L_P L_S} = 1 - \frac{a^2 M^2}{L_P a^2 L_S} = 1 - \frac{L_M^2}{L_P L_S^{'}} = 1 - \frac{1}{\frac{L_P}{L_M} \cdot \frac{L_S^{'}}{L_M}} = 1 - \frac{1}{(1+\sigma_P)(1+\sigma_S)}.$$

Leakage Inductance in Practice

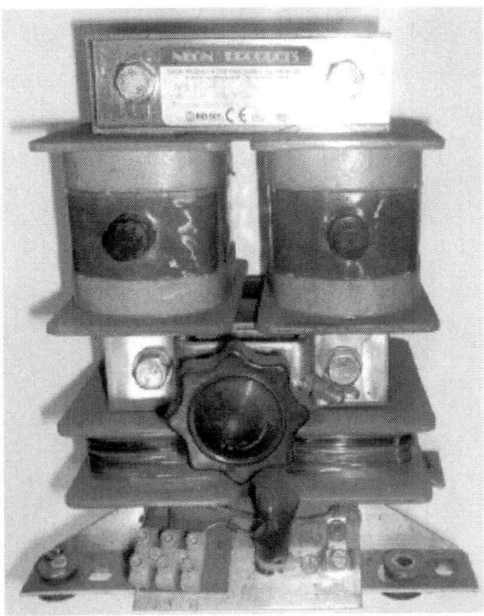

Figure: *High leakage transformer*

Leakage inductance can be an undesirable property, as it causes the voltage to change with loading. In many cases it is useful. Leakage inductance has the useful effect of limiting the current flows in a transformer (and load) without itself dissipating power (excepting the usual non-ideal transformer losses). Transformers are generally designed to have a specific value of leakage inductance such that the leakage reactance created by this inductance is a specific value at the desired frequency of operation.

Commercial transformers are usually designed with a short-circuit leakage reactance impedance of between 3% and 10%. If the load is resistive and the leakage reactance is small ($<10\%$) the output voltage will not drop by more than 0.5% at full load, ignoring other resistances and losses.

High leakage reactance transformers are used for some negative resistance applications, such as neon signs, where a voltage amplification (transformer action) is required as well as current limiting. In this case the leakage reactance is usually 100% of full load impedance, so even if the transformer is shorted out it will not be damaged. Without the leakage inductance, the negative resistance characteristic of these gas discharge lamps would cause them to conduct excessive current and be destroyed.

Transformers with variable leakage inductance are used to control the current in arc welding sets. In these cases, the leakage inductance limits the current flow to the desired magnitude.

Equivalent Circuit

Referring to the diagram, a practical transformer's physical behaviour may be represented by an equivalent circuit model, which can incorporate an ideal transformer.

Winding joule losses and leakage reactances are represented by the following series loop impedances of the model:

- Primary winding: R_P, X_P
- Secondary winding: R_S, X_S.

In normal course of circuit equivalence transformation, R_S and X_S are in practice usually referred to the primary side by multiplying these impedances by the turns ratio squared, $(N_P/N_S)^2 = a^2$.

Core loss and reactance is represented by the following shunt leg impedances of the model:

- Core or iron losses: R_C
- Magnetizing reactance: X_M.

R_C and X_M are collectively termed the *magnetizing branch* of the model.

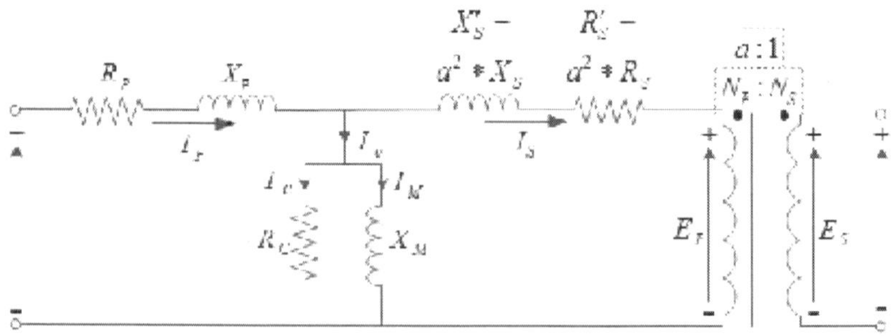

Figure: *Real transformer equivalent circuit*

Core losses are caused mostly by hysteresis and eddy current effects in the core and are proportional to the square of the core flux for operation at a given frequency. The finite permeability core requires a magnetizing current I_M to maintain mutual flux in the core. Magnetizing current is in phase with the flux, the relationship between the two being non-linear due to saturation effects. However, all impedances of the equivalent circuit shown are by definition linear and such non-linearity effects are not typically reflected in transformer equivalent circuits. With sinusoidal supply, core flux lags the induced emf by 90°. With open-circuited secondary winding, magnetizing branch current I_0 equals transformer no-load current.

The resulting model, though sometimes termed 'exact' equivalent circuit based on linearity assumptions, retains a number of approximations. Analysis may be simplified by assuming that magnetizing branch impedance is relatively high and relocating the branch to the left of the primary impedances. This introduces error but allows combination of primary and referred secondary resistances and reactances by simple summation as two series impedances.

Transformer equivalent circuit impedance and transformer ratio parameters can be derived from the following tests: Open-circuit test, short-circuit test, winding resistance test, and transformer ratio test.

Basic Transformer Parameters and Construction

Effect of Frequency

If the flux in the core is purely sinusoidal, the relationship for either winding between its rms voltage E_{rms} of the winding, and the supply frequency *f*, number of turns *N*, core cross-sectional area *a* in m^2 and peak magnetic flux density B_{peak} in Wb/m^2 or T (tesla) is given by the universal emf equation:

$$E_{\text{rms}} = \frac{2\pi fNaB_{\text{peak}}}{\sqrt{2}} = 4.44 fNaB_{peak}$$

If the flux does not contain even harmonics the following equation can be used for half-cycle average voltage E_{avg} of any waveshape:

$$E_{\text{avg}} = 4 fNaB_{\text{peak}}$$

The time-derivative term in Faraday's Law shows that the flux in the core is the integral with respect to time of the applied voltage. Hypothetically an ideal transformer would work with direct-current excitation, with the core flux increasing linearly with time. In practice, the flux rises to the point where magnetic saturation of the core occurs, causing a large increase in the magnetizing current and overheating the transformer. All practical transformers must therefore operate with alternating (or pulsed direct) current.

The emf of a transformer at a given flux density increases with frequency. By operating at higher frequencies, transformers can be physically more compact because a given core is able to transfer more power without reaching saturation and fewer turns are needed to achieve the same impedance. However, properties such as core loss and conductor skin effect also increase with frequency. Aircraft and military equipment employ 400 Hz power supplies which reduce core and winding weight. Conversely, frequencies used for some railway electrification systems were much lower (e.g. 16.7 Hz and 25 Hz) than normal utility frequencies (50 – 60 Hz) for historical reasons concerned mainly with the limitations of early electric traction motors. As such, the transformers used to step-down the high over-head line voltages (e.g. 15 kV) were much heavier for the same power rating than those designed only for the higher frequencies.

Operation of a transformer at its designed voltage but at a higher frequency than intended will lead to reduced magnetizing current. At a lower frequency, the magnetizing current will increase. Operation of a transformer at other than its design frequency may require assessment of voltages, losses, and cooling to establish if safe operation is practical. For example, transformers may need to be equipped with 'volts per hertz' over-excitation relays to protect the transformer from overvoltage at higher than rated frequency.

One example of state-of-the-art design is traction transformers used for electric multiple unit and high speed train service operating across the,country border and using different electrical standards, such transformers' being restricted to be positioned below the passenger compartment. The power supply to, and converter equipment being supply by, such traction transformers have to accommodate different input frequencies and voltage (ranging from as high as 50 Hz down to 16.7 Hz and rated up to 25 kV) while being suitable for multiple AC asynchronous motor and DC converters & motors with varying harmonics mitigation filtering requirements.

Large power transformers are vulnerable to insulation failure due to transient voltages with high-frequency components, such as caused in switching or by lightning.

Energy Losses

An ideal transformer would have no energy losses, and would be 100% efficient. In practical transformers, energy is dissipated in the windings, core, and surrounding structures. Larger transformers are generally more efficient, and those rated for electricity distribution usually perform better than 98%.

Experimental transformers using superconducting windings achieve efficiencies of 99.85%. The increase in efficiency can save considerable energy, and hence money, in a large heavily loaded transformer; the trade-off is in the additional initial and running cost of the superconducting design.

As transformer losses vary with load, it is often useful to express these losses in terms of no-load loss, full-load loss, half-load loss, and so on. Hysteresis and eddy current losses are constant at all loads and dominate overwhelmingly at no-load, variable winding joule losses dominating increasingly as load increases. The no-load loss can be significant, so that even an idle transformer constitutes a drain on the electrical supply and a running cost. Designing transformers for lower loss requires a larger core, good-quality silicon steel, or even amorphous steel for the core and thicker wire, increasing initial cost so that there is a trade-off between initial cost and running cost.

Transformer losses arise from:

Winding Joule Losses: Current flowing through winding conductors causes joule heating. As frequency increases, skin effect and proximity effect causes winding resistance and, hence, losses to increase.

Core Losses:

Hysteresis Losses: Each time the magnetic field is reversed, a small amount of energy is lost due to hysteresis within the core.

According to Steinmetz's formula, the heat energy due to hysteresis is given by

$$W_h \approx \eta \beta_{max}^{1.6}, \text{ and,}$$

hysteresis loss is thus given by

$$P_h \approx W_h f \approx \eta f \beta_{max}^{1.6}$$

where, f is the frequency, η is the hysteresis coefficient and β_{max} is the maximum flux density, the empirical exponent of which varies from about 1.4 to 1 .8 but is often given as 1.6 for iron.

Eddy Current Losses: Ferromagnetic materials are also good conductors and a core made from such a material also constitutes a single short-circuited turn throughout its entire length. Eddy currents therefore circulate within the core in a plane normal to the flux, and are responsible for resistive heating of the core material. The eddy current loss is a complex function of the square of supply frequency and inverse square of the material thickness. Eddy current losses can be reduced by making the core of a stack of plates electrically insulated from each other, rather than a solid block; all transformers operating at low frequencies use laminated or similar cores.

Magnetostriction Related Transformer Hum: Magnetic flux in a ferromagnetic material, such as the core, causes it to physically expand and contract slightly with each cycle of the magnetic field, an effect known as magnetostriction, the frictional energy of which produces an audible noise known as mains hum or transformer hum. This transformer hum is especially objectionable in transformers supplied at power frequencies and in high-frequency flyback transformers associated with PAL system CRTs.

Stray Losses: Leakage inductance is by itself largely lossless, since energy supplied to its magnetic fields is returned to the supply with the next half-cycle. However, any leakage flux that intercepts nearby conductive materials such as the transformer's support structure will give rise to eddy currents and be converted to heat. There are also radiative losses due to the oscillating magnetic field but these are usually small.

Mechanical Vibration and Audible Noise Transmission: In addition to magnetostriction, the alternating magnetic field causes fluctuating forces between the primary and secondary windings. This energy incites vibration transmission in interconnected metalwork, thus amplifying audible transformer hum.

Core Form and Shell Form Transformers

Closed-core transformers are constructed in 'core form' or 'shell form'. When windings surround the core, the transformer is core form; when windings are surrounded by the core, the transformer is shell form. Shell form design may be more prevalent than core form design for distribution transformer applications due to the relative ease in stacking the core around winding coils. Core form design tends to, as a general rule, be more economical, and therefore more prevalent, than shell form design for high voltage power transformer applications at the lower end of their voltage and power rating ranges (less than or equal to, nominally, 230 kV or 75 MVA). At higher voltage and power ratings, shell form transformers tend to be more prevalent. Shell form design tends to be preferred for extra high voltage and higher MVA applications because, though more labour intensive to manufacture, shell form transformers are characterized as having inherently better kVA-to-weight ratio, better short-circuit strength characteristics and higher immunity to transit damage.

Construction

Cores

Laminated Steel Cores: Transformers for use at power or audio frequencies typically have cores made of high permeability silicon steel. The steel has a permeability many times that of free space and the core thus serves to greatly reduce the magnetizing current and confine the flux to a path which closely couples the windings. Early transformer developers soon realized that cores constructed from solid iron resulted in prohibitive eddy current losses, and their designs mitigated this effect with cores consisting of bundles of insulated iron wires. Later designs constructed the core by stacking layers of thin steel laminations, a principle that has remained in use. Each lamination is insulated from its neighbours by a thin non-conducting layer of insulation. The universal transformer equation indicates a minimum cross-sectional area for the core to avoid saturation.

The effect of laminations is to confine eddy currents to highly elliptical paths that enclose little flux, and so reduce their magnitude. Thinner laminations reduce losses, but are more laborious and expensive to construct. Thin laminations are generally used on high-frequency transformers, with some of very thin steel laminations able to operate up to 10 kHz.

One common design of laminated core is made from interleaved stacks of E-shaped steel sheets capped with I-shaped pieces, leading to its name of 'E-I transformer'. Such a design tends to exhibit more losses, but is very economical to manufacture. The cut-core or C-core type is made by winding a steel strip around a rectangular form and then bonding the layers together. It is then cut in two, forming two C shapes, and the core assembled by binding the two C halves together with a steel strap. They have the advantage that the flux is always oriented parallel to the metal grains, reducing reluctance.

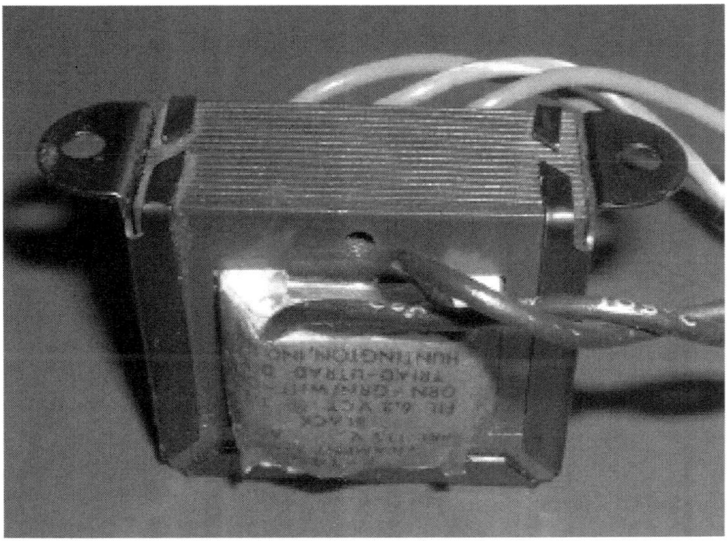

Figure: *Laminated core transformer showing edge of laminations at top of photo*

A steel core's remanence means that it retains a static magnetic field when power is removed. When power is then reapplied, the residual field will cause a high inrush current until the effect of the remaining magnetism is reduced, usually after a few cycles of the applied AC waveform. Overcurrent protection devices such as fuses must be selected to allow this harmless inrush to pass. On transformers connected to long, overhead power transmission lines, induced currents due to geomagnetic disturbances during solar storms can cause saturation of the core and operation of transformer protection devices.

Distribution transformers can achieve low no-load losses by using cores made with low-loss high-permeability silicon steel or amorphous (non-crystalline) metal alloy. The higher initial cost of the core material is offset over the life of the transformer by its lower losses at light load.

Solid Cores: Powdered iron cores are used in circuits such as switch-mode power supplies that operate above mains frequencies and up to a few tens of kilohertz. These materials combine high magnetic permeability with high bulk electrical resistivity. For frequencies extending beyond the VHF band, cores made from non-conductive magnetic ceramic materials called ferrites are common. Some radio-frequency transformers also have movable cores (sometimes called 'slugs') which allow adjustment of the coupling coefficient (and bandwidth) of tuned radio-frequency circuits.

Toroidal Cores: Toroidal transformers are built around a ring-shaped core, which, depending on operating frequency, is made from a long strip of silicon steel or permalloy wound into a coil, powdered iron, or ferrite. A strip construction ensures that the grain boundaries are optimally aligned, improving the transformer's efficiency by reducing the core's reluctance. The closed ring shape eliminates air gaps inherent in the construction of an E-I core. The cross-section of the ring is usually square or rectangular, but more expensive cores with circular cross-sections are also available. The primary and secondary coils are often wound concentrically to cover the entire surface of the core. This minimizes the length of wire needed, and also provides screening to minimize the core's magnetic field from generating electromagnetic interference.

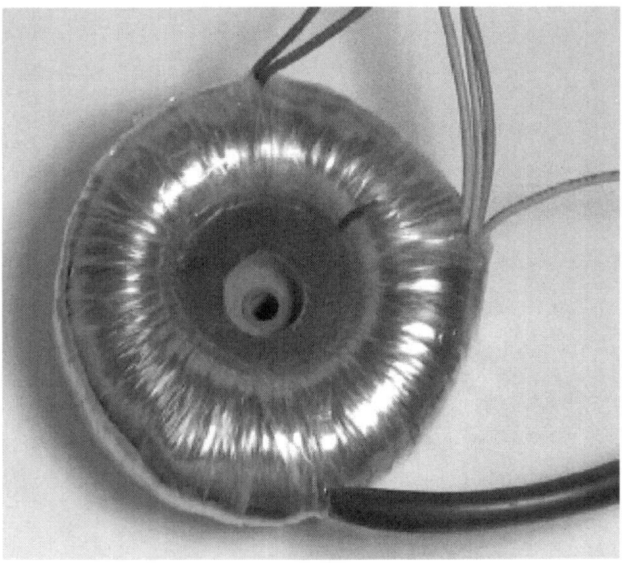

Figure: *Small toroidal core transformer*

Toroidal transformers are more efficient than the cheaper laminated E-I types for a similar power level. Other advantages compared to E-I types, include smaller size (about half), lower weight (about half), less mechanical hum (making them superior in audio amplifiers), lower exterior magnetic field (about one tenth), low off-load losses (making them more efficient in standby circuits), single-bolt mounting, and greater choice of shapes. The main disadvantages are higher cost and limited power capacity. Because of the lack of a residual gap in the magnetic path, toroidal transformers also tend to exhibit higher inrush current, compared to laminated E-I types.

Ferrite toroidal cores are used at higher frequencies, typically between a few tens of kilohertz to hundreds of megahertz, to reduce losses, physical size, and weight of inductive components. A drawback of toroidal transformer construction is the higher labour cost of winding. This is because it is necessary to pass the entire length of a coil winding through the core aperture each time a single turn is added to the coil. As a consequence, toroidal transformers rated more than a few kVA are uncommon. Small distribution transformers may achieve some of the benefits of a toroidal core by splitting it and forcing it open, then inserting a bobbin containing primary and secondary windings.

Air Cores: A physical core is not an absolute requisite and a functioning transformer can be produced simply by placing the windings near each other, an arrangement termed an 'air-core' transformer. The air which comprises the magnetic circuit is essentially lossless, and so an air-core transformer eliminates loss due to hysteresis in the core material. The leakage inductance is inevitably high, resulting in very poor regulation, and so such designs are unsuitable for use in power distribution. They have however very high bandwidth, and are frequently employed in radio-frequency applications, for which a satisfactory coupling coefficient is maintained by carefully overlapping the primary and secondary windings. They're also used for resonant transformers such as Tesla coils where they can achieve reasonably low loss in spite of the high leakage inductance.

Windings: The conducting material used for the windings depends upon the application, but in all cases the individual turns must be electrically insulated from each other to ensure that the current travels throughout every turn. For small power and signal transformers, in which currents are low and the potential difference between adjacent turns is small, the coils are often wound from enamelled magnet wire, such as Formvar wire. Larger power transformers operating at high voltages may be wound with copper rectangular strip conductors insulated by oil-impregnated paper and blocks of pressboard.

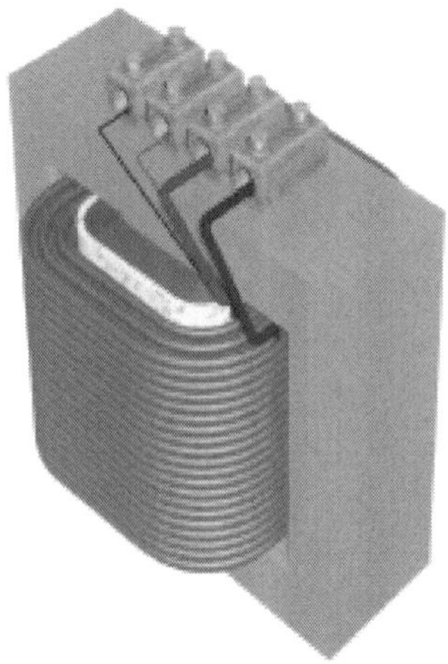

Figure: *Windings are usually arranged concentrically to minimize flux leakage*

High-frequency transformers operating in the tens to hundreds of kilohertz often have windings made of braided Litz wire to minimize the skin-effect and proximity effect losses. Large power transformers use multiple-stranded conductors as well, since even at low power frequencies non-uniform distribution of current would otherwise exist in high-current windings.

Each strand is individually insulated, and the strands are arranged so that at certain points in the winding, or throughout the whole winding, each portion occupies different relative positions in the complete conductor. The transposition equalizes the current flowing in each strand of the conductor, and reduces eddy current losses in the winding itself. The stranded conductor is also more flexible than a solid conductor of similar size, aiding manufacture.

The windings of signal transformers minimize leakage inductance and stray capacitance to improve high-frequency response. Coils are split into sections, and those sections interleaved between the sections of the other winding.

Power-frequency transformers may have taps at intermediate points on the winding, usually on the higher voltage winding side, for voltage adjustment. Taps may be manually reconnected, or a manual or automatic switch may be provided for changing taps. Automatic on-load tap changers are used in electric power transmission or distribution, on equipment such as arc furnace transformers, or for automatic voltage regulators for sensitive loads. Audio-frequency transformers, used for the distribution of audio to public address loudspeakers, have taps to allow adjustment of impedance to each speaker. A centre-tapped transformer is often used in the output stage of an audio power amplifier in a push-pull circuit. Modulation transformers in AM transmitters are very similar.

Dry-type transformer winding insulation systems can be either of standard open-wound 'dip-and-bake' construction or of higher quality designs that include vacuum pressure impregnation (VPI), vacuum pressure encapsulation (VPE), and cast coil encapsulation processes. In the VPI process, a combination of heat, vacuum and pressure is used to thoroughly seal, bind, and eliminate entrained air voids in the winding polyester resin insulation coat layer, thus increasing resistance to corona. VPE windings are similar to VPI windings but provide more protection against environmental effects, such as from water, dirt or corrosive ambients, by multiple dips including typically in terms of final epoxy coat.

Cooling

Figure: *Cutaway view of liquid-immersed construction transformer. The conservator (reservoir) at top provides liquid-to-atmosphere isolation as coolant level and temperature changes. The walls and fins provide required heat dissipation balance*

To place the cooling problem in perspective, the accepted rule of thumb is that the life expectancy of insulation in all electric machines including all transformers is halved for about every 7°C to 10°C increase in operating temperature, this life expectancy halving rule holding more narrowly when the increase is between about 7°C to 8°C in the case of transformer winding cellulose insulation.

Small dry-type and liquid-immersed transformers are often self-cooled by natural convection and radiation heat dissipation. As power ratings increase, transformers are often cooled by forced-air cooling, forced-oil cooling, water-cooling, or combinations of these. Large transformers are filled with transformer oil that both cools and insulates the windings. Transformer oil is a highly refined mineral oil that cools the windings and insulation by circulating within the transformer tank. The mineral oil and paper insulation system has been extensively studied and used for more than 100 years. It is estimated that 50% of power transformers will survive 50 years of use, that the average age of failure of power transformers is about 10 to 15 years, and that about 30% of power transformer failures are due to insulation and overloading failures. Prolonged operation at elevated temperature degrades insulating properties of winding insulation and dielectric coolant, which not only shortens transformer life but can ultimately lead to catastrophic transformer failure. With a great body of empirical study as a guide, transformer oil testing including dissolved gas analysis provides valuable maintenance information. This can translate in a need to monitor, model, forecast and manage oil and winding conductor insulation temperature conditions under varying, possibly difficult, power loading conditions.

Building regulations in many jurisdictions require indoor liquid-filled transformers to either use dielectric fluids that are less flammable than oil, or be installed in fire-resistant rooms. Air-cooled dry transformers can be more economical where they eliminate the cost of a fire-resistant transformer room.

The tank of liquid filled transformers often has radiators through which the liquid coolant circulates by natural convection or fins. Some large transformers employ electric fans for forced-air cooling, pumps for forced-liquid cooling, or have heat exchangers for water-cooling. An oil-immersed transformer may be equipped with a Buchholz relay, which, depending on severity of gas accumulation due to internal arcing, is used to either alarm or de-energize the transformer. Oil-immersed transformer installations usually include fire protection measures such as walls, oil containment, and fire-suppression sprinkler systems.

Polychlorinated biphenyls have properties that once favoured their use as a dielectric coolant, though concerns over their environmental persistence led to a widespread ban on their use. Today, non-toxic, stable silicone-based oils, or fluorinated hydrocarbons may be used where the expense of a fire-resistant liquid offsets additional building cost for a transformer vault. PCBs for new equipment was banned in 1981 and in 2000 for use in existing equipment in United Kingdom Legislation enacted in Canada between 1977 and 1985 essentially bans PCB use in transformers manufactured in or imported into the country after 1980, the maximum allowable level of PCB contamination in existing mineral oil transformers being 50 ppm. Some transformers, instead of being liquid-filled, have their windings enclosed in sealed, pressurized tanks and cooled by nitrogen or sulphur hexafluoride gas.

Experimental power transformers in the 500-to-1,000 kVA range have been built with liquid nitrogen or helium cooled superconducting windings, which, compared to usual transformer losses, eliminates winding losses without affecting core losses.

Insulation Drying

Construction of oil-filled transformers requires that the insulation covering the windings be thoroughly dried of residual moisture before the oil is introduced. Drying is carried out at the factory, and may also be required as a field service. Drying may be done by circulating hot air around the core, or by vapour-phase drying (VPD) where an evaporated solvent transfers heat by condensation on the coil and core.

For small transformers, resistance heating by injection of current into the windings is used. The heating can be controlled very well, and it is energy efficient. The method is called low-frequency heating (LFH) since the current is injected at a much lower frequency than the nominal of the power grid, which is normally 50 or 60 Hz. A lower frequency reduces the effect of the inductance in the transformer, so the voltage needed to induce the current can be reduced. The LFH drying method is also used for service of older transformers.

Bushings

Larger transformers are provided with high-voltage insulated bushings made of polymers or porcelain. A large bushing can be a complex structure since it must provide careful control of the electric field gradient without letting the transformer leak oil.

Classification Parameters

Transformers can be classified in many ways, such as the following:

- *Power capacity*: From a fraction of a volt-ampere (VA) to over a thousand MVA.
- *Duty of a transformer*: Continuous, short-time, intermittent, periodic, varying.
- *Frequency range*: Power-frequency, audio-frequency, or radio-frequency.
- *Voltage class*: From a few volts to hundreds of kilovolts.
- *Cooling type*: Dry and liquid-immersed - self-cooled, forced air-cooled; liquid-immersed - forced oil-cooled, water-cooled.
- *Circuit application*: Such as power supply, impedance matching, output voltage and current stabilizer or circuit isolation.
- *Utilization*: Pulse, power, distribution, rectifier, arc furnace, amplifier output, etc..
- *Basic magnetic form*: Core form, shell form.
- *Constant-potential transformer descriptor*: Step-up, step-down, isolation.
- *General winding configuration*: By EIC vector group - various possible two-winding combinations of the phase designations delta, wye or star, and zigzag or interconnected star; other - autotransformer, Scott-T, zigzag grounding transformer winding.
- *Rectifier phase-shift winding configuration*: 2-winding, 6-pulse; 3-winding, 12-pulse;... n-winding, [n-1]*6-pulse; polygon; etc..

Types

A wide variety of transformer designs are used for different applications, though they share several common features. Important common transformer types include:

- *Autotransformer*: Transformer in which part of the winding is common to both primary and secondary circuits.
- *Capacitor voltage transformer*: Transformer in which capacitor divider is used to reduce high voltage before application to the primary winding.
- *Distribution transformer, power transformer*: International standards make a distinction in terms of distribution

transformers being used to distribute energy from transmission lines and networks for local consumption and power transformers being used to transfer electric energy between the generator and distribution primary circuits.

- *Phase angle regulating transformer*: A specialised transformer used to control the flow of real power on three-phase electricity transmission networks.
- *Scott-T transformer*: Transformer used for phase transformation from three-phase to two-phase and vice versa.
- *Polyphase transformer*: Any transformer with more than one phase.
- *Grounding transformer*: Transformer used for grounding three-phase circuits to create a neutral in a three wire system, using a wye-delta transformer, or more commonly, a zigzag grounding winding.
- *Leakage transformer*: Transformer that has loosely coupled windings.
- *Resonant transformer*: Transformer that uses resonance to generate a high secondary voltage.
- *Audio transformer*: Transformer used in audio equipment.
- *Output transformer*: Transformer used to match the output of a valve amplifier to its load.
- *Instrument transformer*: Potential or current transformer used to accurately and safely represent voltage, current or phase position of high voltage or high power circuits.

Applications

Transformers are used to increase voltage before transmitting electrical energy over long distances through wires. Wires have resistance which loses energy through joule heating at a rate corresponding to square of the current. By transforming power to a higher voltage transformers enable economical transmission of power and distribution. Consequently, transformers have shaped the electricity supply industry, permitting generation to be located remotely from points of demand. All but a tiny fraction of the world's electrical power has passed through a series of transformers by the time it reaches the consumer.

Transformers are also used extensively in electronic products to step-down the supply voltage to a level suitable for the low voltage circuits they contain. The transformer also electrically isolates the end user from contact with the supply voltage.

Signal and audio transformers are used to couple stages of amplifiers and to match devices such as microphones and record players to the input of amplifiers. Audio transformers allowed telephone circuits to carry on a two-way conversation over a single pair of wires. A balun transformer converts a signal that is referenced to ground to a signal that has balanced voltages to ground, such as between external cables and internal circuits.

History

Discovery of Induction Phenomenon

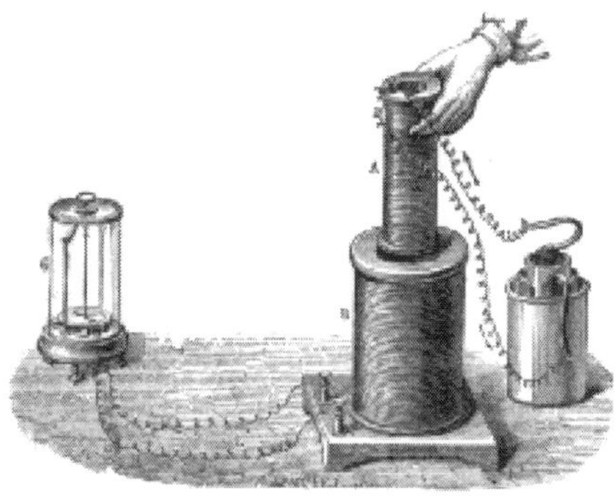

Figure: *Faraday's experiment with induction between coils of wire*

The principle behind the operation of a transformer, electromagnetic induction, was discovered independently by Michael Faraday and Joseph Henry in 1831. However, Faraday was the first to publish the results of his experiments and thus receive credit for the discovery. The relationship between emf and magnetic flux is an equation now known as Faraday's law of induction:

$$|\mathcal{E}| = \left|\frac{d\Phi_B}{dt}\right|.$$

where $|\mathcal{E}|$ is the magnitude of the emf in volts and Φ_B is the magnetic flux through the circuit in webers.

Faraday performed the first experiments on induction between coils of wire, including winding a pair of coils around an iron ring, thus creating the first toroidal closed-core transformer. However he only applied individual pulses of current to his transformer, and never discovered the relation between the turns ratio and emf in the windings.

Induction Coils

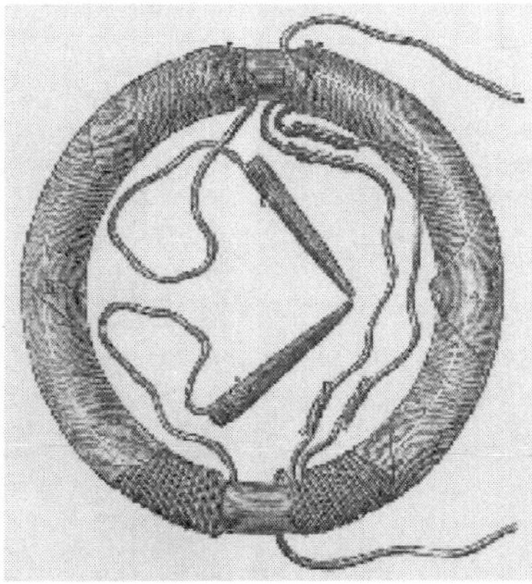

Figure: *Faraday's ring transformer*

Figure: *Induction coil, 1900, Bremerhavn, Germany*

The first type of transformer to see wide use was the induction coil, invented by Rev. Nicholas Callan of Maynooth College, Ireland in 1836. He was one of the first researchers to realize the more turns the secondary winding has in relation to the primary winding, the larger the induced secondary emf will be. Induction coils evolved from scientists' and inventors' efforts to get higher voltages from batteries. Since batteries produce direct current (DC) rather than AC, induction coils relied upon vibrating electrical contacts that regularly interrupted the current in the primary to create the flux changes necessary for induction. Between the 1830s and the 1870s, efforts to build better induction coils, mostly by trial and error, slowly revealed the basic principles of transformers.

Early Devices for Use with Alternating Current

By the 1870s, efficient generators producing alternating current (AC) were available, and it was found AC could power an induction coil directly, without an interrupter.

In 1876, Russian engineer Pavel Yablochkov invented a lighting system based on a set of induction coils where the primary windings were connected to a source of AC. The secondary windings could be connected to several 'electric candles' (arc lamps) of his own design. The coils Yablochkov employed functioned essentially as transformers.

In 1878, the Ganz factory, Budapest, Hungary, began manufacturing equipment for electric lighting and, by 1883, had installed over fifty systems in Austria-Hungary. Their AC systems used arc and incandescent lamps, generators, and other equipment.

Lucien Gaulard and John Dixon Gibbs first exhibited a device with an open iron core called a 'secondary generator' in London in 1882, then sold the idea to the Westinghouse company in the United States. They also exhibited the invention in Turin, Italy in 1884, where it was adopted for an electric lighting system. However, the efficiency of their open-core bipolar apparatus remained very low.

Early Series Circuit Transformer Distribution

Induction coils with open magnetic circuits are inefficient at transferring power to loads. Until about 1880, the paradigm for AC power transmission from a high voltage supply to a low voltage load was a series circuit. Open-core transformers with a ratio near 1:1 were connected with their primaries in series to allow use of a high voltage for transmission while presenting a low voltage to the lamps. The inherent flaw in this method was that turning off a single lamp (or other electric device) affected the voltage supplied to all others on the same circuit. Many adjustable transformer designs were introduced to compensate for this problematic characteristic of the series circuit, including those employing methods of adjusting the core or bypassing the magnetic flux around part of a coil. Efficient, practical transformer designs did not appear until the 1880s, but within a decade, the transformer would be instrumental in the War of Currents, and in seeing AC distribution systems triumph over their DC counterparts, a position in which they have remained dominant ever since.

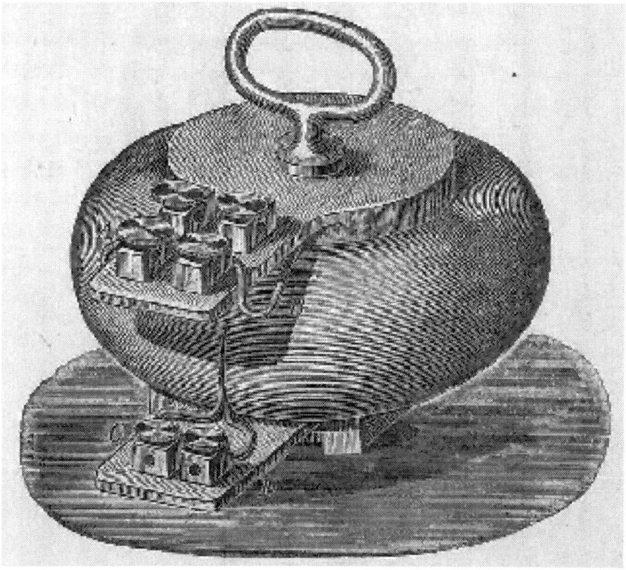

Figure: *Shell form transformer. Sketch used by Uppenborn to describe ZBD engineers' 1885 patents and earliest articles.*

Figure: *Core form, front; shell form, back. Earliest specimens of ZBD-designed high-efficiency constant-potential transformers manufactured at the Ganz factory in 1885.*

Figure: *The ZBD team consisted of Károly Zipernowsky, Otts Bláthy and Miksa Déri*

Closed-core Transformers and Parallel Power Distribution

In the autumn of 1884, Károly Zipernowsky, Ottσ Bláthy and Miksa Déri (ZBD), three engineers associated with the Ganz factory, had determined that open-core devices were impracticable, as they were incapable of reliably regulating voltage. In their joint 1885 patent applications for novel transformers (later called ZBD transformers), they described two designs with closed magnetic circuits where copper windings were either a) wound around iron wire ring core or b) surrounded by iron wire core. The two designs were the first application of the two basic transformer constructions in common use to this day, which can as a class all be termed as either core form or shell form (or alternatively, core type or shell type), as in a) or b), respectively. The Ganz factory had also in the autumn of 1884 made delivery of the world's first five high-efficiency AC transformers, the first of these units having been shipped on September 16, 1884. This first unit had been manufactured to the following specifications: 1,400 W, 40 Hz, 120:72 V, 11.6:19.4 A, ratio 1.67:1, one-phase, shell form.

In both designs, the magnetic flux linking the primary and secondary windings travelled almost entirely within the confines of the iron core, with no intentional path through air. The new transformers were 3.4 times more efficient than the open-core bipolar devices of Gaulard and Gibbs. The ZBD patents included two other major interrelated innovations: one concerning the use of parallel connected, instead of series connected, utilization loads, the other concerning the ability to have high turns ratio transformers such that the supply network voltage could be much higher (initially 1,400 to 2,000 V) than the voltage of utilization loads (100 V initially preferred). When employed in parallel connected electric distribution systems, closed-core transformers finally made it technically and economically feasible to provide electric power for lighting in homes, businesses and public spaces. Bláthy had suggested the use of closed cores, Zipernowsky had suggested the use of parallel shunt connections, and Déri had performed the experiments;

Transformers today are designed on the principles discovered by the three engineers. They also popularized the word 'transformer' to describe a device for altering the emf of an electric current, although the term had already been in use by 1882. In 1886, the ZBD engineers designed, and the Ganz factory supplied electrical equipment for, the world's first power station that used AC generators to power a parallel connected common electrical network, the steam-powered Rome-Cerchi power plant.

Although George Westinghouse had bought Gaulard and Gibbs' patents in 1885, the Edison Electric Light Company held an option on the US rights for the ZBD transformers, requiring Westinghouse to pursue alternative designs on the same principles. He assigned to William Stanley the task of developing a device for commercial use in United States. Stanley's first patented design was for induction coils with single cores of soft iron and adjustable gaps to regulate the emf present in the secondary winding. This design was first used commercially in the US in 1886 but Westinghouse was intent on improving the Stanley design to make it (unlike the ZBD type) easy and cheap to produce.

Westinghouse, Stanley and associates soon developed an easier to manufacture core, consisting of a stack of thin 'E shaped' iron plates, insulated by thin sheets of paper or other insulating material. Prewound copper coils could then be slid into place, and straight iron plates laid in to create a closed magnetic circuit. Westinghouse applied for a patent for the new low-cost design in December 1886; it was granted in July 1887.

Other Early Transformers

In 1889, Russian-born engineer Mikhail Dolivo-Dobrovolsky developed the first three-phase transformer at the Allgemeine Elektricitäts-Gesellschaft ('General Electricity Company') in Germany.

In 1891, Nikola Tesla invented the Tesla coil, an air-cored, dual-tuned resonant transformer for generating very high voltages at high-frequency.

EMF Equation

Electromotive force, also called emf (denoted and measured in volts), refers to voltage generated by a battery or by the magnetic force according to Faraday's Law, which states that a time varying magnetic field induces an electric current.

The electromotive "force" is not a force, as force is measured in newtons, but a potential, or energy per unit of charge, measured in volts.

In electromagnetic induction, emf can be defined around a closed loop as the electromagnetic work that would be transferred to a unit of charge if it travels once around that loop. (While the charge travels around the loop, it can simultaneously lose the energy via resistance into thermal energy.) For a time-varying magnetic flux impinging a loop, the electric potential scalar field is not defined due to circulating electric vector field, but nevertheless an emf does work that can be measured as a virtual electric potential around that loop.

In a two-terminal device (such as an electrochemical cell or electromagnetic generator), the emf can be measured as voltage across the two open-circuited terminals. The created electrical potential difference drives current flow if a circuit is attached to the source of emf. When current flows, however, the voltage across the terminals of the source of emf is no longer the open-circuit value, due to voltage drops inside the device due to its internal resistance.

Devices that can provide emf include electrochemical cells, thermoelectric devices, solar cells, electrical generators, transformers, and even Van de Graaff generators. In nature, emf is generated whenever magnetic field fluctuations occur through a surface. An example for this is the varying Earth magnetic field during a geomagnetic storm, acting on anything on the surface of the planet, like an extended electrical grid.

In the case of a battery, charge separation that gives rise to a voltage difference is accomplished by chemical reactions at the electrodes. Chemically, by separating positive and negative charges, an electric field can be produced, leading to an electric potential difference. A voltaic cell can be thought of as having a "charge pump" of atomic dimensions at each electrode, that is:

A source of emf can be thought of as a kind of *charge pump* that acts to move positive charge from a point of low potential through its interior to a point of high potential. ... By chemical, mechanical or other means, the source of emf performs work dW on that charge to move it to the high potential terminal. The emf ε of the source is defined as the work dW done per charge dq: $\varepsilon = dW/dq$.

Around 1830 Faraday established that the reactions at each of the two electrode–electrolyte interfaces provide the "seat of emf" for the voltaic cell, that is, these reactions drive the current. In the open-circuit case, charge separation continues until the electrical field from the separated charges is sufficient to arrest the reactions. Years earlier, Volta, who had measured a contact potential difference at the metal-metal (electrode-electrode) interface of his cells, held the incorrect opinion that this contact potential was the origin of the seat of emf.

In the case of an electrical generator, a time-varying magnetic field inside the generator creates an electric field via electromagnetic induction, which in turn creates an energy difference between generator terminals. Charge separation takes place within the generator, with electrons flowing away from one terminal and toward the other, until, in the open-circuit case, sufficient electric field builds up to make further movement unfavourable. Again the emf is countered by the electrical voltage due to charge separation. If a load is attached, this voltage can drive a current. The general principle governing the emf in such electrical machines is Faraday's law of induction.

A solar cell or photodiode is another source of emf, with light energy as the external power source.

Notation and Units of Measurement

Electromotive force is often denoted by $\mathcal{E}$ or ε (script capital E, Unicode U+2130).

In a device without internal resistance, if an electric charge Q passes through that device, and gains an energy W, the net emf for that device is the energy gained per unit charge, or W/Q. Like other measures of energy per charge, emf has SI units of volts, equivalent to joules per coulomb.

Electromotive force in electrostatic units is the statvolt (in the centimeter gram second system of units equal in amount to an erg per electrostatic unit of charge).

Formal Definitions of Electromotive Force

Inside a source of emf that is open-circuited, the conservative electrostatic field created by separation of charge exactly cancels the forces producing the emf. Thus, the emf has the same value but opposite sign as the integral of the electric field aligned with an internal path between two terminals A and B of a source of emf in open-circuit condition (the path is taken from the negative terminal to the positive terminal to yield a positive emf, indicating work done on the electrons moving in the circuit). Mathematically:

$$\mathcal{E} = -\int_A^B \mathrm{E}_{cs} \cdot d\ell ,$$

where E_{cs} is the conservative electrostatic field created by the charge separation associated with the emf, $d–l$ is an element of the path from terminal A to terminal B, and '·' denotes the vector dot product. This equation applies only to locations A and B that are terminals, and does not apply to paths between points A and B with portions outside the source of emf. This equation involves the electrostatic electric field due to charge separation E_{cs} and does not involve (for example) any non-conservative component of electric field due to Faraday's law of induction.

In the case of a closed path in the presence of a varying magnetic field, the integral of the electric field around a closed loop may be nonzero; one common application of the concept of emf, known as "*induced emf*" is the voltage induced in a such a loop. The "*induced emf*" around a stationary closed path C is:

$$\mathcal{E} = \oint_C \mathrm{E} \cdot d\ell ,$$

where now E is the entire electric field, conservative and non-conservative, and the integral is around an arbitrary but stationary closed curve C through which there is a varying magnetic field. Note that the electrostatic field does not contribute to the net emf around a circuit because the electrostatic portion of the electric field is conservative (that is, the work done against the field around a closed path is zero).

This definition can be extended to arbitrary sources of emf and moving paths C:

$$\mathcal{E} = \oint_C [\mathrm{E} + \mathrm{v} \times \mathrm{B}] \cdot d\ell$$

$$+\frac{1}{q}\oint_C \text{effective chemical forces} \cdot d\ell$$

$$+\frac{1}{q}\oint_C \text{effective thermal forces} \cdot d\ell ,$$

which is a conceptual equation mainly, because the determination of the "effective forces" is difficult.

Electromotive Force in Thermodynamics

When multiplied by an amount of charge dZ the emf ε yields a thermodynamic work term εdZ that is used in the formalism for the change in Gibbs free energy when charge is passed in a battery:

$$dG = -SdT + VdP + \mathcal{E}dZ ,$$

where G is the Gibb's free energy, S is the entropy, V is the system volume, P is its pressure and T is its absolute temperature.

The combination (ε, Z) is an example of a conjugate pair of variables. At constant pressure the above relationship produces a Maxwell relation that links the change in open cell voltage with temperature T (a measurable quantity) to the change in entropy S when charge is passed isothermally and isobarically. The latter is closely related to the reaction entropy of the electrochemical reaction that lends the battery its power. This Maxwell relation is:

$$\left(\frac{\partial \mathcal{E}}{\partial T}\right)_Z = -\left(\frac{\partial S}{\partial Z}\right)_T$$

If a mole of ions goes into solution (for example, in a Daniell cell, as discussed below) the charge through the external circuit is:

$$\Delta Z = -n_0 F_0 ,$$

where n_0 is the number of electrons/ion, and F_0 is the Faraday constant and the minus sign indicates discharge of the cell. Assuming constant pressure and volume, the thermodynamic properties of the cell are related strictly to the behaviour of its emf by:

$$\Delta H = -n_0 F_0 \left(\mathcal{E} - T\frac{d\mathcal{E}}{dT}\right),$$

where ΔH is the heat of reaction. The quantities on the right all are directly measurable.

Electromotive Force and Voltage Difference

An electrical voltage difference is sometimes called an emf. The points below illustrate the more formal usage, in terms of the distinction between emf and the voltage it generates:

1. For a circuit as a whole, such as one containing a resistor in series with a voltaic cell, electrical voltage does not contribute

to the overall emf, because the voltage difference on going around a circuit is zero. (The ohmic *IR* drop plus the applied electrical voltage is zero). The emf is due solely to the chemistry in the battery that causes charge separation, which in turn creates an electrical voltage that drives the current.

2. For a circuit consisting of an electrical generator that drives current through a resistor, the emf is due solely to a time-varying magnetic field that generates an electrical voltage that in turn drives the current. (The ohmic *IR* drop plus the applied electrical voltage again is zero).
3. A transformer coupling two circuits may be considered a source of emf for one of the circuits, just as if it were caused by an electrical generator; this example illustrates the origin of the term "transformer emf".
4. A photodiode or solar cell may be considered as a source of emf, similar to a battery, resulting in an electrical voltage generated by charge separation driven by light rather than chemical reaction.
5. Other devices that produce emf are fuel cells, thermocouples, and thermopiles.

In the case of an open circuit, the electric charge that has been separated by the mechanism generating the emf creates an electric field opposing the separation mechanism. For example, the chemical reaction in a voltaic cell stops when the opposing electric field at each electrode is strong enough to arrest the reactions. A larger opposing field can reverse the reactions in what are called *reversible* cells.

The electric charge that has been separated creates an electric potential difference that can be measured with a voltmeter between the terminals of the device. The magnitude of the emf for the battery (or other source) is the value of this 'open circuit' voltage. When the battery is charging or discharging, the emf itself cannot be measured directly using the external voltage because some voltage is lost inside the source. It can, however, be inferred from a measurement of the current I and voltage difference V, provided that the internal resistance r already has been measured: $\varepsilon = V + Ir$.

Electromotive Force Generation

Chemical Sources: The question of how batteries (galvanic cells) generate an emf is one that occupied scientists for most of the 19th century. The "seat of the electromotive force" was eventually determined by Walther Nernst to be primarily at the interfaces between the electrodes and the electrolyte.

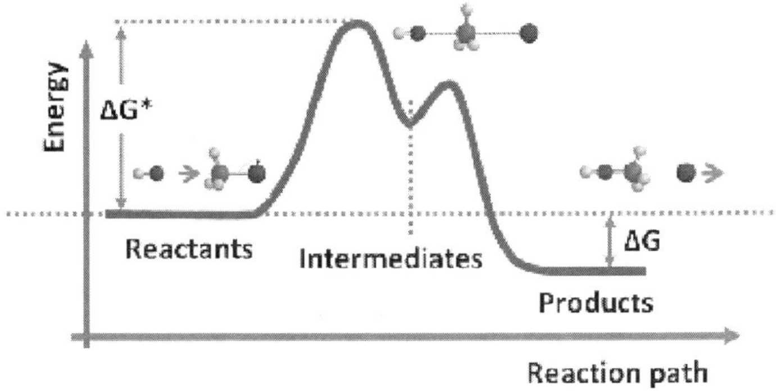

Figure: *A typical reaction path requires the initial reactants to cross an energy barrier, enter an intermediate state and finally emerge in a lower energy configuration. If charge separation is involved, this energy difference can result in an emf.*

Molecules are groups of atoms held together by chemical bonds, and these bonds consist of electrical forces between electrons (negative) and protons (positive). The molecule in isolation is a stable entity, but when different molecules are brought together, some types of molecules are able to steal electrons from others, resulting in charge separation. This redistribution of charge is accompanied by a change in energy of the system, and a reconfiguration of the atoms in the molecules. The gain of an electron is termed "reduction" and the loss of an electron is termed "oxidation". Reactions in which such electron exchange occurs (which are the basis for batteries) are called reduction-oxidation reactions or redox reactions. In a battery, one electrode is composed of material that gains electrons from the solute, and the other electrode loses electrons, because of these fundamental molecular attributes. The same behaviour can be seen in atoms themselves, and their ability to steal electrons is referred to as their electronegativity. As an example, a Daniell cell consists of a zinc anode (an electron collector), which dissolves into a zinc sulphate solution, the dissolving zinc leaving behind its electrons in the electrode according to the oxidation reaction (*s* = solid electrode; *aq* = aqueous solution):

$$Zn_{(s)} \rightarrow Zn^{2+}_{(aq)} + 2e^{-}.$$

The zinc sulphate is an electrolyte, that is, a solution in which the components consist of ions, in this case zinc ions Zn^{2+}, and sulphate ions SO_4^{2-}.

At the cathode, the copper ions in a copper sulphate electrolyte adopt electrons from the electrode by the reduction reaction:

$$Cu^{2+}_{(aq)} + 2e^{-} \rightarrow Cu_{(s)},$$

and the thus-neutralized copper plates onto the electrode. (A detailed discussion of the microscopic process of electron transfer between an electrode and the ions in an electrolyte may be found in Conway.)

The electrons pass through the external circuit (light bulb in figure), while the ions pass through the salt bridge to maintain charge balance. In the process the zinc anode is dissolved while the copper electrode is plated with copper. If the light bulb is removed (open circuit) the emf between the electrodes is opposed by the electric field due to charge separation, and the reactions stop.

At 273 K, the emf $\varepsilon = 1.0934$ V, with a temperature coefficient of $d\varepsilon/dT = -4.53\times10^{-4}$ V/K.

Voltaic Cells

Volta developed the voltaic cell about 1792, and presented his work March 20, 1800. Volta correctly identified the role of dissimilar electrodes in producing the voltage, but incorrectly dismissed any role for the electrolyte. Volta ordered the metals in a 'tension series', "that is to say in an order such that any one in the list becomes positive when in contact with any one that succeeds, but negative by contact with any one that precedes it." A typical symbolic convention in a schematic of this circuit (–| |–) would have a long electrode 1 and a short electrode 2, to indicate that electrode 1 dominates. Volta's law about opposing electrode emfs means that, given ten electrodes (for example, zinc and nine other materials), which can be used to produce 45 types of voltaic cells (10 × 9/2), only nine relative measurements (for example, copper and each of the nine others) are needed to get all 45 possible emfs that these ten electrodes can produce.

Electromagnetic Induction

The principle of electromagnetic induction, noted above, states that a time-dependent magnetic field produces a circulating electric field. A time-dependent magnetic field can be produced either by motion of a magnet relative to a circuit, by motion of a circuit relative to another circuit (at least one of these must be carrying a current), or by changing the current in a fixed circuit. The effect on the circuit itself, of changing the current, is known as self-induction; the effect on another circuit is known as mutual induction.

For a given circuit, the electromagnetically induced emf is determined purely by the rate of change of the magnetic flux through the circuit according to Faraday's law of induction.

An emf is induced in a coil or conductor whenever there is change in the flux linkages. Depending on the way in which the changes are brought about, there are two types: When the conductor is moved in a stationary magnetic field to procure a change in the flux linkage, the emf is *statically induced*. The electromotive force generated by motion is often referred to as *motional emf*. When the change in flux linkage arises from a change in the magnetic field around the stationary conductor, the emf is *dynamically induced*. The electromotive force generated by a time-varying magnetic field is often referred to as *transformer emf*.

Solar Cell

Operation of a solar cell can be understood from the equivalent circuit at right. Light, if it includes photons of sufficient energy (greater than the bandgap of the material), creates mobile electron–hole pairs in a semiconductor. Charge separation occurs because of a pre-existing electric field associated with the p-n junction in thermal equilibrium (a contact potential creates the field). This charge separation between positive holes and negative electrons across a p-n junction (a diode), yields a *forward voltage*, the *photo voltage*, between the illuminated diode terminals. As has been noted earlier in the terminology section, the photo *voltage* is sometimes referred to as the photo *emf*, rather than distinguishing between the effect and the cause.

The light-induced charge separation creates a reverse current through the cell's junction (that is, not in the direction that a diode normally conducts current), and the charge separation causes a photo voltage that drives current through any attached load. However, a side effect of this voltage is that it tends to forward bias the junction. At high enough levels, this forward bias of the junction will cause a forward current in the diode that subtracts from the current created by the light. Consequently, the greatest current is obtained under short-circuit conditions, and is denoted as I_L (for light-induced current) in the equivalent circuit. Approximately this same current is obtained for forward voltages up to the point where the diode conduction becomes significant.

With this notation, the current-voltage relation for the illuminated diode is:

$$I = I_L - I_0\left(e^{qV/(mkT)} - 1\right),$$

where I is the current delivered to the load, I_0 is the reverse saturation current, and m the ideality factor, two parameters that depend on the solar cell construction and to some degree upon the voltage itself, and where kT/q is the thermal voltage (about 0.026 V at room temperature). This relation is plotted in the figure using a fixed value $m = 2$. Under open-circuit conditions (that is, as $I \to 0$), the open-circuit voltage is the voltage at which forward bias of the junction is enough that the forward current completely balances the photocurrent. Rearrangement of the I–V equation provides the open-circuit voltage as:

$$V_{\text{oc}} = m\frac{kT}{q}\ln\left(\frac{I_{\text{L}}}{I_0}+1\right),$$

which is useful in indicating a logarithmic dependence of V_{oc} upon the light-induced current. Typically, the open-circuit voltage is not more than about 0.5 V.

The value of the photo voltage when driving a load is variable. For a load resistance R_{L}, the cell develops a voltage between the short-circuit value $V = 0$, $I = I_{\text{L}}$ and the open-circuit value V_{oc}, $I = 0$, a value given by Ohm's law $V = I\,R_{\text{L}}$, where the current I is the difference between the short-circuit current and current due to forward bias of the junction, as indicated by the equivalent circuit (neglecting the parasitic resistances).

In contrast to the battery, at current levels near I_{L}, the solar cell acts more like a *current source* rather than a voltage source. The current drawn is nearly fixed over a range of load voltages, at one electron per converted photon. The quantum efficiency, or probability of getting an electron of photocurrent per incident photon, depends not only upon the solar cell itself, but upon the spectrum of the light.

The diode possesses a "built-in potential" due to the contact potential difference between the two different materials on either side of the junction. This built-in potential is established when the junction is formed as a by-product of thermodynamic equilibrium. Once established, this potential difference cannot drive a current, however, as connecting a load does not upset this equilibrium. In contrast, the accumulation of excess electrons in one region and of excess holes in another due to illumination results in a photo voltage that does drive a current when a load is attached to the illuminated diode. As noted above, this photo voltage also forward biases the junction, and so *reduces* the pre-existing field in the depletion region.

Bibliography

Arendt Wintrich, Ulrich Nicolai, Werner Tursky, Tobias Reimann: *Application Manual 2011*, ISLE Verlag, Germany, 2011.

Arnold Zankl: *Milestones in Automation: From the Transistor to the Digital Factory*, Wiley-VCH, NJ, 2006.

Bamberger, Robert L.: *The National Energy Strategy: Summary and Analysis,* Congressional Research Service, Library of Congress, Washington, DC, 1991.

Bedford, B. D.; Hoft, R. G.: *Principles of Inverter Circuits*, New York: John Wiley & Sons, Inc., 1964.

Bernard, Finn S.: *The History of Electrical Technology: An Annotated Bibliography*, Garland Publishing, Inc., New York, 1991.

Bishop, R.H.: *Modern Control Systems Analysis and Design Using MATLAB & SIMULINK*, Addison-Wesley, London, 1997.

Bobrow, Leonard S.: *Fundamentals of Electrical Engineering*, Oxford University Press, Delhi, 2003.

Brower, Michael: *Cool Energy: Renewable Solutions to Environmental Problems*, MIT Press, Cambridge, MA, 1992.

Christopher Kilian: *Modern Control Technology*, Thompson Delmar Learning, UK, 2005.

Coleman, Charles: *P. G. and E. of California: The Centennial Story of Pacific Gas and Electric Company, 1852-1952*, McGraw-Hill, New York, 1952.

Desoer, C. A.; M. Vidyasagar: *Feedback Systems: Input-Output Properties,* SIAM, 2009.

Dhawan, B C : *Textbook of Electrophoresis*, Pearl Books, Delhi, 2008.

Donald, G. Fink and H. Wayne, Beaty: *Standard Handbook for Electrical Engineers,* McGraw-Hill, New York, 1978.

Dugdale, J.S.: *Entropy and its Physical Meaning*. Taylor and Francis. 1998.

Dunlop, John T.: *Automation and Technological Change: Report of the Twenty-first American Assembly*, Prentice-Hall, Englewood Cliffs, NJ, USA, 1962.

Edwin, J. Houston and Arthur Kennelly: *Recent Types of Dynamo-Electric Machinery*, P.F. Collier and Sons New York, 1902.

Eveleigh, E.W.: *Introduction to Control Systems Design*, McGraw-Hill, NY, 1972.

Glaeser, Martin G.: *Public Utilities in American Capitalism,* Macmillan Co., New York, 1957.

Goodwin, G.C., Graebe, S.F., and Salgado, M.E.: *Control System Design*, Prentice Hall, NJ, 2001.

Hughes, Thomas P.: *Networks of Power: Electrification in Western Society, 1880-1930*, The Johns Hopkins University Press, Baltimore, 1983.

John, N. Chiasson: *Modeling and High Performance Control of Electric Machines,* Wiley-IEEE Press, New York, 2005.

Khalil, H. K.: *Nonlinear Systems,* Prentice Hall, Upper Saddle River, New Jersey, 2002.

Lander, Cyril W.: "8 *D.C. Machine Control",* Power Electronics, Mc Graw Hill International, London, 1993.

Liptak, Bela G.: *Instrument Engineers' Handbook: Process Control and Optimization*, CRC Press, 2005.

Marder, M. P.: *Condensed Matter Physics,* New York: John Wiley & Sons, 2006.

Mazumder, S.K.: *Power Electronics Handbook*, Academic Press, Burlington, Massachusetts, 2010.

Moorhouse, John C.: *Electric Power: Deregulation and the Public Interest,* Pacific Research Institute for Public Policy, San Francisco, 1986.

Nise, N.S., *Control Systems Engineering*, Addison-Wesley, London, 1995.

Ouellette, Robert: *Automation Impacts on Industry*, Ann Arbor Science Publishers, MI, USA, 1983.

Patterson, Walter C.: *Transforming Electricity: The Coming Generation of Change*, Earthscan, 1999.

Rajput, R.K.: *A Course in Electrical Engineering Materials*, Laxmi Publications, Delhi, 2009.

Rowland, J.R.: *Linear Control Systems*, John Wiley & Sons, NY, 1986.

Smith, Bruce A.: *Technical Innovation in Electric Power Generation, 1950-1970*, Div. Of Research, Michigan State University, East Lansing, 1977.

Ueha, S.; Tomikawa, Y.; Kurosawa, M.; Nakamura, N.: *Ultrasonic Motors: Theory and Applications*, Clarendon Press, UK, 1993.

Willis, H. L., Welch, G. V., and Schrieber, R. R.: *Aging Power Delivery Infrastructures*, Marcel Dekker Inc., New York, 2001.

Index

L

M

N

P

R

S

T

U

V

❑❑❑